PRIVATISATION: THE ASEAN CONNECTION

PRIVATISATION: THE ASEAN CONNECTION

B.N. GHOSH

NOVA SCIENCE PUBLISHERS, INC.
Huntington, NY

Editorial Production: Susan Boriotti
Office Manager: Annette Hellinger
Graphics: Frank Grucci and Jennifer Lucas
Information Editor: Tatiana Shohov
Book Production: Donna Dennis, Patrick Davin, Jennifer Kuenzig,
Christine Mathosian, Tammy Sauter and Lynette Van Helden
Circulation: Maryanne Schmidt
Marketing/Sales: Cathy DeGregory

Library of Congress Cataloging-in-Publication Data

Privatisation: the ASEAN connection / edited by B.N. Ghosh.
    p.   cm.
  Includes index.
  ISBN 1-56072-760-8
1. Privatization—Asia, Southeastern. I. Ghosh, B.N.

HD4295.8 .P73   2000
338.959'05—dc21

                                                        99-055097

Copyright © 2000 by Nova Science Publishers, Inc.
                227 Main Street, Suite 100
                Huntington, New York 11743
                Tele. 631-424-6682   Fax 631-424-4666
                E Mail Novascil@aol.com

Printed in the United States of America

CONTENTS

PREFACE

A great deal of economic success of Southeast Asian economies is attributed to privatisation. Through the mechanism of privatisation, these economies have successfully integrated themselves with dominant metropolitan capitalist countries. The underlying interlinkages have remained vital for the ASEAN miracle. It is rather intriguing for reasons more than one to delve deep into the theory and practice of privatisation, as it applies to the ASEAN countries.

Privatisation was indeed an attempt to introduce the capitalist method of development which could ensure higher efficiency in many ways. However, the concept and mode of privatisation do not have any uniform meaning and application in the Southeast Asian and Western economies. Even among the ASEAN economies, the practice of privatisation in its various forms and structures has not remained the same. Moreover, the priorities and emphasis have also remained remarkably different for these countries. The present volume is purported to bring out these differences in the practice of privatisation. Privatisation has also not been equally motivated, progressive and successful in the ASEAN economies. Besides being economic, it has also in a significant way remained a political issue which has been analysed in terms of duopoly theoretic model in the present volume. The studies presented in the volume are pointers to the fact that in the ASEAN countries, like anywhere else in the world, privatisation exercise could not prove itself to be unmixed blessing. It has given rise to many problematics and issues which the present volume has sought to analyse. All these indeed corroborate the conventional knowledge that a simple change in the ownership of means of production from public to the private hands does not necessarily guarantee higher efficiency and productivity.

The volume analyses the privatisation experiences of five original ASEAN economies including Indonesia, Malaysia, Philippines, Singapore and Thailand. Brunei is a uniue case among the ASEAN countries. It did not encourage privatisation as an engine of economic growth and development. It is, therefore, excluded from the schema of the present study. The present collection of studies is an assortment of both micro and macro aspects of privatisation in the ASEAN region. For obviously impelling reasons, such a line of approach has been found to be significant for the appreciation of the practice of privatisation in these transitional economies. The privatisation experiences of these countries have been studied from a series of interrelated perspectives, and various dimensions of privatisation, e.g. processes and modes, implications and effects, and contemporary issues and challenges, have been elaborated with facts and figures. The relevant developments and associated issues are addressed in such a way that the readers would be in a position to make a comparative analysis of the models of privatisation in these countries. The case studies should be of considerable interests to students, researchers and teachers of the subject.

In finale, I must thank the contributors who in spite of their tight work schedule and other negative externalities have been able to finally create some public goods for the consumption of the academic world. I would also like to thank Ms. Marina Cheah for neatly typing out the manuscript within a very short period of time, and to Ms. Pooni Krishnan for her impeccable secretarial assistance.

B.N. Ghosh, Editor
Universiti Sains Malaysia
11800 Penang

INTRODUCTION
PRIVATISATION: THE ASEAN CONNECTION

The book analyses the privatisation experiences of some of the ASEAN economies. The compilation of papers written by academicians from several countries attempts to delve deep into the various dimensions of privatisation including processes and modes, implications and effects and contemporary issues and challenges. The privatisation experiences of these countries have been studied from a series of inter-related perspectives. The relevant developments and associated issues are addressed in such a way that the readers would be in a position to make a comparative analysis of the models of privatisation in these countries.

Chapter 1

PRIVATISATION: THE ASEAN EXPERIENCE

B.N. Ghosh[*]

Since the eighties, the ASEAN economics, particularly, Singapore, Malaysia, Philippines, Thailand and Indonesia, have been actively engaged in privatisation, deregulation and liberalisation of their economies. These economies had already tested the fruits of marketisation process of which privatisation is an integral part. The ASEAN countries have responded to external constraints and opportunities by opening up their economies. One of the reasons for the enormous economic success of the ASEAN has been their integration into the global system of division of labour (Bowie and Unger, 1997). The external process of capitalist integration has become symbiotic with the internal process of capitalist metamorphosis of the state machinery. All the ASEAN states are more or less not only capitalist in nature but are also very strong and powerful. The *visible hands of state* have been instrumental in the successful capitalist transformation of these economies.

However, although the states are politically powerful, they are found not to be so in the matter of finance and economic prowess. During the pre-privatisation period, the public enterprises exhibited growing losses, overstaffing, suboptimal allocation of resources, and overall declining of economic efficiency in many ASEAN countries (Ng and Wagner, 1989, p. 213).

WHY PRIVATISATION?

There are many reasons for privatisation. These reasons can be classified mainly into two categories: (i) economic, and (ii) non-economic. The basic idea of privatisation in the ASEAN has come from the economic inefficiency including exorbitant running expenditure of public enterprises, lower productivity, higher cost of per capita output, surplus labour and the like. On the other hand, the state exchequers had been feeling the pressure of running the government in the face of growing budget deficit within, and balance of payments deficit without. It was argued that breaking away of monopoly of state enterprises, and introduction of more competitive market forces through privatisation could be helpful for generating economic efficiency, reducing cost and creating more surplus for economic development and growth.

In some cases, not only did the governments want to reduce the financial burden and responsibilities, but also liked to have lesser participation in the management of the economy. Thus, the philosophy underlying the role of state drastically changed from one of a powerful and strong participatory state to a state of minimal participation, though not complete *laissez faire*.

Contrary to the traditional notion, it was argued that state had failed to generate equity in the matter of income and wealth distribution to the comparatively poorer section of the society. *Government failure* in this context, it was argued, could be redressed by the introduction of market forces through privatisation. It was indeed a novel argument which emphasised the fact that through the sale of certain amount of equities of the privatised companies to the poor people, it would be possible to have a more *egalitarian social formation* with lesser concentration of economic power. However, this has to be effected through the proper supervisory power of the state. An interesting fact that one can observe in this connection is that, in the ASEAN countries, the character of state has undergone a slow metamorphosis from powerful and strong state of the pre-privatisation period to one of supervisory state in the post-privatisation period. This is evident from the role of state in the post-privatisation era in the ASEAN countries.

It is often said that many of the ASEAN countries have been dictated for privatisation by some world organisations like, World Bank, Asian Development Bank, IMF and so on. The *structural adjustment philosophy* of the IMF and the World Bank is pretty well-known as a prelude to deregulation, liberalisation and privatisation. These external pressures for privatisation have remained especially decisive in the cases of Philippines and Indonesia (Ng and Toh, 1992, p. 45).

POLITICS OF PRIVATISATION

Privatisation whether slow or rapid has often been influenced by political factors. Privatisation is essentially a political decision, and as such, political factors have remained overwhelmingly more decisive than other factors like economic, social, national, cultural and so on.

Autocentric personal self-interest and ulterior motives are often the pre-dominant considerations for privatisation or no-privatisation of public enterprises in the ASEAN nations as a whole. In this connection, two very important classes of persons who are dominant in the politics of privatisation are politicians (including ministers) and bureaucrats (including top level managers). Needless to say, the politicians are ultimate decision-makers, but nonetheless, civil servants and bureaucrats are also important in the sense that they do not only participate in the policy-making but also provide informatics and data on the operational aspects of public enterprises which are the possible candidates for privatisation. Hence, their roles are very crucial, and often cannot be brushed aside.

A study of privatisation in the ASEAN countries shows that, generally, the politicians are in favour of privatisation because, and if, they can reap some gains out of the privatisation bargain, endow some benefits and advantages to their close relatives, family friends and cronies. The cronies gain in buying the shares of privatised industries at a lower rate and selling at a premium in the future. As a matter of fact, *underpricing of shares* to be sold in the market has remained an important mechanism to benefit the cronies at the cost of huge losses to the state exchequer. The government often wants to reduce its financial burden, and shirk social responsibilities of providing public goods. Another avowed motive of the government may be to better off the economic conditions of less fortunate ethnic groups, as in Malaysia.

However, at times, the government may not be interested in privatisation because it finds that, by so doing, it will lose its monetary benefit, power and control. Thus, the privatisation attempt of Philippines Airlines and Manila Hotel was not a success because the cronies of President Aquino were not ready to surrender the advantages they were deriving from the control of these organisations (Milne, 1991, p. 328). In Philippines, nepotism, favouritism and corruption stood in the way of privatisation of public enterprises. Aquino was quite uninterested in privatisation. The pork barrel politics of survival during Aquino regime was responsible for negative political will for privatisation.

Effective *political will* has been an important factor responsible for rapid rate of privatisation in some of the ASEAN countries including Singapore and Malaysia (Milne, 1991, pp. 329-32). In the case of Malaysia, the agenda for privatisation was close to the heart of the Prime Minister, Dr. Mahathir Mohamad. When a government does not want privatisation of a particular public enterprise, it brings in the excuses of *national interest* and/or *strategic issues* involved (Milne, 1991, p. 324). This happened in the cases of non-privatisation of Philippine National Oil Corporation, and many state enterprises of Indonesia in 1989. In Indonesia, privatisation process is often stalled by the government because the prospective buyers are less-wanted or unwanted rich Chinese business people. Thus, in many countries, and on many occasions, the government may or may not want privatisation for certain stated or unstated reasons or motives.

Another pressure group which has an important direct or indirect role to play in the privatisation is bureaucracy (and top managerial personnel). In general, the bureaucrats are not interested in losing their empires, the control over the public enterprises, which have traditionally remained their citadel of power, prestige and patronage. These enterprises are valuable sources of *rent-seeking* activities. Bureaucratic resistance has been primarily responsible for delays in privatisation in Thailand, Indonesia and Philippines (Milne, 1991, p. 326). In the case of Singapore, the bureaucrats who were in Boards of government enterprises had also disapproved of privatisation at the first instance. In Malaysia too, bureaucracy in general does not have much commitment towards privatisation. But in Singapore and Malaysia, governments being very strong, the bureaucrats lose in the power war with ministers and politicians. In Malaysia, in particular, bureaucracy is too weak to go against the government on any issue whatsoever. Thus, it had to support privatisation process from the outset.

From the foregoing, it becomes clear that the whole process and speed of privatisation in the ASEAN have been considerably influenced by the interactions of a system of *political duopoly* where the government (including politicians and ministers) and bureaucrats are the two main players. The duopoly may be collusive or non-collusive in nature. When both the players agree or disagree jointly to privatisation, the duopoly becomes collusive. But when their interests are diametrically opposite, the duopoly becomes non-collusive. As a matter of fact, the nature of political duopoly has its bearing on the tempo of privatisation. A study of the privatisation process in the ASEAN reveals that there are three distinct interactive political duopoly models of privatisation, and they have their own impact on its progress (vide the chart).

Political Duopoly Models of Privatisation

Model	Country	Nature of Political Interaction	Effect on Privatisation
I	Singapore	Government Proposes Bureaucracy Opposes (**Non-Collusive Duopoly**)	Progressive
II	Malaysia	Government Proposes Bureaucracy Proposes (**Collusive Duopoly**)	Very Progressive
III	Philippines Thailand Indonesia	Government Opposes Bureaucracy Opposes (**Collusive Duopoly**)	Very Slow and Regressive

WHAT IS PRIVATISATION?

The term privatisation is indeed very omnibus. On the one extreme, it may mean denationalisation, and on the other, it may constitute any reform towards marketisation of any government operation. However, although the concept is imprecise, it has at least the following ten applicable connotations:

i) Divestment or sale of government corporate assets including land and property.

ii) At least 50 per cent government shares are sold to private shareholders.

iii) Commercialisation i.e. application of the laws of market.

iv) Corporatisation i.e. changing the legal status of a government organisation to that of a limited liability company.

v) Sale of a government company either partly or wholly in terms of equities.

vi) Privatisation of financing of public goods. The construction and maintenance of, say, overhead bridges may be entrusted to private companies which will charge user fees or levies on the consumers.

vii) Contracting out services to private companies.

viii)Granting of licences, and franchises to private companies for production and/or distribution.

ix) Private sector participation in production, financing or distribution of state-owned enterprises; and

x) Deregulation and liberalisation of processes and procedures.

The nature of the economy, the stage of economic development, the objectives and methods of industrialisation, and similar other factors are important for the choice of the mode of privatisation. Many countries initially approached privatisation through liberalisation (introduction of competition) and deregulation. The ASEAN countries started the exercise on experimental basis by first privatising the small and strategically less important enterprises which were sick and inefficient. Let us have a look now at the broad spectrum of the philosophy and mode of privatisation of five ASEAN economies.

CHOICES OF MODES OF PRIVATISATION

There are indeed many modes of privatisation including divestment or outright sales of public enterprises, joint ventures, management buying out, catering out services, private financing, leasing, franchising and so on.

The choice of the candidates for privatisation is indeed a difficult matter, and is based more on political rather than on economic considerations. However, a few general observations from the ASEAN can be briefly presented here. *First*, privatisation has mainly been introduced in those public sector enterprises which have been running on losses, and are regarded as liabilities. The mode chosen is generally divestment or outright sale. *Second*, divestment has been chosen as the appropriate mode for those enterprises which involve negligible social welfare consideration, and minimum legal impediments or problems. *Third*, strong measures of privatisation, like liquidation and sale, have often been practised in those cases which are not strategic, or which are unimportant from the point of view of national security. *Fourth*, new areas of development or experimentation in cases like transportation, highways, and so on, involving huge lump sum investment have often entrusted entirely to the private sector. However, the government does have some equity participation. *Fifth*, a government often resorts to modes like catering out, licensing, management buy out or financing from the private sector mainly for (i) enhancing efficiency and (ii) relieving its financial burden.

In the early eighties, when the wave of privatisation surcharged the ASEAN economies, many governments became very cautious economically and politically to introduce privatisation. As a first step, they privatised on experimental basis the small enterprises employing only a small number of people and applying simple technique of production. It was thought that privatisation of such enterprises would be safe from political and economic stand points.

Market structure has remained important in the matter of privatisation decision (Bishop and Kay, 1988). Privatisation involves many types and conditions of market organisation and structure. *First*, privatisation has been initially introduced in those lines of business where market fully works, but, the government does not want to compete with the private sector which perhaps is more efficient. Singapore is a classic example of this point. *Second*, there are areas in the government sector which cannot be, or, are not being run on commercial principles. As a result of absence of laws of market, the government is running at a loss, and the financial burden of the government is mounting up. The privatisation of Postal Services or Electricity Generation and Supply are cases in point in Malaysia. *Lastly*, privatisation has also been introduced in those state enterprises in the ASEAN countries, where market failure became conspicuous in the forms of monopoly, public goods and so on. The examples are North-South High Way and Telecommunications privatisation in Malaysia. The idea of privatisation in such cases is primarily based on the belief that it will give way to more and more competition in the system which can apply the principle of *allocative efficiency*.

IMPLICATIONS AND EFFECTS OF PRIVATISATION

It has been argued by many that privatisation has led to higher productivity, enhanced efficiency, lower cost of production and higher profit. For instance, Tan (1991, pp. 12-15) and Md. Sheriff (1991, pp. 186-88) argue that privatisation has been highly beneficial for a country like Malaysia, in the sense that it has raised efficiency through competition (as in the case of TV3 in Malaysia), reduced turn around time (as in KCT) and led to detailed billing and introduction of new services and products (as in Telecom. Malaysia). In many cases, privatisation has been responsible for better engineering efficiency implying an ability to produce more output with lesser inputs, and because of higher efficiency, more resources could be realised for higher production.

However, one can well argue that simple transfer of ownership from the public to the private sector does not automatically generate higher efficiency. Enhanced allocative and productive efficiency may be the result of increased competition, better utilisation of resources, better supervision and control. Privatisation generates some incentives for both the owners and workers which may ultimately be responsible for increased efficiency.

The introduction of the laws of motion of competition helps to do away with many growth-retarding factors, such as, procrastination, rigidities, inelasticities, regulatory tentacles and so on which are responsible for economic slowdown, escalation of costs, and supply constraints. The introduction of market principles in privatised industries is also helpful for reducing cost, wastage and delay. Enhanced competition through privatisation is one of the main factors responsible for increased efficiency. For instance, deregulation in the Indonesian banking sector has made it more competitive, viable and efficient. But at the same time, too much of freedom has landed them into trouble arising out of non-performing loans, as became apparent during the financial crisis of Indonesia in 1997.

It is often argued that privatisation has reduced the administrative and financial burden of the government, and has also diminished the size of the public sector. To many political economists, the reduced role of government in the matter of *social reproduction* is not a salutary sign in a developing economy. The reduced role of government will imply minimisation of social welfare. As a matter of fact, in many ASEAN countries, people have the feeling that privatisation has indeed reduced the burden of the government, but it has increased the burden of the consumers (Ghosh, 1998).

Privatisation might have increased individual economic efficiency to some extent, but it has reduced social efficiency. The cost of the increased efficiency has been too high in terms of market price. The common people are to pay unreasonably higher prices and higher tariffs even for public utilities.

Moreover, it is strongly felt that privatisation in many cases has not led to more competition, but it has generated monopoly power in the hands of a few joint owners of privatised utilities like Telecom and Electricity Generation. Privatisation has indeed converted public monopoly into private monopoly. And the growth of *crony capitalism* is said to be one of the direct consequences of privatisation where the benefits are enjoyed by the relatives and friends of political bosses. In the matter of allocation of shares or granting of contracts, favouritism and nepotism are alleged to have been shown to close political associates and/or blood relations. Political cronyism has been alleged in the cases of Philippines, Malaysia and Indonesia (Ng & Toh, 1992, p. 64).

PRIVATISATION IN THE ASEAN

Indonesia

The progress of privatisation is very slow and not very satisfactory in Indonesia. Bureaucracy is very strong, and it wants the power of control and supervision on the privatised enterprises. Moreover, the enculturated philosophy of socialistic pattern of society stands in the way of large scale privatisation. Many of the state enterprises reveal economic inefficiency, high cost of production and surplus labour. These enterprises, need privatisation; but the road to it is not very clear as yet.

Deregulations and reforms have been suggested as remedial measures from the early eighties. Deregulation measures which were implemented in the later part of eighties included simplification of customs, substitution of tariff for non-tariffs barriers, removal of restrictions on capacity expansion, and simplification of licensing requirements (Pangestu, 1991).

Full scale privatisation was not implemented because of the fear that the local Chinese businessmen and foreigners would buy the industries, and the economic power relations would get distorted. Thus, instead of privatisation, reforms were proposed for various ailing public enterprises. The reforms and deregulations were attempted side by side for the best results. Deregulation of the financing sector was carried on vigorously in the early nineties. But paradoxically, in spite of deregulation, government control became more stringent on the financial sector. As a matter of fact, bureaucratic control has been one of the major factors responsible for the slow progress of privatisation in Indonesia. But despite such controls and deregulations, the performance of the financial sector has remained rather shoddy, and became responsible to some extent for the financial crisis of 1997.

Since the financial crisis of the late nineties, the IMF has been pressing very hard for full scale privatisation of the economy as a pre-condition for the bail out. It is expected that political changes at the high level that have recently taken place in the country will bring about some ideological changes in the matter of economic organisation of industries. There are many instances where public will in the country has revealed its preference for full scale privatisation. The public will may now take precedence over the will of the bureaucrats.

Thus, the post-crisis period may see the flowering of privatisation in Indonesia in the real sense of the term.

Malaysia

Privatisation in both quantitative and qualitative terms has remained very overwhelming in Malaysia (Ng and Toh, 1992, p. 49). Privatisation in Malaysia has been guided by two main considerations. *First*, resource crunch of the government, and *second*, the desire to introduce more and more competition in the economy. There was also the need to reduce the participatory role of state in economic activities so that the private sector can assume greater opportunities for the management of production activities with better efficiency. In Malaysia, guidelines to privatisation were drawn up in 1985 for full scale privatisation to provide dynamism in the economy.

The concept of privatisation that was introduced in Malaysia was indeed very broad. It included management buy-out, contracting out services, leasing, deregulation and debureaucratisation. The whole idea was to introduce corporate culture and ethos in the economy. The techniques of privatisation encompassed both divestiture and non-divestiture programmes. The divestiture exercise which constituted floating of equities of some state-owned enterprises was undertaken in the cases of telecommunications, electricity generation, shipping, airlines operations, postal services and some cement companies.

Privatisation in Malaysia was designed to redistribute wealth and income through allocation of 30 per cent of equities to the *Bumiputras*. A certain percentage of shares was also reserved for the employees, and the remaining shares were sold to the public. Privatisation has also been introduced in the television industry for the sake of competition. Subsequently, privatisation practice has also been extended in the areas of tertiary education through the opening of private educational institutions, and twining programmes with foreign universities. The state universities are now being gradually corporatised. Malaysia's public health services are also being slowly privatised (Ghosh, 1999). The National Heart Institute has already been privatised, and for other state-run hospitals, the practice of catering out services is being introduced in the country. With the adoption of *Privatisation Master Plan*, the process of privatisation is to continue in Malaysia on regular basis to relieve the financial burden of the government. However, it is believed that as the tempo of privatisation increases, the role and power of the state will gradually diminish in the country.

Philippines

The basic objective of privatisation in Philippines was to relieve the financial burden of the government imposed by dodo units of public enterprises. It also aimed at the realisation of maximum cash by selling non-performing assets. The Asset Privatisation Trust (APT) was entrusted with the task of identifying the non-performing government assets which could be sold out to the private enterprises. The APT was mainly responsible for preparing the broad guidelines for privatisation in the Philippines.

The privatisation programme encompassed (i) the disposal of some government corporations, (ii) divesting selected public enterprises to the private sector, and (iii) disposal of some 400 non-performing government assets. Privatisation was regarded as a means to rehabilitate Philippines National Bank and Development Bank which were burdened with non-performing assets.

The Committee on Privatisation (COP) had the responsibility of finding out the suitable ways and means for privatisation. The COP initially recommended for the disposition of 296 public corporations in the following ways: 31 for retention, 140 for privatisation, 45 for regularisation, 15 for consolidation with other government departments and 65 for abolition (Godinez, 1989, p. 270).

The scheme of privatisation included a wide range of activities such as auction and bidding, sale of corporate shares to employees, floatation of shares, negotiated sales, direct debt buyout and so on. Divestment procedure depended on a number of considerations inclusive of the size and nature of the enterprise, the nature of assets, and so on. The process of privatisation is rather slow in the Philippines. The aim that was first set out was that privatisation exercise was to be completed by the end of 1991. But a mid-term report in 1990 pointed out that the progress was very slow due to political uncertainty, natural calamities, weak capital market situation and so on (Low, 1991, p. 36).

A number of factors has slowed down the privatisation process in Philippines. Among the factors, more important were perhaps the disagreements in the government departments, conflicting policies, bureaucratic (and managerial) oppositions, and above all, lack of effective political will and the like. President Aquino was not personally interested in implementing the policy of privatisation. In fact, it is said that she never liked to lead anything, but preferred to follow only. Things did not improve much during the period of President Ramos either. The same old impediments seem to be the formidable constraints even for the present president.

Singapore

The concept of privatisation that is applied in the case of Singapore is the concept of divestment. The Public Sector Divestment Committee proposed divestment of many government companies in Singapore in 1987. The process of divestment involved government companies selling a portion of their equities to various non-government institutions and private companies.

There were various objectives behind privatisation in the case of Singapore. The following were the major objectives:

i)   To withdraw the state from the mundane commercial activities.

ii)   To reduce or stop competition with the private sector.

iii)   To make the stock market broader, more efficient and open to other participating countries.

iv)   To expand the private sector for more competitive efficiency.

v)   To reduce to its minimum the impact of crowding out of private investment from the competitive sector.

Privatisation in Singapore is being performed with a number of asymmetrical exercises. *First*, in some cases of strategic industries like defence, privatisation exercise has been altogether assumed away. *Second*, in the case of some big companies, such as, petrochemical industries, the government's stake in equity has been completely divested. And *lastly*, for important public utilities like Telecom, the government has been proceeding with utmost circumspection, as these involve huge lumpy investment and enormous public concern. In the case of public utilities, like Telecom, it is likely that these industries would retain monopoly status. Therefore, the government wants to have some regulatory control over the public utilities after their privatisation. The government also would like to hold the majority stake in these crucial industries.

It is heartening to note that the government wants to have substantial decision-making power in the strategic privatised industries, and also in those industries which yield externalities. In this context, it is necessary to know the role of the government. In a country like Singapore, the government will have a dualistic role in the face of privatisation. Its role has been reduced in the cases of complete state withdrawal and divestment through non or less participation in production/distribution activities; but in some other cases of privatisation of nationally important and strategic industries, its role has considerably gone up. Whereas the reduced role of the state can be seen in the cases of contracting out services (as in Civil Aviation Services), its heightened role can be observed in nationally strategic industries and public utilities. The state continues to reinvest in many priority areas.

In the realm of *social reproduction* like public health and education, privatisation involves financial but not production activities. Thus, these services after privatisation have shown escalated fees and reduced government subsidies. As a matter of fact, some public utilities after privatisation have ceased to be *public goods* but are emerging as *private goods*.

Thailand

In Thailand, privatisation has been primarily regarded as an attempt to reform the public enterprises. Privatisation in Thailand has taken many forms, such as, sale and liquidation of public enterprises, joint ventures, contracting out, franchising, leasing, and liberalisation (Dhirataykinant, 1991, p. 687). Liberalisation incorporates the notion that public enterprise can be granted more flexibility in decision-making. Thus, a change in the price policy (say) towards full cost pricing can be treated as a privatisation measure. However, in many cases of public enterprises, the existing rules and regulations have not been substantially changed.

The concept of privatisation includes any and every attempt to improve the efficiency of the public sector enterprises. There were in the late eighties at least 25 per cent of the public enterprises which were running into losses and which needed privatisation. Privatisation was introduced in the early years of the Fifth National Development Plan (1982-86). And by the end of the Fifth Plan, 31 small scale public enterprises had been privatised through various ways, including franchising, leasing and sale of equities. Nearly two dozen public enterprises were subsequently liquidated through the sale of shares. Another form of privatisation in Thailand was the participation of the private sector in the management of some inefficient public enterprises. Franchising has been practised in many cases including the catering services of State Railways of Thailand, The Port Authority of Thailand, and Bangkok Mass Transit Organisation. Another mode of popular privatisation has been contracting out services. This mode has been used in the Telephone Organisation of Thailand, Bangkok Mass Transit Organisation, and Electricity Generating Authority of Thailand, among others.

The public enterprises which are regarded as prime candidates for privatisation are basically those which have been running on losses. The Sixth National Economic and Social Plan made it abundantly clear that if public enterprises have continually failed in their operation, they will be the prime candidates for liquidation or sale to the private sector. It is the policy of the government to retain those public enterprises which need huge financial resources and sophisticated technology. It will also retain welfare-oriented, and *cash cow* enterprises from being privatised. But public enterprises in the categories of manufacture, trade and services will be subjected to privatisation, sooner or later.

Government policy advocates strong measures of privatisation for those state enterprises which are not related to national security. The strong measures are liquidation and sale. Weak measures are adopted for other categories of public enterprises. However, so far, only a few public enterprises have been subjected to strong measures. In the same way, divestiture as mode has been very rarely applied in the country. Even the weak measures have not been consistently pursued in Thailand. The whole privatisation exercise in Thailand seems to be half-hearted and non-serious. Some of the loss-making enterprises have been conveniently forgotten, and the legal aspect of privatisation has not yet been given the seriousness that it deserves.

CONTEMPORARY ISSUES AND CHALLENGES

Much of the problematics of privatisation arises partly out of its deleterious effects. Labour unions in many countries, particularly in labour-abundant economies, are not happy about privatisation. The unions feel that privatisation, which essentially will take resort to more capital-intensive method of production, will lead to more unemployment, reduced wage level and diminished bargaining power of the workers. And because of all these, the working class feels that it is becoming more marginalised as a result of privatisation. Thus, though privatisation has improved efficiency in some fields of production, it is alleged to have brought about more social inequalities. The trade-off has been more unfavourable to the working class. It would be indeed a challenge to establish a socially acceptable balance between equity and efficiency. As a matter of fact, labour opposition in many countries like India, Thailand and Malaysia has been the factor for delayed privatisation. In Malaysia, labour, of course, has been given the assurance about their job security, wage protection and sharing of the gains of privatisation.

Simmering discontent is being voiced in many ASEAN countries about the *price effect* of privatisation. In a bid to maximise profit through *surplus extraction*, prices of privatised products and services have been escalating in many industries. This has led to the loss of consumers' surplus, and allocative inefficiency, as price is fixed much above the marginal cost. It is, therefore, a challenge for the privatised industry to maintain a fine balance between consumers' satisfaction with respect to price and quality, and economic efficiency.

In many countries, the legal aspects of privatisation have not been studied in details, and the need for legal changes required to streamline the activities of privatisation has not been properly appreciated. The problem is very acute in Thailand where old laws and rules have been grossly neglected, and new rules have been conveniently superimposed (Dhiratayakinant, 1991, p. 718). The result has been a complete chaos: different officials are interpreting laws differently according to their own whims and convenience, and managerial activities and decision-making processes are to suffer thereby.

Managerial acumen necessary for efficiently managing the privatised industries is indeed very limited in the ASEAN countries: the supply curve of good managers is highly inelastic. Shortages of managers are not only a quantitative but also a qualitative problem. The shortage of managerial personnel is a challenging issue for the success of privatisation in the ASEAN.

As a matter of fact, privatisation was initiated in the ASEAN countries to mitigate partly *government failures* in providing goods and services efficiently at reasonable prices through a competitive system. The introduction of more and more competition was essential to break public sector monopoly through privatisation. However, unfortunately, in many countries, privatisation has resulted in the concentration of market power, allocative inefficiency and monopoly. And all these have created a syndrome of *market failure*. Successful policy of regulation and control of monopoly and prices will, therefore, be a real challenge in the near future. The tension between government failure and market failure in some lines of business activities is perhaps the most dominant issue in the political economy of privatisation in the ASEAN today.

REFERENCES

Bishop, M. and Kay, J. (1988), *Does Privatisation Work? Lessons from the UK*, London Business School, London.

Bowie, Alasdair and Unger, Daniel (1997), *The Politics of Open Economies*, Cambridge University Press, Cambridge.

Dhiratayakinant, K. (1991), "Privatisation of Public Enterprises: The Case of Thailand" in Geeta Gouri (ed.), *Privatisation and Public Enterprise*, Oxford and IBH Publishing Co., New Delhi, 1991.

Ghosh, B.N. (1998), *Malaysia: The Transformation Within*, Longman, Kuala Lumpur.

Ghosh, B.N. (1999), *The Three Dimensional Man: Human Resource Development in Malaysia* (f.c.).

Godinez, Z.F. (1989), "Privatization and Deregulation in the Philippines" in Ng and Wagner (eds.), op.cit.

Low, Linda (1991), *The Political Economy of Privatization in Singapore*, McGraw Hill Book Co., Singapore.

Md. Sheriff (1991), "Privatisation", in Lee, K.H. and Nagraj, S. (eds.), *The Malaysian Economy Beyond 1990*, Persatuan Ekonomi Malaysia, Kuala Lumpur.

Milne, R.S. (1991), "The Politics of Privatisation in the ASEAN States", *ASEAN Economic Bulletin*, Vol. 7, No. 3.

Ng, Chee Yuen & Toh, Kin Woon (1992), "Privatization in the Asia-Pacific Region", *Asian Pacific Economic Literature*, Vol. 6, No. 2.

Ng, Chee Yuen and Wagner, N. (1989) (eds.), "Privatisation and Deregulation in ASEAN", *ASEAN Economic Bulletin*, March, Vol. V, No. 3.

Pangestu, Mari (1991), "The Role of the Private Sector in Indonesia", *The Indonesian Quarterly*, No. 1.

Tan, C.H. (1991), "Privatisation in Malaysia and Singapore: A Comparison", *Journal of Southeast Asian Business*, Vol. VII, No. 2.

Chapter 2

PRIVATISATION: THEORY, PRACTICES AND ISSUES

*G.S. Gupta**

INTRODUCTION

Most countries in the world today are mixed economies, where public and private sectors co-exist. The public sector comprises of administrative departments (like agriculture, industry, commerce, finance, human resource development, defence, law, etc.), department enterprises (like railways, postal and radio telecommunications, and television broadcasting, ordnance factories, etc.) and public sector enterprises (PSEs) (like oil companies, airlines and several other essential goods-producing firms). These enterprises are managed by the Central Government, State and Union Territories government, as well as at the local government levels. While the central government runs enterprises in many activities, the state department enterprises are mostly confined to road

* The paper is a revised version of the one presented as an invited paper at the national workshop on Economic Liberalisation: Consumer, Investor and Environment interests, conducted by the Consumer and Education Research Centre, Ahmedabad during November 1-3, 1996. The author is grateful for useful suggestions from the workshop participants.

transportation, electricity, education and health. The department enterprises of local bodies are mostly concerned with road transportation, water supply and maintenance of roads. Besides these, there are public sector banks, government owned long-term financial institutions, and regulating organisation (like RBI, DFHI, SEBI, etc.) which govern both the public and private enterprises under their jurisdiction. These departments/organisations thus regulate the economy, and provide goods and services to the people.

In consequence to the declared policy of the "socialist pattern of society", and the resultant emphasis on equity, poverty eradication, employment generation, and development, the public sector has expanded significantly until the Reagan-Thatcher era of supply side economics. In India, for example, besides the large number of huge administrative departments and departmental enterprises, insurance, banking and financial institutions, there are 245 central PSEs and over 1,000 state level PSEs in India. In 1993-94, they together accounted for about 29% of GDP at factor cost, 42% of the country's gross capital formation, and only 1.23% of our gross savings. During 1994-95, the central PSEs alone had Rs.1,61,311 crores worth of capital employed and net profit of Rs.7,214 crores, yielding a return (ROI) of only 4.47%, even less than the interest rate cost. Their gross sales during that year stood at Rs.1,87,126 crores, with gross total assets of Rs.3,33,355 crores, resulting into an asset turnover ratio of just 0.53. The data on state level public enterprises (SLPEs) are available only with a lag. Though their number is larger than the central PSEs, capital invested in them is even less than 50% of the latter. As on March 31, 1992, there were 954 SLPEs, excluding the state electricity boards and state transport corporations, and their investment was around Rs.38,000 crores. Barring a few exceptions, the net profit from all SLPEs in each state has been negative. Malaysia's industrial progress accelerated with the emergence of non-financial public enterprizes (NFPEs) during the 1970s. Investments in the new projects of the NFPEs were considerably substantial such that the country became one of the largest NFPEs sectors amongst non-socialist economies. Public investment surged to about 17.7% of GNP during 1971-80, compared to only 9.9% during 1966-70. The global recession of the early 1980s caused sizeable current account deficits and the government revenue could no longer sustain the high rate of public investment. Total investment reached a substantial 35.7% of GNP during 1981-85, with public investment accounting for about 17.6%.

The PSEs are spread in practically all kinds of manufacturing as well as service sectors, ranging from vegetable oils to steel making and from hoteling to air transport services. While many of these were initially found in the public sector, several of these were acquired due to a range of reasons, including sickness in the private sector and the lack of an appropriate exit policy. While some of the PSEs are operating in the monopolistic market, the others are dealing in fairly competitive markets. Among the former, some are "natural monopolies", the rest are created through artificial barriers. These are run both on commercial as well as non-commercial motives.

Public sector exists in all countries but its relative size varies significantly across the world. An examination of the data would reveal that the big state ownership and the low growth rate tend to move together. For example, PSEs account for about 18% of output in Africa, their share is around 13% in low income countries, 10% in Asia, and 5% in industrialised countries. In Africa, PSEs account for about 28% of all capital formation, 17% of the total credit, and 16% of the labour force, in contrast to 21%, 10% and 3%, respectively in middle income developing economies, which include the Asian tigers.

The philosophy of the "socialist pattern of society" has produced an economy which is experiencing many economic ills. These include large unemployment (in the midst of many vacancies), severe poverty, sizeable income inequalities across regions and households, significant price fluctuations both of goods and stocks, fiscal deficits, trade deficits, large external debt, fluctuating growth, etc. These ills have provided some evidence against our ideology of promoting the public sector. Besides, there is a world wide trend towards privatisation, popularised by Margaret Thatcher since 1979 and Ronald Reagan since 1981. In addition, the World Bank and IMF are prescribing privatisation as the most powerful medicine to the economic ills of all less developed countries (LDCs). All these developments have prompted our policy-makers to move towards privatisation.

THEORY

What is privatisation? It means rolling back the government role in the economy. This can be attempted through various approaches, viz.

- True privatisation
- Proxy/cold privatisation
- Green field privatisation

The first approach includes transfer of ownership from the public (anonymous bureaucrats and politicians) to the private (known individuals) hands through either sales of assets or of equity shares, contracting out some of the activities of PSEs to private parties, and closure of PSEs. Under the second method, either a Memorandum of Understanding (MOUs) is signed between the government and the PSE management, where in the management is made free from the government controls but it is expected to perform as per the agreed understandings, or an erstwhile departmental run PSE is corporatised. Under the third method, an erstwhile reserved industry/sector is declared open for the private sector and the regulations like licensing, entry conditions, etc. are relaxed. Thus, the various approaches to privatisation vary in terms of the degree to which they mean privatisation.

Privatisation is known by different names around the world. For example, it is called "de-nationalisation" in U.K., "dis-incorporation" in Mexico, "prioritisation" in Australia, "asset sales program" in New Zealand, "transformation" in Thailand, "people-isolation" in Sri Lanka, and "dis-investment" in Pakistan.

Why privatisation? There are several theories, not mutually exclusive, of privatisation. These include

- Efficiency (in production)
- Property rights/Incentives
- Contestability
- Human Capital
- Technology/Innovation

- Opportunities to individuals
- Fiscal dimensions
- Fiscal support
- Poor performance of PSEs
- Focus

Under PSEs, there is a dichotomy between the owner (The President / King of the country) and the management (floating bureaucrats and politicians). The property rights theory argues that the non-owner management have poor incentives to perform as compared to the owner management. In a recent interview to Business Today (Oct. 1996), Mr. Russy Mody, Chairman, Air India and Indian Airlines, had this to say: "I see a history of mismanagement. Rather a situation where there is no accountability, no punishments, no rewards, no participation, no performance ...... the problem is not one of inferior quality of personnel .... what is different is the work ethos, and that has to do with several factors. The first is that of ownership....... "

The contestability theory, advanced by Prof. W.J. Baumol in 1982, argues that the production efficiency is more under competition than under monopoly. In particular, monopoly leads to "dead weight loss" to the society:

Figure 1: Dead Weight Loss Under Monopoly

Q_M = Monopoly output
Q_C = Competitive output
P_M = Monopoly price
P_C = Competitive price
_ABC = dead weight loss

However, privatisation does not always mean competition. For example, if the Ahmedabad Electricity Company is bought by Torrent, it would mean no competition. Also, competition would be missing even if more than one firm exists if all of them collude either through a cartel or tacit understanding. The possibility for such a collusion would be high if the product is standard. It is the fear of excess capacity, i.e. fear of not getting enough customers, which exist only if there are other competing suppliers either of the same product or of close substitute products, which forces the firm to care for the quality and the affordable price to consumers, which, in tern, guarantees the production efficiency (P=MC).

The human capital rationale for privatisation suggests that in the public sector, recruitments are based more on political acceptance than on skills, while quite the opposite is the case in the private sector. If so, PSEs have less efficient (and excess) personnel than the private sector enter prises. The innovation theory is advanced on the ground that the new technology is infused and new markets are found easily by multinationals, and so they must be encouraged. Privatisation is also recommended on the ground of providing greater choice and opportunities for the private enterprises so as to encourage private investment and thereby foster economic growth. In U.K., one of the key objectives of privatisation was to create capital assets for middle class households, thus creating a large constituency for privatisation. Many people have argued that the public sector has become so large that the government is unable to manage them. Thus, a focus on selected enterprises/sectors is desirable. The poor performance of PSEs is yet another cause of worry. Though there is no solid proof that performance is subject to ownership, yet many people argue for privatisation even on this count. The last but not the least reason for privatisation is the need for funds by the government to honour its other commitments/priorities, including infrastructure investments, debt-servicing, rural development, poverty alleviation programmes, etc. and to reduce fiscal deficit.

There are theories against privatisation as well. These include the principle of equity, public good and the last resort. The private owners of enterprises are often the wealthy individuals and they tend to add more and more wealth overtime through their organisations. The proportion of non-owners is rather large, and they tend to suffer due to private ownership of enterprises. Also, private enterprises usually set high (profit-maximising) prices and thus the benefits of their products may not be available to poor sections of the society. For this reason, allocative efficiency is more under public sector than under the private sector. Also, due to the sheer size of non-owners, privatisation programme is socially and politically difficult to implement.

The theory of public goods, goods which are non-rival and non-exclusive in consumption (like national defence, justice, national broadcastings over radio and television, pollution control, public roads, etc.), suggests that these goods must be supplied by the government only. Even the chief proponent of laissez-faire, Adam Smith, argued for these goods to remain under the public domain. The principle of last resort suggests that if some private firm is sick and cannot be closed due to the absence of an exit policy, it has to be nationalised.

There is a theory (natural monopoly) which recommends monopoly over any other form of market structure. Natural monopoly exists when there are significant economies of scale over the range of output, which is sufficient to cater to all demands for that product. Such a situation arises when there are large fixed costs (even sunk costs) and small average variable cost. Examples of products enjoying natural monopoly include public utilities, like water, gas, power, communication, sanitation, roads and means of transportation. In fact, such products have to be not only produced by a single firm but also will have to be subsidized lest they lead to inefficient production (P>MC) and the dead weight loss to the society. If a natural monopolist is the private firm, then the government must regulate it such that the maximum price for its product is set equal to its marginal cost and then it is provided a subsidy equal to its loss (= □ P_c BAC).

Figure 2: Regulation of Natural Monopoly

While the public sector route was initially adopted for natural monopolies in Britain and other European countries, the strategy of regulated monopoly was followed in the United States.

It is argued that competition could be infused even in some of the natural monopoly's products through sub-dividing their products. For example, electricity generation, transmission and distribution could be separated, and if so, electricity generation is not subject to natural monopoly. Similarly, railway track operation, passenger transport and goods transport could be separated, and then the latter two components are free of natural monopoly. By the same reasoning, ports operation and sea transport, airports operation and air transport could be bifurcated and thereby part of these activities may be made free of natural monopoly. Incidentally, note that if an activity is divided by region, there may be need to cross subsidize the operations in the non-profitable regions by those in the profitable ones.

PRACTICES

Nationalisation was the popular strategy until the late Seventies. Britain took the lead in privatisation in 1979 and many countries followed her in due course. About 10,000 enterprises are reported to have been privatised around the world.

"From the modest start with a small number of British Petroleum shares in 1979, to the major privatisations of seven years later, the programme climbed an exponential curve on which each year's sales figures easily dwarfed those of the previous year. The sequence which included British Gas in December 1986, British Airways in February 1987, Rolls Royce in June 1987 and British Airports Authority in July 1987 saw the privatisation of many important sections of the public sector within the space of eight months" (Pirie, page 255). Telecommunication (1984), the water industry (1989), electricity (1990), etc. have also been privatised. It is estimated that the British treasury raised £65 billion through these processes, which would have eased its fiscal position considerably.

Outside of Britain, privatisation has made good progress in Asia. In Sri Lanka, Ceylon Transport Board has been privatised, some sick textile mills have been sold, National Milk Board has been corporatised, State Fertilizer Corp., Tobacco Industries Corp. and National packaging Materials Corp. have been dissolved, and so on. Similar has been the trend in Bangladesh, Pakistan, Malaysia, Singapore, New Zealand, Thailand, Russia, South Korea and Philippines. Several countries in Latin America have witnessed substantial privatisation. These include Costa Rica, Brazil, Mexico and Argentina. Many African countries have accepted the virtues of privatisation but they are still experiencing difficulties in its implementation. In the United States, privatisation has been extensive at local and state levels, though little progress has been achieved at the central government level. Many US cities contracted out many of their services to private parties. These include operation and management of hospitals, residential garbage collection, operation and maintenance of bus services, management of museums, parks, and swimming pools, repairing of roads, controlling traffic, providing ambulance service, etc. Some state governments have contracted out maintenance of prisons to private companies. De-regulation of various kinds have been introduced at all governments levels, including federal government.

In India, interest in privatisation program began ever since Shri Rajiv Gandhi assumed the prime ministership in October 1984 and its momentum was picked up with the New Industrial Policy of July 1991. Several PSEs have already been transferred to the private sector and the efforts are on for a few more. The former includes ACC Babcock, Allwyn Nissan, Auto Tractors, East Coast Breweries and Distilleries, Goa Telecommunications, Goa Time Movers, Haryana Breweries, Hindustan Allwyn's refrigeration division, Orissa Mining Corporation's charge chrome plant and Rajasthan State Tanneries. The latter consists of Indian Iron and Steel Company, Bharat Electronics Ltd., Scooters India, Great Eastern Hotel, and UP State Cement Corporation. Many state governments have contracted out bottling and/or transportation of raw-materials or finished goods to the private sector for their department run liquor production units. Some local governments have privatised cleanings of roads, providing street lights, etc.

The central government has so far conducted seven rounds of dis-investments in PSEs. The number of PSEs affected stand at 40 and the amount of money raised at Rs. 10,718 crores. This constitutes about 15% of the total shares of the 40 enterprises, and a mere 3% of the gross assets of the central PSEs. Due to lack of an exit policy, no PSE has been closed so far. However, as many as 59 central and 70 state PSEs have been referred to BIFR. 26 of these have been dismissed as non-maintainable, rehabilitation proposals have been sanctioned for 29, and two central and one state PSEs have been declared as no longer sick. Under the NRF, an amount of Rs. 542 crores was released during 1993-94 and Rs. 261 crores during 1994-95, and about 75,000 workers have opted for voluntary retirement under this scheme.

During 1994-95, 99 PSEs had signed MOUs. Of these 95 have turned in their self-evaluation, indicating better than the targeted performances. Some units, like Mahanagar Telephone Nigam Ltd. (MTNL) and Videsh Sanchar Nigam Ltd. (VSNL), have been corporatised. In July 1991, at one stroke, the reservation for public sector was reduced from 17 to 8 (and subsequently to 6) industries, all the remaining industries were de-licensed except 18 (subsequently, slashed to 14), and 34 industries (subsequently, included software industry also) were notified for 51% foreign equity participation and foreign technical know-how on automatic basis. Approvals for larger participation than 51% need processing through the Foreign Investment Promotion Board (FIPP) for case by case consideration. Even in reserved categories, some activities have been privatised. For example, in railways, catering and wagon ownership have been thrown open to the private sector. The Board of Industrial and Financial Reconstruction (BIFR) was established in 1987 and currently it is entrusted with the responsibility of examining the cases of sick industrial units both in the public as well as the private sector. The National Renewal Fund (NRF) was found in February 1992 to assist employees in re-training, re-deployment and counselling, and in funding voluntary retirements. A number of liberalisation schemes have been introduced in the financial sector, including the winding up of the Controller of Capital Issues and the permission of private banks through licensing from the Reserve Bank of India. In Malaysia, the privatisation programme has been implemented on a case to case basis. Malaysian Airline Systems (MAS) was privatised in 1985 and Malaysian International Shipping Corporation (MISC) in 1987, both through partial divestment of government equity via public issue. Sports Toto was privatised in 1985 through sale of 70% of its shares to two private companies. The North-South Highway and the Kuala Lumpur Roads and Interchanges were "contracted out" in 1988. TV3 was allowed to float in 1984 through private sector to compete with government owned TV1 and TV2. Proton was established in 1983 under the joint sector venture with two Mitsubishi companies. Syarikat Telekom Malaysia (STM) and Tenaga Nasional Bhd (TNB) were corporatised in early 1990s. The privatisation programme not only involved selling the nation's jewels but also speeding up of infrastructure development and yielding high corporate taxes. It is believed that privatisation has brought some advantages in terms of performances efficiency, competition and autonomy, and thereby the high rates of national savings and investment.

It is estimated that an amount of US $ 270 billion has been raised through privatisation through out the world during its first 15 years (1979-1994) and that, in general, the privatised units have improved their performances.

Thus, privatisation has been effected in various ways all over the world. It has generally resulted into improved profitability/product quality. However, it has not been without problems. The significant ones include

- Choice of PSEs for privatisation
- Opposition from employees
- Pricing of assets/equity
- Extent of dis-investment
- Mode/preference of selling
- Political instability

Efforts have been made and some progress has been achieved, but one doubts if a completely satisfactory solution will ever be found to these issues. In particular, overwhelming concerns are with regard to the foreign participation (especially in the consumer goods sector), dis-investments in favour of financial institutions rather than public, retention of management controls which is unlikely to lead to efficiency improvements, and the reversals of decisions by the prospects of new government. The experience suggests that it is easier to induct the private sector in new enterprises even if they are in the core or strategic area (e.g. refinery) but attempts to closure are opposed by employees.

Issues

Privatisation raises several issues, which can be grouped under two categories:

- Whether to privatise a particular industry/PSE?
- How to privatise the chosen industry/PSE?

The decision on de-reservation/delicensing of a particular industry hinges on the assessment of the significance of that industry in terms of its product in the economy, its price to the consumers, as well as on the nature and size of the economies of scale operating in that industry, among other factors. These factors are not easy to agree upon, and thus such decisions tend to be subjective/political. Incidentally, if dereservation is decided, government must ensure private participation lest the product disappear from the market (e.g. infrastructure). Also, if the de-reserved industry happens to be a natural monopoly, then private monopoly alone must be floated and well regulated lest it results into inefficient production and dead weight loss to the society. With regard to privatisation decision on a particular PSE, Dr. Prajapati Trivedi (1993) has suggested that a unit should be privatised if it is making loss, which is illegitimate (i.e. not due to price control), and it cannot be turned around under the public sector. However, it is not easy to decide on the turn aroundability of a firm. Further, if a PSE is making profit, it does not necessarily mean it is well managed and should not be privatised. If privatisation could lead to improved efficiency, it must be done. The experience suggests that privatisation is generally good. Pirie (1988) (p.255) has this to say: "The accumulated experience of privatisation in Britain has taught an important lesson: there is no part of the public sector which cannot be helped by privatisation".

Public goods have to remain in the public sector, while private goods can be considered for privatisation. However, it is not feasible to privatise all PSEs engaged in private goods production simultaneously. Thus, privatisation must follow some sequence. The Arjun Sengupta Committee (1986) had recommended the privatisation of the units in the non-core sector. May be such units could be taken up first. Thus, PSEs in the consumer goods sector could be recommended for immediate privatisation. Also, the ones running into heavy illegitimate losses could be privatised early, profit-making units could be privatised only under financial stringency. privatisation of manufacturing units could precede that of units rendering services, which may precede that of regulating bodies. There is no clear rational answer either to the question whether to privatise a unit or not or to the question of sequence to be followed. Thus, it lot depends on ideology, politics and above all on pragmatic considerations.

How to privatise? This raises several issues.

- Which approach is the best for which unit?
- Are various approaches substitutes/complementary?
- How to motivate politicians/ bureaucrats/ employees/ towards privatisation?
- When to sell assets/equity?
- How to value assets/equity?
- What % of equity to sell?
- Whom to sell: Home buyers, multinations, expatriates, NRIs?
- Does privatisation fetch sustainable revenue?
- How to close in the absence of exit policy/voluntary retirement scheme?
- How to sequence privatisation?
- Would dis-investment crowd out private investment?

There is no definite answer to any of these questions. However, certain suggestions have been advanced. MOU is recommended before putting up a unit for sale. Thus, MOUs and sales are considered complementary rather than alternatives for privatisation. South Korea has followed this practice in several cases. However, MOUs are not easy to design and implement. Selling out of large PSEs creates both political as well as economic problems. On the one hand, the powers of politicians and bureaucrats are axed and the fear is expressed in terms of loosening of social obligations. On the other hand, employees are scared of job losses, wage cuts and longer working hours, consumers are concerned about possible price hikes, the prospective buyers fear subsidy cuts, and the media is worried about loosing sensational news. Besides, the decisions on the timings of sale and the selling price of a unit are not easy to arrive, as the latter fluctuate overtime and is unpredictable.

Dis-investments have their own problems, like the pricing of the equity, method of marketing, and the extent of dis-investment. Stock prices of unlisted companies are not known and they are not easy to determine optimally. Market flotation of shares is possible for listed companies but the timing of flotation is crucial due to market fluctuations, which may be significant. Trial and error methods, multi-round dis-investments and selling to public institutions, etc. are resorted to absolve these problems. However, such acts are condemned as poor privatisation.

Contracting out of some activities raises the issue of deciding on the activity, its price, client, ensuring future quality, sustainability, etc.. The closure of PSEs requires exit policy, which does not exist. Corporatisation of otherwise departmental enterprises raises political issues, as it impinges on the powers of legislators and bureaucrats.

There is no consensus as to the buyer of assets/equity. The highest bidder cannot be the criterion. If it is the home buyer, he must be capable of running the unit successfully. If it is the foreign buyer, it must not make huge profits and take it to its home country. Some people have argued against selling assets to any one, including nationals. They say, it is like selling "family silver to pay for grocery". While selling yields revenue only once, owning provides income for ever.

Sequence of the privatisation programme is also not quite clear. While investors want blue chips, government desire to off-load sick units first. However, there is almost a consensus with regard to the core and non-core sectors, and industry, services and regulations. The recommendation is in favour of privatising non-core and the manufacturing units first, followed by services, and finally, if at all, consider entrusting private parties to regulate specific activities. Fear is also expressed if privatisation would crowd out the investment in new ventures by the private sector. Initially yes, but in the long-run, it will depend upon the profitability of the privatised units.

Thus, while privatisation may be a good strategy, it is neither a panacea for all troubles of PSEs nor it is easy to implement. Accordingly, it is both an economic as well as a political matter.

SUGGESTIONS AND CONCLUSIONS

Of the various forms of ownership, the government (public) ownership is under attack. Accordingly, the privatisation programme is well under way and it is already a source of major economic consequences. In all its varieties, it aims to improve the performance of PSEs. Unfortunately, there is no formula to choose the unit or the method of privatisation for the chosen unit. The experience suggests that each case is unique with regard to the product profile, efficiency level, interest group, etc. and requires a unique remedy. However, there is a general consensus that the sequence must proceed from monopolies to competitive units, from industries to utilities, and from there to services and regulatory bodies. The PSEs involved in the supply of social services and public goods should continue remaining in the public sector. Sick units in the private goods (e.g. textiles, hotels, transportation, etc.) market must be seriously considered for privatisation. MOUs may precede selling of assets. Globally successful privatisation has inevitably been preceded by the restructuring of PSEs through changes in management, technology and finance mix. Contracting out of more and more activities may be resorted to over time. Dis-investment of small fractions of equities could merely serve the purpose of funds, large fractions of equity needs to be sold out for ensuring improvements in efficiency. Selling of small proportions of equity is devoid of new (private) participation in management and thus significant dis-investments (51% or more) are recommended. The British government disinvested 51% of its equity from British Telecom in the first instance for this reason. Indian government has disinvested small proportions of equities and that too in favour of mostly financial institutions. This has hampered the development of capital market and creation of capital assets for middle class households. It is argued that dis-investment programme should be executed so as to encourage autonomy in management with accountability, broad-based ownership, and improved competition, and thence the increased profitability. The discounted cash flow (DCF) technique and/or the open tender system are recommended for valuation of assets/equity. Sick and non-turn-aroundable units have no alternative but to close down. The workers of such units must be re-trained for new jobs and/or compensated through the National Renewable Fund.

Political will, stability of the government, proper communications, and transparency in intentions and dealings will go a long way in providing the much needed impetus to the privatisation programme. Finally, it must be emphasised that the success of the privatisation programme hinges a great deal on the education of the masses, timely dialogues among the stake holders, and healthy development of the capital market, among other factors.

REFERENCES

Barberis, N. et. al. (1996): How Does Privatisation Work? Evidence from the Russian Shops, *Journal of Political Economy,* Vol. 104, No.4, pp. 764-91.

Business Today (1996): Privatisation Paradigms, Jan. 22-Feb.6, pp. 68-81.

Government of India, Ministry of Finance, Eco. Division, (1996): *Economic Survey 1995-96.*

Government of India, Min. of Industry, Dept. of Public Enterprises (1996): *Public Enterprises Survey 1994-95,* Vol. I.

Gupta, Anand P. (1996): Political Economy of Privatisation in India, *Economic and Political Weekly,* Sept. 28, pp. 2687-94.

Kalirajan, K.P. and Shand, R.J. (1996): Public Sector Enterprises in India, Is Privatisation the only Answer? *Economic and Political Weekly,* Sept. 28, pp. 2683-86.

Kumar, Suresh (1991): Issues in Privatisation - Indian Scenario, in Geeta Gouri, ed. *Privatisation and Public Enterprise, The Asia Pacific Experience,* Oxford, IBH, New Delhi, pp. 163-68.

Mani, Sunil (1995): Economic Liberalisation and the Industrial Sector, *Economic and Political Weekly,* May 27, pp. M-38-50.

Pirie, Madsen (1988): *Privatisation: Theory, Practice and Choice,* Wildwood House, London.

Snaker, T.L. and Reddy, Y.V. (1991): Privatisation of Activities and Enterprises in the Public Sector in India, in Geeta Gouri, ed. *Privatisation and Public Enterprise, The Asia Pacific Experience,* Oxford, IBH, New Delhi, pp. 547-81.

Syed Azizi Wafa and Mohamed Irshad (1997): Privatisation in Malaysia, in the Second Asian Academy of Management Conference Proceedings *Towards Management Excellence in the 21st Century Asia,* Universiti Sains Malaysia, Penang, pp. 181-195.

Trivedi, Prajapati (1993): What is India's Privatisation Policy?, *Economic and Political Weekly,* May 29, pp. M-71-76.

Chapter 3

PRIVATISATION EXPERIENCE IN INDONESIA

Mohamed Eliyas Hashim

INTRODUCTION

Since the mid 1980s, there has been significant redirection of economic policies in Asia Pacific region towards exposing the public sector to competition. This has been particularly evident among four members of ASEAN countries (Indonesia, Malaysia, the Philippines and Thailand) and the newly industrialised countries comprising South Korea, Taiwan and Singapore where increasing attention has been given to privatisation, deregulation and liberalisation

To push ahead with privatisation, committees to draw up guidelines and design master plans were set up within various countries in the region. In Singapore, a public sector divestment committee was established in January 1986 and was charged with the responsibility of formulating a program for the divestment of government linked companies and to make recommendations on the implementation of the program. In Malaysia, guidelines on privatisation were drawn up in 1985. Accordingly, the Fifth Malaysian Plan (1986-1990) gave a greater role to the private sector to provide dynamism in the economy. This was followed by the release of the country's privatisation master plan 1991 wherein the techniques of the privatisation were specified and the services and entities to be privatised and restructured identified. In the Philippines, the

Asset of Privatisation Trust was set up to divest a wide range of public enterprises; particularly those nationalised during the Marcos year. In Indonesia, the government has placed the main emphasis on deregulation rather than on disposing of assets.

In this paper I propose to describe the experience of privatization through the process of deregulation in Indonesia. In my approach, I will touch on the broader principles and not on particular companies due to lack of enough information. I will also touch on deregulation as a process toward privatisation in Indonesia.

BACKGROUND OF PRIVATIZATION IN INDONESIA

At the time of the independence, the Indonesian economy was characterized by imbalance in the allocation of the resources amongst various sectors – a situation inherited for the Dutch. The Sukarno administration, known as the old order of the government, was inspired by the socialist notion that central economic planning was the best policy direction (Ketu. T. Mardjana, 1993: 53). It was thought that state owned enterprises were the main instrument to achieve the national objective of the balanced economic development. The new order government president, Soeharto in 1969 introduced substantive liberalization of the economy including trade and industrial reforms. The policy approach adopted by the new order government contrasted sharply with heavily interventionist policies of the Sukarno government (Mari Pangestu, 1989: 219).

In 1982, there were 212 state-owned enterprises (SOEs) with the major sector being industry (54) agriculture (51) and finance (52). In terms of value added, the industrial (21 per cent) and financial sectors (43 per cent) dominate, whereas in terms of capital formation the highest share went to electricity, gas and water, industrial (26 per cent) and agricultural (11 per cent) sectors. The largest contributors to the project are finance (75 per cent) and the industry sectors (17 per cent). In contrast, in areas where the government participation declined, there has been a decline in budget allocation. In 1983 – 84, 22 per cent of the development budget was allocated to industry and mining sectors. The beginning of the rephrasing and postponing of the several projects in 1993 through austerity drive, government has reduced its role and by 1991 - 92, only

4 per cent of the development budget was allocated to this sector. Government capital participation was essentially government subsidies or funds used to finance state owned enterprises. The substantial decline in share and negative growth indicated government policy since the oil price decline to reduce subsidies to the state owned enterprises (Mari Pangestu, 1993: 253 - 265).

The overall performance of the SOEs has not been encouraging. The return on investment of SOEs has remained low and was estimated to be around 3 per cent in 1987. This can be compared with the general return to invest in the economy at about 13-22 per cent between 1982-1988 and the cost of the capital over 10 per cent per year. The bulk of the profit was concentrated in a few sectors, mainly banking and some of the SOEs in the industry sector. The level of the profit is still low compared with the investment needs.

The financial performance of course failed to capture the general performance of SOEs. The performance of SOEs was affected by factors which were external to the enterprise and can act favorably or unfavorably on the performance. Government policy can often constrain the operations of SOEs. On the other hand, policies such as the exclusive right of the operation, preferential access to funds and immunity against bankruptcy put SOEs in a favourable position compared to the private sector competitors.

Growing realization of the burden of SOEs has led to several policy changes since 1988. Two decrees introduced during the October 1988 - June 1989 period established a set of financial soundness measures covering profitability, liquidity and solvency, which are used to rank the individual SOEs. To date most of the SOEs have been classified into four categories: very sound, sound, less sound and unsound based on financial data from 1985-1988. The Ministry of Finance and the line ministries use the soundness criteria and consideration of the types of goods and services provided by the SOEs to determine the appropriate corporate restructuring option. Several different options are set out: (1) change in legal status; (2) sale of stock on the stock exchange; (3) direct placement of stock; (4) consolidation or merger; (5) sale of company to third party; (6) establishment of a joint venture; (7) liquidation (Mari Pangestu, 1993: 274 - 275).

In Indonesia, the public sector is the largest employer. Government formulates economic, social and political goals. However, there was inefficiency all around. Therefore, Indonesia expressed interest in deregulation or privatization as the alternative strategy to achieve the objective of economic growth and development. Moreover, privatization may promote competition among newly privatized firms to reduce cost and to provide better quality goods and services. There are widespread inefficiency and resource misallocation in the import-substitution industrialized strategy. The state-owned enterprises fail to achieve social economic objectives with lack of managerial efficiency, poor performance, low quality of goods and services and misallocation of resources. Inefficiency created budgetary burden for the state owned enterprises.

What is Privatization?

Privatization is a term which as often been described as "more than an umbrella term" or as "an ugly word but a beautiful concept". Although the idea of privatization is not very new, the usage of the term varies considerably. After reviewing current literature on the subject, it is interesting to note that the term can have different definitions from different perspectives.

Many governments embraced privatization in order to relieve the burden of the national budget, maximise consumer choice and improve the quality of the goods and services (William T.G 1991:03). A number of observers view privatization as a relaxation of government restriction, which include permission of minority private ownership in state owned enterprises, the appointment of private managers to the positions of managerial responsibilities in the state owned enterprises and the participation of private concerns in enterprises previously considered a state monopoly (Raymond Vernon, 1988:02). Thomas Callaghy and Ernest Wilson defined privatization as any action that serves to "dilute or eliminate government equity ownership or managerial control of an enterprises". (Thomas Callaghy and Ernest Wilson 1988:80). They argue that this type of privatization involves the transfer of company assets from the government as owner to the private sector receiver. This type of privatisation, sometimes, is that government does not sell all its equity but sell some portion of it to either to one or several buyers. It also has another form that government transfers the managerial control to the private sector. Ravi Ramamurti argues that privatization is the sale of all or part of a government's equity to the private sector (Ravi Ramamurti, 1992:225) Steve

Hanke defined privatization is a transfer of assets and service functions from public to private hands. He emphasized activities ranging from selling state owned enterprises to contracting out public services to private contractors. (Steve Hanke, 1987:4)

From an economic point of view, Calvin Kent defined privatization as the transfer of the functions for which the government previously held a monopoly into the hands of the private sector. These functions are performed by private sector at prices that clear the market and reflect full costs of production whereas they were performed at zero or below full cost prices by the government (Calvin Kent 1987:4). Paul Starr viewed privatisation as a policy movement and a process that shows every sign of reconstituting major institutional domains of contemporary society. He defined privatisation as a shift of individual movements from the whole to the part--- that is, from public action to private concerns. (Paul Starr 1989:15). Starr goes further by defining privatization as another kind of withdrawal from the whole to the part; a transfer of ownership to the private sector of a good formerly accessible to the public sector at large. Marc Bendick, Jr. defined privatisation as shifting to non-governmental hands some or all roles in producing a good or service that was once publicly produced or might be publicly produced (Marc Bendick, Jr. 1989:98). T. Kolderic argues that governments perform separate functions, either of which---or both---could be privatised. (T. Kolderic 1986:290). The first function he defined is provision and the second one is production. Production is administrative action to produce that good and service, whereas provision is the policy decision to provide a good or service. V. V. Ramanadham argues that privatization is denationalisation in the sense of transferring ownership of the public enterprise to private hands. Another idea in vogue is liberalization and deregulation which unleash forces of competition (V.V. Ramanadham 1989:4). Paul Cook and Colin Kirkpatrick view privatisation as a range of different policy initiatives intended to change the balance between the public and private sector. They distinguish three main approaches to privatisation: a change in the ownership of the enterprise, liberalization or deregulation and a transfer of good or service from the public to private sector while the government retains ultimate responsibilities for supplying the service.

According to the literature on privatisation, privatisation is a process of transfer of asset from the public to private sector. The state may decide to keep all equity and delegate management of the enterprise to the private sector, or it may choose to sell a portion of its assets and retain majority or minority ownership; in other words, establishing a joint venture between the public and private sectors. Under the privatization arrangement, the government is expected to liberalise protected markets and encourage competition. Privatisation is thus assumed to increase efficiency and improve the quality of the goods and services. In the developing countries, privatisation is viewed as deregulation, liberalisation, denationalisation, selling state owned enterprises to the private sector and transferring the management of the enterprise to the private hands. Indonesia adopted this type of privatization.

Forms of Privatization

Privatisation is a measure that has been implemented by the several governments world wide in both developed and developing countries. The are different forms of privatization in different countries. Harry Hatry conducted a survey that lists different forms of privatization such as subsidies, grant, and franchises, contracting out, self-help volunteers, use of regulatory and taxing authority, reducing demand for service, obtaining temporary help from the private sector and forming ventures between the public and private sectors. (Harry Hatry 1983:10-100). However, there are a few of the forms being used in both developed and developing nations: contracting out, voucher, sales of assets by the government to private sector, joint venture, subsidies, load shedding, private payment, management privatization and liberalisation or deregulation.

Contracting-out is the simplest form of privatization. It is widely used in the developing countries where the private sector is involved in the provision of certain goods and services but government remains in charge of all major activities. Sales of assets or equity are known as joint-venture form of privatization. Divestiture is a total sale of all or part of the company to private sector: there is an actual change of ownership of an enterprise from the public to private sector. Equity could be easily sold to the public because of the buying power of the people in developed nations. However, the sale of the equity in whole or part is a very tedious task in the developing countries where capital markets are either non-existent or underdeveloped. Denationalization could involve the sale of the enterprise as a complete entity or as a joint venture between the public and private sectors. Subsidies are designed to provide profit opportunities to private firms by subsidising some of their production inputs---those governmental sector would like to see employed. The liberalization or the deregulation of the entry into the activities previously restricted to public sector enterprises is a very common form of privatization in Third World countries. This form removes all or some restrictions in entering particular market in order to increase competition, hence, giving more choices to the consumer. Liberalization of import/export industries, for instance, could help promote competition and thus stabilise the prices of imported goods in the marketplace and thus diffuse political tension between privileged groups and majority of the people. In the case of management privatization, the government of a particular state owned enterprise invites the private sector, with its expertise and know-how. But government still retains complete ownership of the state-owned enterprise (Jacques V. Dinavo, 1995: 6-10). In Indonesia, the common forms of privatisation are selling state-owned enterprises to the private sector, joint venture, transferring management to the private sector, liberalisation and deregulation.

FORMS OF PRIVATISATION IN INDONESIA

In a narrow sense, privatisation involves transfer of ownership to the private sector. However, many professional economists do suggest that it does not necessitate the sale of government assets but rather accommodates management of the private sector. The accommodating private management includes deregulation and de-bureaucratisation measures which can influence the public companies. The government of Indonesia has adopted three forms of privatisation: first, by transferring government ownership (fully or partially to the private sector). In this case, there is a shift of power from state control to a private control. Second, by deregulation of the economy. This is concerned with relaxation of the regulation and statutory monopoly power. Third, by privatisation in terms of liberalisation, which refers to relaxing the restraints of newcomers in the economy by allowing private entry into the business of public enterprises and allowing private sector yardsticks to be utilised in the management of the public sector.

WHY DOES STATE NEED PRIVATIZATION?

In developing economies, state-owned enterprises (SOEs) are losing money. States have been spending substantial sums of money to subsidize these enterprises. Gray Cowan argues that industries can be managed more effectively and good services can be rendered more efficiently by private than by the government and, at lower cost to public (L. Gray Cowan, 1987: 7). Ramanadham observes that state-owned enterprises should be reorganized into a private enterprise when it has a comparative disadvantage in making a contribution to the national well-being. Alternatively, public enterprise should be preferred to other forms if it proves to be a superior means of making a contribution to the national well-being (Ramanadham, 1989: 14-15). Most of the professional economists had agreed that privatization leads to the competition, and achieves much greater efficiency and produces much better quality goods and services than the SOEs. Most of the scholars of privatization have emphasized on cutting the size of government budgets by privatizing SOEs. Competition is crucially important to stimulate efficiency. Vernon argues that the threat of entry is sufficient to inhibit firms from earning monopoly rents. In evaluating privatisation, there are some important criteria that need to be looked at, including competition, efficiency, quality, reliability, accountability and legitimacy. Privatization does increase competition in the market in which the newly privatized enterprise operates. As competition increases, it enhances quality and improves performance. Competition ensures the highest quality at the lowest price. According to Smith, competition is 'an invisible hand that caused producers, while they pursued their own self interest, to maximize the well-being of all' (A. Smith, 1976: 456).

In contrast, the state-owned enterprises are not usually driven by the desire to make profit and do not face any competition with other firms. The managers of the SOEs are more interested in the size of their budgets and the number of the employees, and not necessarily with the efficiency and the quality of the goods and services.

Increasing efficiency can be viewed in two ways. First, from a micro or enterprise perspective it is assumed that privatization will force companies to be more commercially oriented, will foster greater competition and will encourage individual initiative on the basis of entrepreneurship. A monopolistic company, either private or state, tends to be inefficient because it lacks the pressure of competition. The second, privatization can improve efficiency from the government and public enterprise's point of view. Market forces, which privatization basically relies on, would influence the government to free state enterprises form political interference and bureaucratic hindrance. This, in turn, could result in the reduction of the cost at the enterprise level due to breakdown of hierarchical and bureaucratic process. Similarly, at the government level, increased efficiency and decreasing national budget spending would follow from the reduction in the number and the size of the public enterprises. It may stop the drain on government budget that stems from inefficiency of public enterprises.

The concept of privatization can be viewed in two contexts: macro and micro perspectives. Macro privatization takes into account the new dividing lines of state and market. Divestiture of government ownership and liberalisation of economy is the manifestation of this proposition. The role of the government shifts from a producer state to a regulator state, and ultimately to a facilitator state. Following this paradigm, the state becomes unnecessary for the provision of goods and services. Rather, the government should handle directly policy consideration towards facilitating measures that would promote companies performance and economic growth of the country. Micro privatization is concerned with dynamic modern management at the enterprise level. It aims at better performance of, and fund generation form, public enterprises, through relinquishing power to manage and judging managers' achievements against an appropriate performance measurement. Thus, both macro and micro privatizations are aimed at competition, providing greater managerial autonomy and stimulating entrepreneurial creativeness to achieve efficiency at the enterprise level and in the economy as a whole (I Ketut T. Mardjana, 1993).

Some of the well-known economists of the country argued that many of the state- owned enterprises have failed in discharging their task of being the spearhead of modernization by generating resources for further investment, or to be the pioneer in the industrialisation processes of the country. They also accused some of those state owned enterprises of being more likely a burden to the government budget than a generator of new resources (Pandi Radja Silalahi, 1987: 158-160).

Therefore, the Indonesian economic policy has adopted privatization as policy instrument to correct the country's economic imbalance through the process of deregulation. There is no clear cut official definition of the restructuring in Indonesia. The government undertook restructuring policies in 1980s, when the previous forms of public enterprise were reorganized into a new form, known as PN (Perusahaan Negara). In 1989, in turn, the PN was divided into three forms of public enterprises, (the *Perjan, Perum* and the *Persero*). In this context, restructuring took the form of rearranging, or reorganizing the former public enterprises. During the last decade, the government has been seeking to restructure the economy by opening up business activities to market control rather than government intervention or more specifically, by shifting the basis of the economy from oil to non-oil exports. In the recent Indonesian public enterprise reform, restructuring policy consisted of a set of strategies. It covered reorganization of the state enterprises, divestiture or selling of government assets and transfer to private sector concept into enterprise management. It shows that the restructuring and privatization are inseparable.

In brief, privatization can address issues of the positive impact of market forces and competition, and negative consequence of political meddling on the behaviour and performance of enterprise and economy as a whole. Pelkmans and Wagner suggest that two conditions must be considered when aiming to improve companies' efficiency: First, government control and interference have to be abolished, and secondly, privatised companies must be exposed to increased competition (Pelkmans & Wagner 1990: 19). While there is general consensus about the ability of privatisation to remove political control and to encourage competition, there is scope for confusion in the broad and differing terms for various methods of privatisation used in a range of countries.

Indonesian public enterprise 'restructuring' is mixed up with 'privatisation' concepts.

REASONS FOR PRIVATIZATION IN INDONESIA

Specific reasons for privatization in Indonesia are not clear but financial pressure, economic pressure, non-economic pressure and external pressure are considered crucial for privatization.

Financial Pressure

Financial pressure is an important reason for policy changes in Indonesia. Government has financial difficulties, budget deficits, balance of payment deficits, and shortage of funds in public enterprises. The fall in oil price resulted in budget austerity, and the needs for Indonesian government to look for a better system. Moreover, government usually seeks to reduce its expenditure or to secure additional sources of revenue. Public enterprises are restructured because there is lack of profit, and also inefficiency. The poor financial performance of the public enterprise meant that there was a continual useless flow of government funds to state-owned enterprises. This, in turn, had adverse effects on fiscal policy (national budget) and monetary policy (government borrowing, crowding out effect and balance of payment problem). The increase in public borrowing, in turn, placed the country under greater influence of international lending agencies.

Economic pressure

Public enterprises are not efficient and there is a general feeling of frustration and disappointment with the public policy. There is no competition among the enterprises which enjoy monopolistic power. For the employees in public sectors, there is no motivation, no incentive or pressure in order to influence or increase the productivity of the public sector. Goods and services are of shoddy quality.

Non-Economic Pressures

The desire to achieve greater equity and to enhance motivations are important non-economic pressures. In Indonesia in March 1990, the President Suharto suggested to a group of thirty-one business leaders that a portion of the equity of their conglomerates should be sold to co-operatives. However, there is a fear of the Indonesian government on privatisation because privatisation project may be given to the wealthy persons who are the Chinese ethnic minority (Ng Chee Yuen and Toh Kin Woon, 1992: 45).

International Pressure

World Bank and IMF have been exerting pressure on developing countries to privatize their large public sectors. The World Bank and IMF were putting the pressure on the Third World Countries that were experiencing severe financial crisis in the 1970s to reduce the role of the state in the public enterprises and to sell those enterprises that were operating at a loss to the private sector. These institutions are helping the developing countries with the structural adjustment programs. They are encouraging competition and efficiency in developing countries to foster economic growth. But some argue that the international institutions are politically motivated in the Third World Countries. Indonesian economy was helped by the international institutions like World Bank, IMF and USAID. They suggested Indonesian government to introduce several policy reforms with regard to incentive structure and trade regime, regulatory framework and administrative control, and the financial and foreign investment policies in order to improve overall investment climate for manufacturing firms, and to encourage the growth of more efficient manufacturing firms (Thee Kian Wie, 1995: 141).

The Globalisation of World Trading System is supposed to bring a large impact on product and services. To improve competitiveness, the quality and quantity of the products and services need to be increased. Therefore, in order to enable Indonesian global competition, World Bank has recommended to eliminate various existing transformation obstacles. The World Bank has stated five categories of obstacles in the Indonesian economy. These categories are the cartel practice, price control, restriction of entry and exit, special license or obstructions in business administration as well as the domination of the government in a certain sector. The facing of global competition, avoiding unhealthy competition and creating a free market mechanism are important agendas to benefit from global competition. For the purpose of global competition, to improve efficiency and productivity, the World Bank suggested that the Government should give autonomy to the state-owned enterprises management to enable them in playing the role as development agent and to stipulate strategic decisions in achieving an optimum target. One of the alternatives in improving the performance of state owned enterprises was the privatisation program *(Indonesian Economic Review*, No. 182 / 1997: 13).

External pressures on developing countries come from multi-national institutions or bilateral agencies such as the International Monetary Fund (IMF), the World Bank and the United State Agency for International Development (USAID). External pressures often involve transference of ideology, which can be encouraged by internal pressure (shortage of the government funds). The ideology of free market competition is believed to be better in the hands of private sector enterprises than through the operation of public enterprises. Babai argues that "Of the large cast of actors that have provided the external stimulus toward privatisation in developing countries, two international organisations stand out: the World Bank and the International Monetary Fund (IMF). In recent years, the Bank and the Fund have issued a stream of reports that assign much of the blame for the backwardness and instability in developing economies to excessive government intervention. Running through such reports is a common theme: the state needs to place greater reliance on the market as the essential mechanism of allocation and distribution and, in the process, must make more room for the private sector" (Babai, 1988: 254).

The mission of the USAID is clear. As the A.I.D.'s policy determination states: "Privatization is a key intervention in support of A.I.D.'s [Agency for International Development's] overriding goals of stimulating economic efficiency. This policy determination sets forth privatization as an important mission activity for enhancing efficiency in sectors and/or markets of concern to A.I.D. and seeks to encourage innovation which is often the result of creative risk taking. (USAID 1991:1

Indonesia receives substantial loans and grants from these international institutions in pursuing development. Therefore, this type of policy pressure is very likely in Indonesia. The USAID, for example, places experts in Indonesia as government advisers and gives grants in order to help Indonesia speed its privatization program.

Another Western institution is HIID (Harvard Institute for International Development). It provides technical assistance in formulating new public enterprise performance evaluation and criteria on the basis of case-by-case assessment for each type of public enterprise. The combination of these types of pressure might have move the Indonesian economy, previously a stronghold of state intervention, towards competitive market (I Ketut T. Mardjana, *1993*: 58-59).

PRIVATIZATION IN THE PROCESS OF RESTRUCTURING

The issue of the alleged inefficiency of public enterprises has always attracted public attention. The government itself has legitimised concern about the inefficiency of public enterprises. In a Complete Cabinet Meeting on December 30, 1986 the President instructed all ministers to increase the level of productivity and efficiency of the public enterprises in their departments. Three years later, after intensive evaluation of each public enterprise, the Indonesian Minister of Finance explained in the press release that the critical problems faced by the Indonesian public enterprises were: (i) the weakness of financial structures ; (ii) lack of managerial capability; and (iii) absence of efficiency and productive methods, and lack of managerial flexibility in the decision making process.

Consequently, because of the inefficiency of many public enterprises combined with shortage of government funding, present core government policies were designed to enhance the efficiency and productivity of public enterprise management. The approach used in this policy reform consisted of (i) company restructuring; and (ii) simplification of decision making process.

Two decrees: October 1988- June 1989 are a set of financial soundness measures covering profitability, liquidity and solvency, which are used to rank the individual SOEs. To date, 189 out of 212 SOEs have been classified into four categories: very sounds, sound, less sound and unsound based on financial data from 1985-1988. The soundness criteria and consideration of the type of goods and services provided by the SOEs are in turn used as criteria to determine the appropriate corporate restructuring option for the SOEs by the Department of Finance and the line ministries.

Company restructuring, which is covered in the Minister of Finance Decree No. 740/KMK.00/1989, was planned to be conducted through six approaches, as follows:

- Changing the legal status of public enterprises into a status that is likely to be conducive to efficient and productive operations (e.g. from a public law basis to a business law basis).
- Contracting out the enterprise to a third party (public or private enterprises) with the purpose of increasing market shares, technological/operational capability and managerial efficiency.
- Consolidating or merging the enterprises to increase working capital, in order to increase market share and competitiveness.
- Splitting-up the enterprise into two or more productive enterprises, in order to strengthen internal control and to increase business services.
- Going public through the capital market, if the company is able to comply with the requirements of the capital market, or otherwise, the direct placement of shares (i.e. not through the capital market). Going public intended to improve the company and simultaneously extend the people's participation through ownership of shares.
- Joint ventures with private sector businesses to extend market shares, operational capability and improve capital returns.

The method of company restructuring undertaken in any particular case, would obviously have effects on the future management of the enterprises. Changes in their legal status (from the *Perjan* to the *Perum* or to the *Persero*, or from the *Perum* to the *Persero)* would bring public enterprise into the commercial arena, and consequently would lessen government intervention. Consolidation, mergers, or splitting-up policies would have simplifications on the range of control of the management. Management contracts, going public, direct placement of shares and joint ventures would all open the opportunity to third parties to be involved in controlling the enterprise. It would also tend to make public enterprise more transparent and open to public scrutiny. This, in turn, creates further pressure on the government to ease its controls over public enterprises, and pressure for public enterprises to run their business with commercial orientation. Otherwise, third parties would not want to be involved in managing the enterprise or wish to buy shares in the enterprise.

In addition, the process of company restructuring mentioned above is not likely to be greatly different in practice from the concept of privatisation. It covers transfer of ownership, contracting out, splitting-up consolidation, and liberalism by allowing the private sector to be a partner in joint-ventures. Hence, what is here called company restructuring is, by definition, a process of privatization. More specifically, the above restructuring strategies involved: divestment policy, organisational changes and managerial reforms. These were intended to increase levels of efficiency or productivity by introducing public enterprises to the greater market orientation.

The Decree of the Minister of Finance No. 741/KMK.00/1989 strengthens the policy of company restructuring. It was concerned with simplification of control systems, and covered: (i) corporate plans; and (ii) shortening the policy decision-making process. Both of these methods provide ways for the government to relax its controls over public enterprises.

Measures to improve the management of SOEs were introduced in the 1989-1990 period. First was the requirement for SOEs to prepare long term (five years) strategy, annual budget and annual corporate plan to be used by management comprising the Board of Directors, Board of Commissioners and Supervisors, line ministries and Department of Finance. Second, financial compensation for commissioners/ supervisors and directors of SOEs was to be made more flexible. This was to be related to the job description of the individual ; performance criteria of the SOEs such as soundness and profitability; and size of the SOE based on assets (Mari Pangestu, 1991: 32).

The Minister of Finance reported that among the 178 existing State-Owned Companies in 1995, 49 of them were classified in the category of very healthy, and 43 companies in the category of healthy, 37 companies were classified as less healthy, and 49 in the category of not healthy *(Indonesian Economic Review* No. 182 1997: 13).

POLICY AND PRACTICE OF PRIVATIZATION

Privatization in the state-owned enterprises has been in practice in Indonesia for quite some time. The government has approved production/profit-sharing between Pertamina (the state oil company) and foreign companies, user pays charges on toll roads that are conducted by PT Jasa Marga (state road enterprise) and the private companies have been allowed to build toll roads as well as to operate them jointly with PT Jasa Marga. They also join operations involving PT Perikanan Samudra Besar (the state fishery company) and PT Bali Raya (a private company).

The government policy, in recent years, on the public enterprise has been made clear by the Presidential Instruction No. 5/1988. The instruction containing the following was directed to sixteen ministers, containing the following (i) guidelines on how to improve the level of efficiency and productivity in public enterprises. (ii) a delegation of power to undertake further action from President to Ministry of Finance. There are two decrees: public enterprise restructuring and simplification of the control. Reform in public enterprise sectors (or privatization of public enterprise management or ownership) orienting it towards more competitive market and more effective control has thus been legitimised (I Ketut T. Mardjana, 1993: 52). Privatization through the stock market, according the World Bank, inclined to be more competitive since the prevailing regulation on listing will enable the reduction of government interference.

Substantive deregulation of SOEs was undertaken at the beginning of the new order period. In a 1986 cabinet instruction, managers were given more autonomy. In a 1987 Presidential instruction on the reorganization of the status of SOEs was also undertaken whereby SOEs were to be converted from their designation as *Perusahaan Negara* (PN) or State Corporations to three new categories: *Perusahaan Jawatan* (Perjan) or Government Agencies, *Perusahaan Umum* (Perum) or Public Corporations and *Perusahaan Perseroan* or Limited Liability Companies.

The conversion of status was aimed at increasing the flexibility of operations of the SOEs and thus to facilitate the long term aim of the government to sell part or all of its shares in government limited liability companies. SOEs justified under public goods welfare arguments will remain as one of the other categories.

The conversion process took longer than expected not just because of procedural matters such as revaluation of assets, but due to reluctance of line ministries to relinquish control to the Department of Finance. Of the 21 SOEs owned by the central government, the largest number (155) were in the limited liability category, (122) wholly owned and 33 joint ventures and are spread out over the agriculture estates, manufacturing, mining and services (airlines, state trading companies) sectors.

In terms of sectoral breakdown, there has been a shift from government to private ownership of basic needs such as food and textiles, and other sectors such as printing and publishing, rubber products, pottery and China glass products, cement and other non- metallic minerals. For the food, beverages and cement sub-sectors, despite the increased role of private sector, the share of SOEs is still around one third (Mari Pangestu, 1991: 29-31).

DEREGULATION AS A FORM OF PRIVATIZATION

Deregulation is a form of privatization. In Indonesia, the main attention in privatization process is deregulation, which is from public enterprises to private enterprises. During the period of 1986-1995, Indonesia adopted a series of deregulation measures covering the whole aspects of the economy to increase efficiency. From micro economic point of view, in Indonesia, deregulation has three meanings. 1) Lessening of the barriers to the market entry. Many strategic activities previously preserved by the state are opened for private participation. This is known as liberalisation. The government avoids using the term liberalization that has a negative meaning in the political context. 2) Reducing the rules and constraints governing the activities of the business sector. 3)

Transferring public ownership to the private sectors (Anwar Nasution, 1991: 12).

During the oil boom years, Indonesian industrialization policy was oriented towards import substitution and increasingly protectionism. Since the mid-1970s, the development of broad industrial base including upstream and strategic industries, was mainly based on steel, cement and fertilizers industries. When oil price declined in early 1980s, the government's response was initially ambivalent. But subsequently, the policy formulation became more streamlined. The government undertook appropriate macroeconomic stabilization measures. Many government projects were postponed and expenditure was reduced, tax reform was introduced to increase government revenues. 50 per cent devaluation of the Rupiah was undertaken in 1983. Government granted subsidy to SOEs in the form of capital participation.

Moreover, in 1993, deregulation of the banking was introduced to control of deposits. The regulation increased the competition faced by the state banks. It also reduced the source of cheap funds for liquidity and credit, and forced State Banks to compete with private banks for deposit funds. Industrial and trade policies became more proctectionist. In late 1992, the regulated import management system was introduced, through which imports of certain categories could only be done by one of the importers. During 1993 – 1995, the number of the importers were increased. They were given monopolistic power as state trading companies. Another type of import license, the producer – importer category gave the right to import inputs to the producer of the product. This type was applied for SOEs particularly in steel and tin. When oil prices declined drastically in 1986, the government introduced substantive reforms. In April 1985, a form of deregulation was privatization of customs operations. In May, 1986 a new and improved duty drawback system was introduced. Exporters could obtain a refund on the duty paid out on imports used to produce exports or to get exemptions from paying duties. Exporters were defined to be producers who exported 85 per cent or more of their total production.

The foreign investors were allowed 90 per cent foreign ownership in exports oriented investments, utilization of low interest export credits, and joint ventures with 75 per cent more of Indonesian equity. In October 1986, the swap ceilings were removed. Many non-tariff barriers were removed and replaced by tariffs in October 1986 and January 1997. The approved import management system was also rationalized during that time. In June 1987, the investment and capacity licensing requirements for domestic firms were substantially deregulated. The categorization of licenses was considerably broadened in order to encourage diversification within the same type of product (Mari Pangestu, 1989: 227-229).

In July 1987, the system of textile quota allocation to Indonesian textile and garments exporters was also improved. The main changes were aimed at reducing the discretionary powers of officials and reducing unnecessary administrative procedures and costs (Mari Pangestu, 1987: 527). In December 1987, measures to reform capital market were announced. Deregulation of the capital market was aimed at reducing government interventions in the operation of stock exchange, such as limiting the rate of increase of prices, and to introduce over-the-counter trading. Foreigners were allowed to purchase shares in Indonesian capital market.

The simplifications of licenses for opening hotels were also introduced. Joint ventures were to be treated as domestic companies if 51 per cent of the equity was Indonesian or if 20 per cent of the shares were sold in the capital market. Joint ventures could export their own products as well as exports from other companies. Export licenses were eliminated except for quota items.

In October 1988, the financial sector increased competition between banks, thus increasing efficiency and reducing intermediation costs. Eventually, it could reduce interest rate and increase the availability of investment funds, which were crucial for the future growth of the economy. The deregulation included removing restrictions on limiting the number of the banks, both foreign and domestic. New domestic banks were allowed to operate, foreign exchange licenses were opened, new foreign banks also could enter as joint ventures (up to 85 percent equity) and the geographical and product (saving deposits) restrictions faced by existing foreign banks were removed. State enterprises were also allowed to place deposits in non-State-Banks.

In November 1988, the deregulation that was introduced was related to shipping, distribution of the goods by foreign investors and non-tariff barriers. Regulations on routes and licensing of inter-island shipping were removed and the requirement to use domestically produced ships was relaxed. Foreign investors were also allowed to distribute their own goods by setting up a joint ventures distributing company.

In December 1988, deregulations in the capital markets and financial services were introduced which allowed opening of a private stock exchange in cities other than Jakarta, and improved transaction in securities at the Jakarta stock exchange. The regulations of financial services such as hire-purchase, venture capital, leasing, brokerage, credit cards and consumer credit were rationalized and clarified (Mari Pangestu, 1989: 229-231).

The Effects of Deregulation

From 1986 to 1990, deregulation was apparently helpful for economic growth in Indonesia. In fact macro economic performance in 1989 was stronger than during the heyday of oil boom, Growth rate of GDP was about 7.4 per cent. Investment picked up strongly with new approvals, and a large number of jobs was created during this process of recovery. The current account deficit was within the tolerable range measured in terms of the financing possibilities.

Micro economic performance was equally encouraging. Export of non-oil products reached its peak to exceed oil and gas export in 1989. Export value and diversification grew up product-wise and destination-wise. The share of labour intensive products in total export of manufactured product increased at the cost of resource-intensive products, implying a harmony between the growth and the need to create large number of new jobs. The number of new manufacturing establishment also increased. Moreover, newly improved investments became increasingly export oriented. Deregulation and marketization were among the important factors behind the encouraging trend of performance of the Indonesian economy until 1990 (Djisman S. Simandjuntak, 1991: 368-369). Deregulation brought efficiency and better allocation of resources to the Indonesian economy during 1986 to 1990.

The rationale for removing control, raising interest rate and introducing competition in financial sector was that rising interest rate and increasing inefficiency of the financial system would lead to an increase in saving. By June 1990, the government granted licenses to establish 35 new domestic private banks, 12 new joint-venture banks, 194 new village financial institutions, and more than 400 new branches of offices of the banks. The interest rate served to channel savings into higher earning sectors, increased rate of return on investment and enhanced the productive capacity of the economy. January 1990, regulation required domestic private and state banks to lend 20 per cent of their portfolio to medium and small scale enterprises and corporations. October 1988 regulation introduced a maximum lending limits to insiders: owners, members of the board, executive directors and employees of the banks. The capital account liberalisation led to capital inflows that could cause overshooting of the real exchange rate. The foreign exchange has been relatively free ever since 1986. The system is free of restricting payment transfers for current external transaction. Foreign nationals and Indonesian citizens are free to open accounts in Indonesia in the Rupiah or foreign currencies with banks which are authorised to deal with foreign exchange transactions. The significant steps taken to increase competitive advantage of manufacturing industry and agricultural sector in international market place came with the removal of import licensing control and reduction in protective tariffs (Anwar Nasution, 1991: 18-21).

The growth rate of GDP reached a peak of 7.4 per cent in 1989 compared with 2 per cent in 1985. Non-oil exports increased at about 30 per cent in the 1987-1988 period and by 19 per cent in 1989. Growth in non-oil exports, however, slowed down in 1990. The aim was for the private sector investment to reach 55 per cent of total investment by the end of the Five Year Plan (1993 - 1994). Approved domestic and foreign investments more than doubled compared with 1988. For the period January-September 1990, approved domestic investment had reached up to Rp. 47.1 trillion (US$25 billion) and approved foreign investment had reached US$7 billion compared with Rp. 15.7 trillions and US$3.5 billion in 1988. Growth of bank credit was much higher for private national banks than state banks and other types of banks. As a result, the share of credit from state banks declined from 78 per cent to 60 per cent in the 1983-1990 period and it was all absorbed by the national private banks whose share increased from 12 per cent to 32 per cent in the same period. Growth rate of deposits for national private banks was much higher than that of state banks and the share of deposits of state banks declined from 64 per cent to 53 per cent in the 1983-1990 period while that of private national banks increased from 24 per cent to 41 per cent in the same period. The share of deposits at foreign banks also declined. Thus, deregulation which opened up competition between state and private banks did in fact push the growth of private banks higher.

After 1983 deregulation, several of the state banks did undertake reorganisational exercise, the most notable one being the largest state bank, BNI 1946, which laid off 600 people and undertook a massive ongoing reorganization effort including computerization. As for the capital market, up to August 1990, the number of listed companies increased to 114 (compared with 24 Jan in 1988) with market capitalization reaching Rp. 15.1 trillion or US$8 billion (Mari Pangestu, 1991: 33-34).

Banking deregulation has led to increased competition between existing banks as evidenced by increased advertising and promotion, product differentiation such as the higher incentives related to savings deposits, opening of new branches and interest rate competition. Three joint venture banks, two Japanese and one French, were approved and over twenty new domestic private banks obtained approval. Several major companies such as Zebra Taxis and Bakrie Brothers went public and there had been a substantial increase in the stock market activity with a high level of foreign interest.

In 1996, the economic growth of Indonesia was 7.82 per cent, (lower than 1995 growth) which reached 8.21 per cent, but higher than the average target of 7.10 per cent during the Sixth Five Year Development Plan (Pelita VI). This high growth occurred due to macro economic stability and continuously improved business climate through deregulation, which thereby increased the aggregate demand through investment activities. During these last six years, the development of state-owned companies has shown quite respectable work performance result. The total assets in 1990 amounting to Rp. 179.15 trillion, increased to Rp 312.80 trillion in 1995. In the meantime, the profit had also increased, from Rp 8.3 trillion in 1990 to Rp 9.3 trillion in 1995. In fiscal year of 1994 - 1995, the state had obtained funds of Rp 1.9 trillion from income tax of State-Owned Companies, which increased to Rp 2.0 trillion in the following year. While the non-tax income of Rp. 1.4 trillion in 1994 – 95 reached up to Rp 1.5 trillion in the following year. The government's capital participation at State Owned Companies was gradually declining. In the fiscal year of 1991 – 1992, it amounted to Rp 872 billion, but in 1993 – 1994, it was only Rp 126 billion.

In 1994 - 1995, the participation of the government's capital again increased. This was caused by the new participation in the industrial sector and addition of capital participation in the general services and banking sectors. But in general, it can be said that the capital participation of the government in the state owned enterprises is reducing, which in 1995 - 1996 was only Rp 79.2 billion. Since 1992, the government started to gradually reduce its assistance to State-Owned Companies. This indicates that the government started to reduce its interference in the activities of state owned companies. This was to push those companies to be more independent in its business (*Indonesian Economic Review,* No. 182, 1997: 11-13).

One can observe an increase of efficiency after the processes of deregulation, reorganization, liberalization and privatization. The level of the efficiency increase can be gauged from the return on investment, total factor productivity, sales etc. The sales increased up to 18.5 per cent per year and the profit increased almost 40 per cent per year (a 10 per cent per year increment in state owned enterprises as national income/profit) (*Economy and Finance in Indonesia,* Vol. XLI, No 2, 1993: 225-246).

OBSTACLES AND ISSUES IN THE PROCESS OF PRIVATIZATION

Privatization efforts in Indonesia still have several problems such as lack of transparency and accountability, lack of specification of the goals, conflict between growth and efficiency, lack of clear exit mechanism, conceptual problems, ideological and political problems, fear of distributing projects to non indigenous hands (Chinese), and so on.

The lack of transparency is reducing the accountability of the enterprise. Establishment of the enterprise and its substantial expansion are left wholly to the management. In 1975, state oil company was unable to pay its debts according to schedule due to over expansion. Defining relationship between SOEs and government agency and overseeing it is a core problem. If the enterprise is operating according to outside agency, then there is little role for management. Otherwise, if the management operates with total freedom then one gets into the accountability problem. The right balance is difficult to achieve. The most progressive reform does not delink totally a state enterprise from government. The government usually retains some important decisions such as the price, output or providing captive markets such that it is difficult to isolate factors contributing to the performance of SOEs.

Lack of specification of a clear goal can also mean that managers can "hide" the lack of performance by pointing out conflicting goals. The most off-cited conflict is between the function of a SOE as an "agent of development" and the efficiency goal. For instance, in 1989 as part of the increased concern for distribution, 1-5 per cent of SOE profits was allocated to the development of the "weak" economic sector. In the past it was difficult to close down a SOE: there is no clear exit mechanism and in fact, there is a presumption that the government will always come to the rescue. Thus, the possibility of liquidation as an option under the recent evaluation of SOEs and restructuring moves, is an encouraging sign.

There are also conceptual problems. There is no clear agreement on which sectors should remain with the state and which are to be privatized. Recently there has emerged a less clear definition of "strategic industries", and a new body has been created: Agency for the Development of Strategic Industries that needs to be retained by the government. Ten SOEs, including steel, were placed under this body. They are PT Krakatau Steel, PT Borna Bisma Indra, PT Barata Indonesia (railway), PT INKA (railway), PT IPTN (aircraft), PT PAL (shipping), PT Pindad (railway), Perum Dahana, PT Inti (telephone), and production unit of *Lembaga Elektronika Nasional* – LEN (Electronic).

At present the Ministry of Finance is committed to the privatization exercise. It is likely to meet with a lot of resistance. As such, the process will be a gradual one and perhaps that is the wisest path to follow when complexities and problems are associated with the process. One present issue is ideological and political in nature. While the need for improving the performance of SOEs has been realized as an important objective, there is wide divergence of views regarding the extent to which the SOE sector should be changed. For a long time, divestiture of ownership has been resisted with several types of arguments. An ideological rationale comes from those who are against any move to a more competitive market oriented system. A related political problem is that SOEs are implicitly assumed to be owned by non-indigenous, especially

Chinese business groups, and the fear is that the ownership of the domestic private sector will be in the hands of the Chinese. In addition, it is also perhaps feared that it could end up under the ownership of groups close to the power centre (Mari Pangestu, 1991: 37-40).

The central issue was perceived to be mainly about transferring government assets from the public to the private sector. This issue is sensitive because it relates to the Indonesian Constitution of 1945, which was hardly ever mentioned in the past. Consequently, debates extended to the ideology, politics and economics of the public enterprise sector. Many economists and business people argue that the problems of inefficiency of public enterprise in Indonesia are fundamentally derived from excessive government intervention, treating public enterprise as an extra arm of the government to discourage initiative and innovation, and to dampen the entrepreneurial spirit of the managers. State enterprises tended to become dependent on government subsidy, and subsequently burdened the national budget. It was suggested that government subsidies to public enterprises should not be maintained; otherwise development would stagnate. Accordingly, privatisation was seen as an appropriate method for solving these problems.

Counter arguments came from those who favoured a state-dominated system. They related their arguments to the ideology of the state and considerations of specific ethnic groups, especially Chinese conglomerates. In terms of ideology, privatisation of owned enterprises would move the economic system towards the capitalist system. This would not fit with Article 33 of the Constitution that legitimates a strongly controlled sector. Another argument against privatization was that public enterprises were assumed to be the fortress of the indigenous people (*benteng pribumi*). Transferring ownership out of government hands would mean that the economic power in the country would be held by a small group of people who were in the main Chinese Indonesians (*non-pribumi*).

The argument for privatization seems to be influential, and is supported by at least four major factors. First, there is an international tendency to move form control by the state to control by market forces, which to some extent has an effect on Indonesia. Second, the government has experienced a lack of funds to finance national development. Third, as the role of the private sector becomes stronger, its voice becomes more powerful. Fourth, the press has been successful in crystallizing the issue in the society and has covered it openly. Also there has been as shift of philosophy from the interpretation of 'control' previously taken to mean' belonging to', to the interpretation of 'control' which recently meant 'supervised by' the State. Since the beginning of the 'New Order' Government era, the economic system has moved from the 'guided economy' to a 'democratic economy'. Foreign and domestic investment is encouraged , and was formally legitimised by various Acts. The concept of state ownership, contained in the Constitution, began to be openly contested in discussion. According to the Constitution, controls are necessary for those branches of production that are considered vital to the state and affect the life of most people.

The two statements above suggest that a clear formulation of the terms 'strategic' or 'vital' is essential. It will be necessary to make clear distinction between the industries that should be retained in government hands and the businesses that preferably should be operated by the private sector, or a firm classification of the industries that public enterprise should operate on a commercial basis and the ones still needing government participation. Nonetheless, political consideration linked to the Chinese conglomerate may constitute a potential barrier to privatization, or at least, could cause a different form of privatization than a straight transfer of state ownership. Privatization of ownership means a transfer of assets and controlling rights from the public to individuals. The potential problem of a small group of people controlling a major portion of the economy is still a sensitive issue. This, then, is a dilemma facing Indonesia concerning the program of privatization. The government faces budget constraints; selling public assets would result in revenue and there would no longer be the need for funds from government to public enterprise as subsidies. However, selling public assets to the Chinese may raise political problems.

These political implications may hang over as there are no official term of 'privatization' used in Indonesia. The issue is obviously politically sensitive. Yet, the government's response on privatization policy has been clear. Public policy reform or public enterprise administration, which takes the form of company restructuring and simplification of control systems, has been launched and aimed at efforts to enhance the efficiency and effectiveness of public enterprise management.

CONCLUSION

The process of privatization has been experiencing the conflict between ideological and political issues. According to privatization literature of Indonesia, government does not dare to use the term privatization. State owned enterprises are still dominant contributors to the economy of the country. Since the fall in oil prices in 1982, the role of private sector as a source of the growth has become increasingly important. The decline in oil revenues implies that government can no longer function as the main contributor to the growth of the economy.

Economic and financial difficulties during the 1980s, plus international influences especially from the Western Development Agencies, have pressured the government to review public enterprise policy. The privatization concept, both in terms of divestiture and management, was launched in order to bring companies into a new environment of less government control and to allow enterprises to compete at the marketplace. The response of the Indonesia government has been more toward deregulation to enhance the role of the private sector. At the same time, reliance on market controls would mean reducing bureaucratic controls.

Privatization is a long process. Due to complex operational issues related to privatization process ranging from management and organisational issues to valuations of assets, transparency of sale, availability of funds in the stock market, it is difficult to analyse the success and failure of privatization in Indonesia.

However, in general, the Indonesian economy has benefited from the deregulation exercise which has removed many obstacles and bottlenecks. A strategic planning is required for the privatization program to be fully implemented in Indonesia. Such strategic planning, should in principle contain which companies area able to be privatized, and what is the benefit intended to be achieved through this privatization program.

REFERENCES

Anwar Nasution, (1991), "Recent Economic Reforms in Indonesia". *Indonesian Quarterly*, XIX/1 .

A. Smith, (1976), *An Inquiry into the Causes of the Wealth of Nations,* (London: Liberty Classics), 456.

Babai , D. (1988), "The World Bank and the IMF: Rolling Back the State or Backing Its Role". in *Promise of Privatization:A Challenge for American Foreign Policy*, (ed.) R. Vernon,, New York: The Council on Foreign Relation, Inc.

Berg, E. (1987). "The Role of Divestiture in Economic Growth". in *Privatization & Development*, (ed.), S.H. Hauke, San Francisco: The Institute for Contemporary Studies.

Calvin A. Kent, (1987), "Privatization of Public Functions: Promises and Problems," in *Entrepreneurship and the Privatizing of Government*, (ed.) Calvin A. Kent (New York: Quorum Books) 4.

Djisman S. Simandjuntak, (1991), "Process of Deregulation and Privatization: The Indonesian", Experience: *Indonesian Quarterly*, XIX/4.

Harry Hatry, (1983), *A Review of Private Approaches for Delivery of Public Services* (Washington, D.C.: Urban Institute), 10-100.

I Ketut T. Mardjana, (1993), Public Enterprise in Indonesia: Restructuring or Privatisation. *Indonesian Quarterly*, XXI/I .

Jacques V. Dinavo, (1995), *Privatisation in Developing Countries: Its impact on Economic Development and Democracy.*

Kolderic, T. (1986), "The Two Different Concepts of Privatization," *Public Administrative Review* (July/August): 285-290.

L. Gray Cowan, (1987) ,"A Global Overview of Privatization," in *Privatization and Development*, ed. Steve H. Hanke (San Francisco: International Center for Economic Growth Press), 7

Mahmud Thoba, (1993), Privatisasi dan Efisiensi ; Teori dan Kenyataan Empiris, *Ekonomi dan Kewangan Indonesia.* Vol. XLI No. 2, Jun. Lembaga Penyelidikan Ekonomi dan Masyarakat , Fukultas Ekonomi, Universitas Indonesia, Jakarta.

Marc Bendick, Jr., (1989), "Privatising the Delivery of Social Welfare Services: An Idea to be Taken Seriously," in *Privatisation and the Welfare*

State, eds. Sheila B. Kamerman and Alfred J. Kahn, Princeton, N. J.: Princeton University Press, 98.

Mari Pangestu, (1989), "Economic Policy Reforms in Indonesia", *Indonesian Quarterly*, XVII/3.

Mari Pangestu, (1987), "Deregulation and Reregulation: Where are we Going?" *Indonesian Quarterly*, XV/4

Mari Pangestu, (1991), "The Role of the Private Sector in Indonesia: Deregulation and Privatization", *The Indonesian Quarterly*, XIX/1 .

Mari Pangestu, (1993) "The Role of the State and Economic Development in Indonesia", *The Indonesian Quarterly*.

Ng Chee Yuen and Toh Kin Woon, (1992), "Privatization in the Asian – Pacific Region", *Asian-Pacific Economics Literature* Vol. 6 No. 2, pp. 42-68.

Pandi Radja Silalahi, (1987), "Privatisation of the State-Owned Enterprises", *Indonesia Quarterly*, XV/2 .

Paul Cook and Colin Kirkpatrick, (1988) *Privatisation in Less Developed Countries,* New York: St. Martin's Press, p. 3.

Paul Starr, (1989), "The Meaning of Privatization," in *Privatisation and the Welfare State*, (eds.) Sheila B. Kamerman and Alfred J. Kahn (Princeton. N.J.: Princeton University Press, p. 15.

Pelkmans, J. & Wagner, N. (1990), "The Economics of Privatization and Deregulation: Lessons from ASEAN and the EC". in *Privatisation and Deregulation in Asean and the EC: Making Market More Effective*, (ed.) J. Pelkman and N. Wagner, Singapore: Institute of South ASEAN Studies, 3-28.

Ravi Ramamurti, (1992), "Why Are Developing Countries Privatizing?" *Journal of International Studies* 23: 225.

Raymond Vernon, (ed.),(1988), *The Promise of Privatization: A Challenge For U. S. Policy* (New York: Council on Foreign Relations Books, 1988), 2.

Steve H. Hanke, (ed.), (1987), *Privatisation and Development* (San Francisco: International Centre For Economic Growth Press, p. 4.

Suryadi, (1997), "Privatization of State Owned Companies: The Globalization Era", *Economic Review*, No. 182, Pt. Bank Negara Indonesia (Persero) BK

Thee Kian Wie, (1995), "Economic Reforms and Deregulation in Indonesia" *Indonesian Quarterly*, XXIII/2.

Thomas M. Callaghy and Ernest J. Wilson III, (1988), "Africa: Policy, Reality or Ritual?" in R. Vernon (ed.) (New York: Council on Foreign Relations Books), *ThePromise of Privatization. A Challenge to US. Policy,*

USAID (1991), *Implementing AID: Privatisation Objectives* (Unpublished), Washington.

V. Ramanadham, (ed.), (1989), *Privatisation in Developing Countries* (London: Routledge, 4.

Vernon, R. *The Promise of Privatization: A Challenge for U.S. Policy,* New York.

William T. Gormley, Jr., (ed.), (1991), *Privatization and its Alternatives,* Madison: University of Wisconsin Press, p. 3.

APPENDIX 1

Summary of Reform Measures

Reform	Main Contents	Effects
Financial:		
1983 June1 Banking Regulation	- Remove interest rate control for State Banks - Reduce Liquidity Credit - Remove credit ceilings	- Rise in deposit rates - Some fall in intermediation costs - But liquidity credits in fact increased
1986, October	- Removal of ceiling on Central Bank Swap	
1988, October 21 (PAKTO)	- Open up licences for new banks, including joint ventures - Lending limits regulation - Reserve requirement lowered	- Opening up many banks and joint ventures - Intense competition between banks - Rising interest rates and failing spreads initially
1987, December (PAKDES)	- Deregulation of capital markets - Reduce govt. role in stock exch. - Foreigners can buy stock	
1988, December (PAKDES)	- Further capital markets deregul. - Deregulation in insurance industries. - Rationalisation of financial services sector	- Sharp increase in capital Markets activity and index - Many major co. going public

Fiscal:				
1984, April Tax Reform	-	Remove with holding tax and intro. VAT	-	Increased government revenues
	-	Rationaliz. Of income and sales tax		
Trade and Shipping:				
1985, March Tariff Rationalizati on	-	Range reduction from 0 – 225% to 0-60%	-	Some reduction in protection
	-	Number of tariff Levels reduced from 25 to 11		
1985, April Customs Reform (INPRES NO. 4)	-	Removal of Customs Dept. in Goods Clearance	-	Reduced subst. Average time of imports and exports clearance
	-	Appointment of Private Surveyor SGS		
	-	Removal of restrictions on choice of international carrier	-	Important psychological effect
1986, May (PAKEM)	-	Duty drawback and bypass monopoly	-	Improve duty drawback process and
	-	Armslenght transactions and computerized processing	-	Important factor to incr. Exports

Resource: The Role of The Private Sectors in Indonesia: Deregulation and Privatization. By Mari Pangestu

APPENDIX 2

Indonesia: Macroeconoic Indicators, 1980-89

	1980	1981	1982	1983	1984	1985	1986	1987	1988	1989
1. Rate of growth of GDP (per cent, 1983 prices)	8.5	7.2	-0.3	8.9	6.7	2.5	5.9	4.8	5.7	6.3
a) Oil and LNG GDP	2.3	1.5	-14.0	14.2	13.1	-7.2	4.9	1.6	-0.6	3.8
b) Non-oil/LNG GDP	10.9	9.3	4.2	7.4	4.9	5.5	6.2	5.6	7.4	6.9
2. Inflation rate (%)	16.0	7.1	9.7	11.5	8.8	4.3	8.8	8.9	5.5	6.0
3. Bank lending rate	13.5	13.5	13.5	26.3	18.6	21.3	23.1	23.9	24.0	22.54
4. Budget expenditure as % of GDP	23.9	23.8	22.9	23.6	21.6	23.6	21.3	21.6	20.9	21.8
5. Oil revenues as % of Government total revenue	72.6	72.9	66.7	70.3	73.3	64.1	43.6	53.4	43.8	31.3
6. Budget deficit as % of GNP	3.5	2.0	2.7	1.8	0.7	0.4	3.1	2.2	5.2	5.
7. Terms of trade (1983=100)	93	108	105	100	99	106	80	84	71	-
a) Export price	62	76	78	100	109	110	85	116	133	-
b) Import price	66	71	75	100	109	104	106	138	189	-
8. Oil and gas as % of total exports										

	81.3	82.1	82.4	76.3	73.2	68.4	55.9	49.9	40.0	39.2
9. Current account deficit (US$ million)	-3.006	566	5334	6338	1,856	1,923	3,911	2041	1,552	-
10. Real effective E.R. (1980-1982 = 100)	4.0	0.6	5.9	8.2	2.3	2.4	5.5	3.0	1.9	-
11. External debt repayments as % of										
a) Routine budget exp.	88.4	99.7	110.9	95.8	96.1	94.6	72.8	56.7	54.0	56.4
	13.0	13.0	17.0	29.0	28.0	27.8	37.3	46.9	52.8	52.2
b) Exports	8.1	8.5	11.6	19.6	19.6	24.0	37.3	33.9	36.3	31.2
i. Amortization	4.3	4.7	5.9	8.0	8.0	10.90	21.2	19.9	22.5	-
ii. Interest	3.8	3.8	5.7	11.6	11.6	13.1	16.1	14.0	13.8	-
12. OECD import price of crude oil (cif, US$/Barrel)	32.29	36.34	33.94	28.29	28.29	27.45	15.04	17.90	14.84	17.68

APPENDIX 3

Indonesia: Balance Of Payments (In Million US Dollars)

Year	1975	1980	1985	1986	1987	1988
Current acc.	-1,164	2,754	-1,950	-4,099	-2,023	-1,552
Export, fob.	6,869	22,609	18,567	14,396	17,219	19,509
Oil	5,052	16,530	12,549	7,740	8,570	7,832
Non Oil	1,817	6,079	6,018	6,656	8,649	11,677
Import, fob.	-5,468	-13,456	-12,705	-11,938	-12,297	-13,831
Oil	-853	-3,391	-2,560	-2,181	-2,225	-2,103
Non Oil	-1,339	-10,065	-10,145	-9,757	-10,072	-11,728
Transportation and travel	-853	-2,131	-1,717	-1,454	-1,250	-1,081
Investment income	1,339	-3,048	-3,311	-3,211	-3,660	-4,092
Oil	-970	-1,964	-1,705	-1,321	-1,248	-1,158
Non Oil	-369	-1,084	-1,606	-1,890	-2,412	-2,934
Government, n.i.e.	-26	-108	-125	-25	-128	-137
Other services	-347	-1,112	-2,619	-1,767	-1,907	-1,920
Special Drawing Rights (SDR) Capital account	0	65	0	0	0	0
Private capital	285	1,574	1,807	4,365	3,677	2,372
Official capital	-1,493	-630	68	1,291	1,596	407
Loans and grants	1,778	2,204	1,739	3,074	2,081	1,965
PL-480	1,757	2,079	1,695	3,026	2,057	1,951
Errors and emissions	21	125	44	48	24	14
Balance of payments	-104	-2,057	-810	-810	-444	-741
Monetary movement	-983	2,336	-544	-544	1,210	321
IMF position	983	-2,336	544	544	-1,210	321
Foreign liabilities	34	-31	-10	-10	-14	5
Foreign assets (increase = -)	101	-22	0	0	0	0
	848	-2,283	554	554	-1,196	316

Resource: Bank Negara Malasia

APPENDIX 4

CONTRIBUTION OF STATE OWNED COMPANIES TO THE STATE'S INCOME
(Billion Ruppiah)

SPECIFICATION	1989/90	1990/91	1991/92	1992/93	1993/94	1994/95	1995/96
1. Income tax							
- Total	2,556.0	3,489.0	4,006.8	5,050.0	14,758.	18,355.	20,520.
- State Owned Companies	1,093.0	1,438.3	1,450.0	1,600.0	9	1	0
- Percentage	42.0	41.2	36.2	31.7	2,000.0	1,927.5	2,020.1
2. Non-Tax Income					13.6	10.5	9.8
- Total	2,096.0	2,383.2	2,71.7	2,993.1			
- Dividen/DPS/BLP of State Owned Companies	958.0	1,096.0	1,311.2	1,053.2	3,8955, 3	5,997.2	7,801.1
- Percentage	45.7	46.0	48.3	35.2	1,516.6 38.9	1,393.1 23.2	1,477.7 18.9

DPS = Overall Development Funds

BLP = Government's Profit Share

(Source: State Speech of the President of the Republic of Indonesia.)

APPENDIX 5

The Progress of Usaha BUMN in Indonesia until 1990/ 1991

Information	1988/89	1989/90	1990/91
1. Total Manufacturing	213	212	205
2. Finance			
a. Total activities	125,239	178,170	202,438
b. Sales	35,710	42,440	49,174
c. Income before tax	3,297	5,310	5,913
3. Economic Role (RP Milyar)			
a. Tax			
b. Tax/BUMN outcome	1.839,3	2.661,4	4.005,8
c. Non-tax	1.198,6	1.198,6	1.450,0
d. Dividen/DPS/BLP	1.568,8	2.062,1	2.357,8
	636,3	811,0	915,2
4. Workforce (million people)	1,006	1.145	1,145
5. BUMN Health Level			
a. Excellent	35(18,5%)	58(31,5%)	72(38,7%)
b. Good	25(13,2%)	38(20,7%)	35(18,8%)
c. Moderate	37(19,6%)	29(15,8%)	29(15,6%)
d. Ill	92(48,7%)	59(32,1%)	50(26,9%)

Resource: Pidato Kenegaraan Presiden RI, 199 and RI Financial Department, in Bidik J. Rachbini Prisma, 1992

Chapter 4

PRIVATISATION, MARKET POWER AND ALLOCATIVE INEFFICIENCY

B.N. Ghosh

INTRODUCTION

Most of the developing countries, and particularly the countries of East Asia, have undertaken capitalist method of industrialisation by permitting liberalisation, opening up of the economy and by introducing private ownership of the means of production, or what is popularly known as *privatisation*.

MEANINGS AND FORMS OF PRIVATISATION

There are indeed various meanings of privatisation. First, privatisation may simply mean the private ownership of means of production. Second, privatisation also stands for not only private ownership of means of production but also complete private control over policies, organisation and operations. Third, privatisation can also mean the transfer of an organisation to a few persons or an organised body of persons. This type of arrangement is also called corporatisation. Fourth, privatisation may involve joint ownership by the private sector and the public sector. This is also known as the joint venture programme. In a joint venture type of privatisation, both the partners have the tacit understanding that capitalist philosophy will hold sway. In Malaysia, most of the privatised industries and organisations have joint venture type of privatisation. Another type of privatisation, which one can think of, is a system of development of industries when economic development is introduced in a nascent economy. The capitalist method of industrialisation in macro perspective is also sometimes known as industrialisation through the private sector. In such a philosophy of development, the role of government or public sector is gradually reduced to virtual nothingness and the private sector becomes increasingly powerful. The state becomes a representative or agent of the capitalist, and itself becomes capitalist. This is often referred to as the Marxist notion of state. This type of state has already emerged in Malaysia and privatisation of this genre is gradually spreading its tentacles over the macroeconomic set-up. In privatisation, what is more important is the philosophy of profit maximisation and not simply the private ownership of means of production.

GROWTH OF MARKET POWER

Market power of monopoly power is the ability to have control over the output supply and prices of the product in the market. Market power grows directly with profit that is generated by the industry and also with the market share of output supply. Market power is very much related to the nature of organisation of industries. In a perfectly competitive market, the possibility of earning supernormal profit is totally bleak and it is also not possible for a firm or organisation to have any control over the prices of the product. And since each firm is supplying a very small fraction of the total output, its market share is unlikely to be high and crucial. Thus, in a highly competitive system, the market power is very unlikely to grow on.

Things are however, diametrically different under monopoly where, by definition, competition is conspicuous by its absence. Monopoly is able to create supernormal profit. The profit cannot be competed away due to entry barriers and legal protection enjoyed by monopoly. A monopolist has, therefore, complete control over the supply of the product and its price. And obviously, its market share is the highest. Because of all these facilities or properties that characterise a monopoly, it can generate market power. There are many models to estimate market power. In the Kalecki model, the market power which is called the degree of monopoly power (λ) can be estimated as:

$$\lambda = \frac{p-mc}{p}$$

(where, p=price and mc=marginal cost)

As a matter of fact, the greater is the difference between the price and the marginal cost, the higher becomes the degree of monopoly power.

The growth of market power is associated with high price of the product, low consumers' surplus, high profit for the monopolist, and concentration of economic power and growth of inequalities. More often that not, a growing market in the context of monopoly may be associated with declining efficiency. When price becomes higher than marginal cost, there occurs allocative inefficiency for the society.

PRIVATISATION IN MALAYSIA

In Malaysia, the concept of privatisation has been used in a very comprehensive manner to include even licensing to participate and also contracting out services. Privatisation has the following main connotations (see, Jomo, 1994). Privatisation includes: (i) the public issue or sale of shares of a state-owned public company, like the Malaysian Airlines System, (ii) a joint venture scheme like the Perbadanan Otomobil Nasional (Proton) and many others of the same type, (iii) contracting out public services such as garbage disposal services, parking services and so on, (iv) introduction of competition in the case of previously controlled monopoly practices like the privatisation of TV3 services in the Malaysian television, (v) sale or divestment of state concerns such as the incorporation of Tenaga Nasional Berhad, (vi) the placement of shares with institutional investors, as in the case of the sale of MAS stock to the Brunei government, and (viii) programmes to introduce private financing into construction projects, such as the North-South Highway and the like.

Privatisation in Malaysia started in the late sixties and early seventies. So far, some 400 enterprises have been privatised in Malaysia. At the initial stage, the tempo of privatisation was on a very low scale and it was experimental. The relative role of public sector vis-à-vis the private sector has undergone sea-saw changes over the years in Malaysia. Since the seventies, the state in Malaysia has become capitalist and it publicly declared the objective of profit maximisation. At one time, it was also competing with the local capitalists to gain market share, higher command over resources, competitive supremacy and control over the economy.

But in actual practice, the performance of state enterprises was becoming unsatisfactory. The idea of privatisation was influenced by a number of factors in the past. First, it was the aim of the state to industrialise the country at a fast rate in order to raise the standard of living of the people. Second, the state itself wanted to become more efficient and stronger to have more effective control over men and materials. This was imperative after the racial riots in 1969. Finally, the state wanted to suppress the growth of ethnocentric Chinese capitalism which was based on the principle of unequal exchange and was accentuating socio-economic inequality. During the initial stage of industrialisation in the seventies, the Malays who constituted 50 per cent of the population, had only 2 per cent of the economic wealth whereas the Chinese who constituted 40 per cent of the population had 45 per cent of total economic wealth. It was, therefore, necessary to limit the growth of domestic ethnic capitalism, but at the same time, ensure a high rate of growth of the economy and reduction in racial inequalities. The answer was the introduction of privatisation through multinational corporations from abroad.

Subsequently, privatisation encompassed the whole gamut of enterprises including many crucial national industries, telecommunications, power generation and infrastructure. In most cases, joint venture type of privatisation has been translated into practice and the state retains the equity participation. The basic objectives of such an arrangement were to: (i) ensure the control of the state, (ii) accord some opportunities to Bumiputra share holders to go up on the ladder of socio-economic capillarity and to compensate them against the injustice meted out to them earlier, (iii) create a class of successful entrepreneurs through the joint venture scheme which offers an interactive process of learning the intricate tricks of business philosophy, (iv) extract surplus by the state which can be ploughed back for the purpose of economic development, (v) to make the state enterprises more viable, efficient and productive, and (vi) reduce poverty and income inequality among the ethnic groups.

PROBLEMATICS OF PRIVATISATION

What is the impact of privatisation in Malaysia? It is claimed by many (among others, see Tan, 1991, pp.12-25, and Sheriff, 1991, pp.186-88) that privatisation in Malaysia has been highly beneficial. They believe that privatisation has firstly raised efficiency through competition (as in the case of TV3) and has led to reduction in turn-around time (as in KCT), detailed billing and introduction of new services (as in Telecom), and time reduction in the completion of the projects (as in the case of Labuan Water Supply Project).

Secondly, economic growth has also been facilitated by many factors in the wake of privatisation like the increase in engineering efficiency, i.e. the ability to produce more output with lesser inputs. And because of more efficiency, more resources could be released for higher production. Privatisation has also been responsible for various built-on transfer (BOT). Thirdly, privatisation has made it possible to reduce the size of the public sector and relieves the burden of the government in administrative and financial matters. Lastly, privatisation has been able to achieve the objectives envisaged in the New Economic Policy (NEP), like reduction in poverty, achievement of economic equity among the ethnic groups, and increasing Bumiputra participation in the national drama of development.

However, none of the points stated above is free from controversy. Let me analyse the points one by one:

i.   As for efficiency, two questions are often raised. First, whether efficiency has at all increased or not is a debatable point. I shall discuss more on this point later. Secondly, if at all any efficiency has been gained, it is at what cost? Many people believe that some amount of efficiency might have been achieved but the cost has been unwarrantedly high. Detailed billing and introduction of new products/services by Telecom do not necessarily mean efficiency. In some cases, the efficiency gained might have resulted from structural changes, new motivations, reforms and all that but not necessarily due to privatisation.

ii.   Has privatisation really expanded competition? The TV3 case is a solitary example. Moreover, TV3 cannot be thought of as a competitive bid. The purpose and products being different, it cannot be regarded as competition *per se*. Even if it is deemed as such, it remains at the most a monopolistic type of competition. As a matter of fact, many Malaysian economists are of the opinion that the privatisation has indeed reduced competition and has given rise to monopolistic market morphology as in the case of telecommunications, water supply, power generation and so on. Privatisation has simply converted public monopoly into private monopoly (Jomo, 1994, p.275) and has benefited the shareholders who have political linkages and not the common people.

iii.   There is no evidence that the so-called improved efficiency and performance has positively contributed to economic growth. Sheriff (1991, pp.186-88) and Tan (1991, pp.12-25) believe that privatisation has resulted in higher rate of economic growth in Malaysia. However, their impressionistic views have not been adequately substantiated. It is sometimes argued that by means of cross-subsidy made possible by higher tariffs on services provided by privatised sectors such as Telecom, North-South Highway and so on, privatisation has made possible higher growth. The argument is feather-bedding. As Jomo has pointed out, there is no mechanism to use these private resources by the government for cross-subsidy. To my mind, economic development or growth has become possible in Malaysia because of large volume of FDI, better foreign technology, surplus from the export sector and the like. A mere change in the ownership of production has not really done the trick.

iv.   It is said that privatisation has reduced the administrative and financial burden of the government and has also reduced the size of the public sector. While it may be true to some extent, it is not always a salutary sign to reduce the role of government in a growing economy. This will mean that the government does not get the opportunity to perform its responsibilities of welfare maximisation, and social welfare is going to be reduced. As a matter of fact, many concerned people strongly feel that privatisation in Malaysia has reduced the burden of the government but has increased the burden of the common people who are now to pay higher prices and higher tariffs for the public utilities.

v.   The claim that privatisation has been helpful to achieve the NEP objectives is a false claim. Although it has been able to achieve 30 per cent equity participation for Bumiputra, it has not directly contributed to poverty alleviation, employment distribution and inter-ethnic income (wealth) equality. These problems are still persisting in Malaysia. To a growth economist, there is no direct and proximate linkage between privatisation and these socio-economic variables. Rather, there are possibilities that the syndrome of socio-economic of inequalities gets aggravated and class differentiation gets accentuated under privatised (capitalist) process of development.

Privatisation, after all, is not a panacea. It has had some inherent problems of its own, which get manifested in the course of time. A privatised industry is generally run on higher and higher capital intensity. Malaysia is not an exception. If one looks at the Malaysian manufacturing sector, which is private sector-dominated, one can observe that capital intensity between 1970 and 1985 went up more than three times (see supra, Ch.15, Table 15.1). The increased capital intensity (the higher organic composition of capital) leads to higher value-added per worker and makes possible the extraction of larger amount of surplus value. Moreover, the introduction of high tech-method of production results in technological unemployment in the country by reducing the demand for labour. However, fortunately, this has not happened in Malaysia particularly because of higher output effect of capital intensive industries. The fear of unemployment is also not haunting because the economy is already a labour-deficit economy.

What is happening in Malaysia is that the prices of products in privatised public utilities like water, electric power, telephone, communication services (like roads) have been continuously rising up. Whenever the cost is increasing, the tariffs are also increasing, but many suspect, at a higher rate. Tenaga Nasional's case is revealing in this connection (see Tables 20.1 and 20.2).

Tenaga Nasional (TN) made continuously higher profit till 1994 and subsequently due to higher cost of purchase of power from other sources on the advice of the government; the total profit has declined in recent years. But the interesting points that cannot be overlooked by discerning readers are that: (i) since 1992 till 1994, the per unit cost of electricity generation continuously went down, but TEN's per unit revenue and profit consistently went up, and (ii) in 1995 and 1996, per unit cost looked up but per unit revenue and profit also went up. Profit after tax has remained substantially high for Tenaga Nasional excepting a few years.

TABLE 1: PROFITS OF TENAGA NASIONAL
(RM MILLION)

Year	Profit before tax	Profit after tax
1992	1404.1	1140.4
1993	1835.7	1519.9
1994	1986.4	1728.0
1995	1624.7	1249.1
1996	1028.1	689.6

Source: Tenaga Nasional (Annual Report), p.10

TABLE 2: PER UNIT REVENUE AND COST OF ELECTRICITY
(CENT)

Year	Per unit revenue	Per unit cost	Profit per unit
1992	18.50	13.40	5.10
1993	19.50	12.80	6.70
1994	20.44	12.50	7.94
1995	21.18	17.50	3.68
1996	22.14	20.33	1.81

Source: Tenaga Nasional (Annual Report), p.11

As a result, consumer surplus, if at all any, has been reduced. The consumers cannot go elsewhere as there no competitive suppliers. The consumers cannot dispense with these services which have almost inelastic demand, and which are essential in nature. Thus, privatisation has created monopoly and monopoly power in the country. These basic services should have more competitive supply market. It is true that because of the lumpy and heavy nature of investment and infrastructure, some of these basic services create natural monopoly. Nevertheless, the introduction of competition in these lines of business should not be impossible in a fast growing economy. The growth of a countervailing power would be a welcome strategy. As monopolists, the suppliers of these services have complete control over prices and outputs, and the market share is almost 100 per cent. In the case of telecom products, some of these services like handphones are of course allowed to be supplied by other competitive producers. This is indeed a very welcome move and should have been extended to the services of basic telephone lines and connections. However, because of the strong market power, these privatised companies have been earning huge amount of profit to the extent of several billions annually and the rate of return is extremely high the like of which is not generally experienced in competitive market economies. For instance, Petronas doubled its profit to RM12 billion in 1996 from 6 billion in 1995 and Proton made a profit of RM1 billion in 1996, Telecom's profit which was RM563 million in 1990 went up to RM1.9 billion in 1996, and similar is the story of other privatised industries in Malaysia.

The role of the government is a bit embarrassing as an equity holder in such companies and as an overall co-ordinator of the economy. Whenever the tariff is to be increased, the government has to accord the permission to do so after being satisfied of the reasons for the proposed tariff increased. Under such a situation, it is indeed difficult for the government to escape from *rent-seeking behaviour*. It should be noted that the government is co-ordinating the functions primarily as the capitalist and there is no better information system in the hands of the government to challenge the cost calculus presented by the privatised companies. The government has to rely on the information on cost and other heads of expenditures as provided by the company. It is often not realistically possible for the government to challenge the logistics. Such an action very often is neither pragmatic nor congenial for business-government relations.

Nobody, therefore, seems to be responsible to check the increase in marginal cost that is proposed to justify the marginal increase in tariff. As a matter of fact, in the case of pure public goods, the marginal cost of supplying the services to an additional person is always zero by definition. But the companies supplying such goods do charge prices on the basis of full cost plus profit margins. It appears that there is no control over cost and costing. Who takes care of the caretaker? It is stated that the government uses the extracted surplus from out of these privatised public utilities to develop the rural services through the method of cross-subsidy. This is indeed salutary, if at all it can be translated into reality, to create a balance between political disequilibrium of the urban consumers and political equilibrium of the rural consumers. Such an action can indeed completely exonerate the government from the charge of being a hard-headed capitalist to a benevolent socialist. But is it possible in reality?

What about social efficiency of privatised industries? This is indeed a debatable issue in Malaysia. Three strands of arguments are prevailing at present. First, it is argued by some quarters that although privatised firms charge higher tariff, it is worth paying that in view of their improved services and better quality products. For instance, if one compares Telecom products and services of seventies, one will appreciate that these are much better now as compared to those of the seventies. The services are now more quick and efficient, and facilities are much better. Second, others argue that both products and services have improved no doubt but the charges are unreasonably higher. Lastly, some will argue that after reaching a peak, the services and efficiency for the consumers are now going downhill and the tariffs are continuously moving up. The case that is often cited in this connection is the case of the postal department in Malaysia. Since there are different strands of opinions and different types of privatised industries, it would been hazardous to pronounce adjustment on this slippery issue. But it seems to be reasonable to say that the private industries supplying pure or mixed types of public goods might have been giving rise to allocative inefficiency, as the prices far exceed their marginal cost. The escalation of costs, of course, may be influenced by a number of exogenous factors. For instance, for TENAGA Nasional, a large part of the increase in the cost is due to the fact that it has to purchase electric power from a private company whose cost of production is higher than

TENAGA's own cost. However, having said all that, it would be imperative to identify those industries, which are having allocative inefficiency, and it would be the responsibility of the government to take appropriate actions in those cases.

There are many other problems besetting the privatised industries in Malaysia. These industries take the advantages of the country's infrastructure but do not pay any attention to the training programme for improving the skill of its manpower. This was the complain made by Malaysia's the then Finance Minister, Dato' Sri Anwar Ibrahim, in June 1997. He made the point that privatised industries are making huge amount of profit; they are concerned only with profit maximisation but neglect the responsibility of manpower and infrastructure development. In privatised industries, the philosophy of *value added* becomes a predominant consideration. This may prevent the maximisation of social welfare and socially desirable goods or goods for the masses (wage goods) may not be produced in adequate amount. Many of the privatised firms in Malaysia are bringing out high tech and costly goods for the export market. The vast majority of the people who form the low paid working class cannot afford to buy these goods which are often produced by them in their factories. There is, thus, a growing sense of *alienation*. For instance, the workers in the Proton automobile factory lament that they cannot afford to buy Proton cars produced by them.

The growth of state capitalism may exacerbate rather than ameliorate the situation. The state may often act as an intermediary between the general public and the privatised industries and in the process of intermediation, it often tends to compromise popular interest for the benefit of the capitalist sector of which it is a part. In this connection, many may be able to cite the case of land deals in Malaysia. It is often alleged that the state buys land at a cheaper rate from the public and sells the same to housing companies at a higher rate. The state thus performs the role of merchant capitalist to extract surplus. Although there is nothing wrong in such deals provided the land has remained fallow for a long-time and belongs to an unproductive rentier class which has possessed the land through the means of unearned increment and, provided the profit from out of that land deal is spent on the creation of public goods or for the maximisation of social welfare function.

Privatisation has also been contributing to many internal contradictions and conflicts. Many small privatised firms cannot effectively compete with the large firms in the matters of technology, economies of scale and resource-use efficiency. The large firms through their strategy of concentration and centralisation of capital are engulfing the small firms by means of take-over, amalgamation and merger. This is alleged to have been happening in Malaysia. Through this process, competition is gradually reduced and large-scale conglomerative monopoly power gets accentuated. And as the monopoly power develops, the social efficiency consideration becomes the first casualty and there develops a contradiction between the objective of privatisation and its actual manifestation.

REFERENCES

Jomo, K.S. (1994), *Malaysian Economy in the Nineties* , Pelanduk Publication, Kuala Lumpur.

Ghosh, B.N. (1998), *Malaysia: The Transformation Within,* Longman, Kuala Lumpur.

Sheriff, Mohd. (1991), "Privatisation" in Lee, K.H. and Nagraj, S. (ed.) (1991), *The Malaysian Economy Beyond 1990,* Persatuan Ekonomi Malaysia, Kuala Lumpur.

Tan, C.H. (1991), "Privatisation in Malaysia and Singapore: A Comparison", *Journal of Southeast Asian Business,* Vol. VII, No. 2.

Chapter 5

FROM PRIVATISATION TO CORPORATISATION: THE STATE RESPONSE TO THE CHANGING DEMAND FOR HEALTH CARE SERVICES IN MALAYSIA

Moha Asri Abdullah & Mohd. Isa Bakar

INTRODUCTION

Economic development and rapid industrialization process directly and indirectly influence lifestyle of individuals, community and society. History has proven that this process has been occurring in many societies throughout the world across without referring to all ethnics, religions, physical appearances, cultures and backgrounds of populace. In many cases, industrialization and modernization processes result in the movement of people, increase in the rate of urbanization, transformation in the composition of demography, their practices and activities as well as status and quality of health. Malaysia, in this regard is not an exception. Rapid economic growth and continuing expansion of industrial and manufacturing activities over the last two or three decades have brought about many changes and influenced the quality and life style, the rise in particularly per capita income and the status of health among the multiethnic societies in the country. The process of transformation in the structure of economic activities from the predominantly agricultural and its related activity to the urban-industrial activities have brought about comfortability and luxurious lifestyle to Malaysian population. Changes in the patterns of diseases among various communities are also noticeable.

Apparently, in addition to the sustained economic growth, the development of new urban areas and an enlargement of the middle class group have largely contributed to the rapid growth of corporate investment in the Malaysian private hospital. All these have had a considerable impact on the existing health care practices and the role of government in the provision of health care services as well as public policy on the health care system in the country as a whole. Indeed, issues such as whether the health care system should be corporatized or otherwise and the potential benefits and potential contradiction in view of protecting the interests of consumers in the country must be carefully and thoroughly studied and analyzed. In this relation, rapid growth of corporately owned private hospitals has also posed services implications on the existing complexity of the issues and subsequently provide greater challenges on the entire health care system in Malaysia. This chapter therefore attempts to vertically review the balance between economic growth and its implications on quality of health among the population in Malaysia, changes in the patterns of diseases contraction among communities, the role of government in the provision of health care system as well as issues and challenges in the pressures for corporatization of health care provision in the country.

ECONOMIC GROWTH, QUALITY OF HEALTH AND CHANGES IN THE PATTERN OF DISEASE

Economic Growth

Before the recent economic crisis, Malaysia has been relatively experiencing a phenomenal economic growth for the past three decades. During the period of 1971-1990, for example, the Malaysian economy has been expanding at a rate of an average of 6.7 percent per annum. During this period, Gross Domestic Product increased almost four-fold, that is from 21.5 billion to

RM79.1 billion (in 1978 prices). From the late 1980s till now, Malaysia become one of the most rapidly growing economies in the world. During the period between 1990-1995, for instance, her economy has been growing at an average rate of 8.4 percent per annum (Malaysia 1996).

One of the most prominent characteristics in the high rates of overall growth is that it is closely associated with the rapid growth of the manufacturing sector. Growth in manufacturing output increased at an average annual rate of 13.3 percent between 1991 and 1995, surpassing the Sixth Plan target of 12.2 percent. Between 1991 and 1995, the non-resource based industries, a group, achieved a higher annual growth rate of 18.3 percent, while resource-based industries grew at 9.1 percent per annum. Continuing increase in the manufacturing outputs over the last two decades has consequently transformed the structure of the Malaysian economy. This transformation can be observed from the declining share of agricultural sector (including forestry and fisheries sub-sectors) in the Malaysian Gross Domestic Product (GDP) i.e. from 30.8 percent in 1970 to about 14.9 percent in 1994 and 16.4 percent in 1995. In the reverse, the share of manufacturing sector to GDP has increased substantially from 13.4 percent in 1970 to 31.4 percent in 1994 and 39.8 percent in 1995 (see Table 1). It is further expected that the sector's share will reach 66.2 percent by the year 2000 (Malaysia 1996).

TABLE 1: MALAYSIAN GDP COMPOSITION (PERCENT) BY ECONOMIC SECTOR 1970-2000

	ECONOMIC SECTOR	1970	1980	1990	1995	2000
1.	Agricultural, livestock, forestry & fishery	30.8	23.4	14.4	16.4	18.4
2.	Mining & quarrying	6.5	5.0	7.7	8.9	10.0
3.	Manufacturing	13.4	20.5	21.3	39.8	66.2
4.	Construction	3.9	4.5	2.8	5.2	8.5
5.	Electricity, gas & water	1.9	2.2	1.5	2.8	4.6
6.	Transportation, storage & communication	4.7	6.3	5.4	8.7	14.5
7.	Whole sale & retail	13.3	12.4	8.8	14.5	22.3
8.	Finance, insurance, real estate & business services	8.4	7.8	7.7	12.8	20.9
9.	Government services	11.1	12.5	8.4	11.6	14.9
10.	Other Services	2.5	2.6	1.6	2.4	3.7
	TOTAL	100.0	100.0	100.0	100.0	100.0

Source: **Ministry of Finance,** *Annual Economic Report* **(various issues), MALAYSIA 1993 and 1996.**

The increased amount of investment in manufacturing sector is said to be the main impetus towards high growth rate of the sector. During the period of 1991-1995, private investment along reached RM84 billion, exceeding the Sixth Plan target of RM80 billion. The amount of approved investments totaled RM116.2 billion, representing an increase of 98.3 percent as compared to the amount approved during the Fifth Malaysian Plan (1986-1990). This is an indication of the continued attractiveness of the country as a location for foreign and local investments (see Malaysia 1996).

With the rapid growth in the manufacturing sector, its share the largest total employment of the all economic sectors at about 24.6 percent. Demand for labor in the sector also grew at 9.0 percent per annum between 1991 and 1995 with the total employment at 2.1 million by the end of 1995. In tandem with the trends in investment and output, the subsectors with high rates of employment growth were the electrical and electronic products, wood and wood based products, petroleum refineries, transport equipment, plastic products and fabricated metal products, with growth rates ranging from 10 percent to 23 percent per annum. Concomitant with this growth, exports of manufactured goods also increased at an average rate of 25.8 percent per annum. This rate is much higher as compared to 19.8 percent during the period of 1986-1990.

The share of manufactured exports total exports increased from 58.8 percent in 1990 to 79.6 percent in 1995. The principal source of export earning was the electrical and electronic products industry with a share of 65.7 percent of manufactured exports in 1995. The strong growth performance of the electrical and electronic products industry, with a growth rate of 19 percent per annum, was mainly attributed to the large increase in production and demand for refrigerating and air-conditioning machinery, as well as radios and television sets. Despite the significance of electrical and electronic products in total exports, analysis of export trends showed that diversification and expansion of the export base has taken place. Although the newly emerging export-oriented industries such as transport equipment, chemical and its related-products, and furniture are relatively small in proportion, but they have recorded high rates of growth. Among the domestic market-oriented industries, the fabricated metal products, basic iron and steel, and non-metallic products industries, registered double-digit growth rates in output of 36 percent, 15.7 percent and 12.8 percent per annum respectively. Indeed, the growth of these industries were linked to the rapid process of industrialization in the country and expansion of related-activities such as the construction, services and the implementation of infrastructure-related projects.

Quality of Health

Rapid economic growth in the country has given the opportunity for the government to pay more attention on the health care of the population. Other than the increase in the government expenditure on the development of health care over the years which will be highlighted in the next few sub-sections, the provision of infrastructures and other basic health facilities has lifted up Malaysia as one of the best few countries recognised by the *World Health Organization* (WHO), (see Moha Asri 1997). Up to the end of 1994, it was estimated that less than 5 percent of the total population in the country who live in the remote areas which are located over three miles from the health facilities such as health centre or clinic centre. The setting up of rural health infrastructure and the successful implementation of promotive and preventive health care programmes are among the most effective measures that determine the wider accessibility and outreach of the health services to the community.

The changes and improvement in the status of health among the population in Malaysia as compared to other Asian countries can be seen in Table 2 below. Comparatively, Malaysia just second behind South Korea in terms of the percentage of total population with access to health care, safe water and sanitation, but far higher rate of accessibility than any other countries in the Table 3. In addition, it is found that the trend of health indicators for Malaysia is moving towards improvements. For example, infant mortility rate (calculated for every 1,000 live birth) in Malaysia has sharply reduced from 30 to 12 during 1980-1994. Life expectancy at birth also among the highest i.e 71 years. Meanwhile, the ratio of the number of population per medical doctor has also declined dramatically.

This can be seen in Table 3, indicating that the number of medical officers has increased from 2,757 persons in 1976 to 10, 238 persons in 1995, while for the ratio of medical officer polulation increased from 1:4,552 to 1:1,275 during same period.

TABLE 3: MEDICAL OFFICER - POPULATION RATIO IN MALAYSIA 1976-1995

Year	No. of Medical Officer	Ratio per population
1976	2,757	1:4,352
1980	3,514	1:3,738
1985	4,939	1:3,174
1990	7,012	1:2,533
1993	8,279	1:2,301
1995	10,238	1:1,275

Source: Ministry of Health, *Annual Report* (various issues), Kuala Lumpur.

According to the reports from Ministry of Health, the death rate of every 1,000 persons has declined sharply from 12.8 percent in 1957 to 4.8 percent in 1993, while infant mortality rate has reduced from 75.5 per 1,000 live birth in 1957 to 10.6 percent in 1993. Mother death rate while giving birth has also declined from 2.82 for every 1,000 births to 0.20 percent during the same period (see Table 4).

TABLE 4: HEALTH INDICATORS AMONG THE MALAYSIAN COMMUNITY 1957-2000

Indicator (per 1,000 persons)	1957	1976	1985	1990	1993	2000e
Birth Rate	46.2	31.7	30.3	27.0	27.1	22.9
Death Rate	12.4	6.2	5.5	4.9	4.8	3.8
Infant Mortality Rate	75.5	30.7	24.0	13.1	10.6	5.4
Child Death Rate	10.7	2.6	2.0	0.9	0.9	0.1
Mother Death Rate (while giving birth)	2.8	0.8	0.6	0.2	0.2	0.1

Note: e - Estimation

Source: Ministry of Health, *Annual Reports* (various issues), Kuala Lumpur

Changes in the Pattern of Diseases in the Community

The process of industrialization and modernization experienced by Malaysia has given considerable impacts on the pattern and types of diseases among the community. In general, it is observed that rapid process of industrialization and modernization has remarkably reduced communicable diseases, while non-communicable diseases has statistically increased. These changes are comparatively similar to those in developed countries. These changes are reflected in the declined rate and number of cases of old and traditional diseases which had become the major threats to the population's health for more than two decades. Instead the emerging of relatively new types and modern diseases is quite alarming.

The Declining Types of Old Diseases

Observation on reports from Ministry of Health indicates that communicable decease such as tuberculosis, measles and whopping cough, leprosy, malaria and to a less extent cholera that had been widely spreaded and affected over the years, have been drastically reduced. This reduction is directly related to the improvement in the health development programs and health care initiated by the government since the Independence. In addition, the public has been widely informed and updated on the causes, dangers and impacts of those diseases on the community at large.

The declined rate of these diseases can be seen on the basis of available data. In 1970, a total of 12.1 death cases caused by tuberculosis for every 100,000 population in Peninsular Malaysia was registered. This figure declined to 1.6 death cases in 1970. In terms of the number, it had been reduced from 1,069 to 286 persons. Based upon this trend, tuberculosis is expected not to be a big threat to the Malaysian population by the year 2000 (see Table 5). In conjunction to the reduction in the death case caused by tuberculosis, the number of tuberculosis cases among individuals is also declined i.e. from 49.11 cases in 1975 to 35.28 cases in 1995.

TABLE 5: NUMBER AND RATE OF DEATH CAUSED BY TUBERCULOSIS IN PENINSULAR MALAYSIA 1970-1990

Year	No. of death	Rate of death per every 100,000 persons	Tuberculosis case for every 100,000 persons
1970	1,069	12.1	na
1975	831	7.7	49.11
1980	596	5.4	41.33
1985	484	3.1	36.76
1986	413	2.6	na
1987	436	2.6	na
1988	399	2.8	na
1989	370	2.6	na
1990	286	1.6	na
1995	23	0.0	35.28
2000e	5	0.0	na

Note: e - Estimate

Source: Ministry of Health, *Annual Reports* (various issues), Kuala Lumpur.

Changes in the pattern of diseases can also be seen with the decline in the leprosy cases that had been once most the dangerous diseases for the community. Table 6 presents the declined cases from 6,445 in 1986 to 1,112 in 1995, while the rate of cases occurring is from 4.0 to 0.2 per 100,000 people for the same period. By the year 2000, this kind of disease is expected to have disappeared in the country.

TABLE 6: NUMBER AND PERCENTAGE OF THE LEPROSY PER EVERY
100,000 PERSONS IN MALAYSIA 1986-2000

Year	No. of cases	Rate of Disease
1986	6,445	4.0
1987	6,364	3.9
1988	5,723	3.4
1989	5,031	2.9
1990	4,149	2.4
1991	3,439	1.9
1992	2,989	1.7
1993	2,520	1.4
1995	1,112	0.2
2000e	none	none

Note: e - Estimate

Source: Ministry of Health, *Annual Reports* (various issues), Kuala Lumpur

Economic growth and industrialization processes have also given considerable impacts on the number of cases and rate of cases of measles and whopping cough. In the case of measles, it is found that a total of 5,163 death cases for every 100,000 persons in 1985 was registered, but it later had decreased to only 517 cases in 1993 and 197 in 1995. This figure has reduced from 32.9% to 2.7% in 1993 and 0.3% in 1995. The same trend is observed in the whopping cough i.e. from 150 cases in 1985 to 18 cases in 1993 and only 4 cases in 1995 producing a negligible rate for any cause to worry. (See Table 7).

TABLE 7: NUMBER AND RATE OF MEASLES AND WHOPPING COUGH (PER EVERY 100,000 PERSONS) IN MALAYSIA BETWEEN 1985-1995

Year	Measles		Whopping Cough	
	No. of cases	Rate	No. of cases	Rate
1985	5,163	32.9	150	0.95
1986	4,697	29.2	68	0.42
1987	5,429	32.9	121	0.73
1988	2,304	13.6	27	0.15
1989	1,028	5.9	25	0.14
1990	563	3.5	23	0.14
1991	275	1.6	20	0.11
1992	378	2.0	25	0.13
1993	517	2.7	18	0.09
1994	429	1.9	11	0.03
1995	197	0.9	4	0.00

Source: Ministry of Health, *Annual Reports* (various issues), Kuala Lumpur.

Development and improvement in the health care programs has also brought about a reduction in malaria fever among the population in the country. Malaria fever is a major threat particularly among the local population especially those who live in the rural areas. Available statistics indicate that during the period of 1957-1966, an estimated of 300,000 malaria cases had occurred every year. However, the cases have been dropped to 49,526 and 39,890 in 1985 and 1993 respectively, while it was further reduced to only 29,213 cases in 1995. A large proportion of malaria fever case that are currently still communicable can be found in Sabah which consist of 73% of the total cases in 1993 and 81% in 1995.

The rate of incident for malaria fever diseases, as is noticed, a total led to 313.6 cases for every 100,000 persons in 1985 and was then dropped to 209.4 cases and 86.1 cases in 1993 and 1995 respectively (see Table 8). By the year 2,000, it is expected that the case will be further reduced to 3,091 with the rate of 21.0.

TABLE 8: MALARIA FEVER (FOR EVERY 100,000 PERSONS) IN MALAYSIA 1985-1995

Year	No. cases	Rate of cases
1985	49,526	313.6
1986	42,710	265.1
1987	33,151	200.6
1988	50,721	299.4
1989	65,283	375.8
1990	50,500	284.3
1991	39,189	223.1
1992	36,853	197.9
1993	39,890	209.4
1994	29,213	193.2
1995	11,398	86.1
2000e	3,091	21.0

Note: e = Estimate

Source: Ministry of Health, *Annual Reports* (various issues), Kuala Lumpur.

The Increasing Types of Some Diseases

Economic growth, development and expansion in health services and health care have not necessarily protected the community from the threat of certain diseases especially some of those communicable diseases. This is obviously shown in the cases of dengue and dengue-related fever in the country. In 1985, there were 367 dengue and dengue related fever in Malaysia. This number was confined to the rate of 2.32 cases for every 100,000 persons. However, the number of dengue and dengue-related fever had increased quite alarmingly to 1,924 cases in 1990, 3,436 cases in 1993 and 5,214 cases in 1995. Simultaneously, the rate has also risen from 18.04 cases to 21.94 cases for every 100,000 persons in 1993 and 1995 respectively. Looking at the trend, the cases are expected to rise to 8,168 with the rate of 29.31 by the year 2000.(See Table 9).

TABLE 9: DENGUE AND DENGUE-RELATED DISEASES (FOR EVERY 100,000 PERSONS) IN MALAYSIA 1985-1995

Year	No. of cases	Rate of cases
1985	367	2.32
1986	1,408	8.74
1987	2,025	12.25
1988	1,428	8.42
1989	1,470	8.46
1990	1,924	10.83
1991	3,070	17.48
1992	2,753	14.79
1993	3,436	18.04
1994	4,893	19.93
1995	5,214	21.94
2000e	8,168	29.31

Note: *e* = Estimate

Source: Ministry of Health, *Annual Reports* (various issues), Kuala Lumpur.

The Increasing Trends of Non-Communicable and Modern Diseases

Apparently, modernization processes of the country has either directly or indirectly resulted in the increase of non-communicable diseases and other communicable modern diseases. This situation is reflected in the types of non-communicable diseases that threaten adult population such as hearth problems, hypertension or high-blood pressures, cancer, HIV carrier and AIDS diseases. These are other than the increase in the road accidents which are directly related to higher life style, and improved quality of life resulting from robust modernization process in the country.

Data from the Ministry of Health indicates that several types of cardiovascular deceases (heart and high-blood pressures related diseases) have dramatically increased during the 1980s and 1990s. In 1975, there were 16,347 patients who were admitted to the hospital caused by various types of cardiovascular diseases. These numbers increased to 19,472 and 66,530 in

1980 and 1990 respectively. The total number of cases continued to rise i.e. 83,858 patients in 1993 and 115,981 patients in 1995 and is expected to reach 268,000 by the year 2000. Following the increase in the number of admitted patients, death cases caused by cardiovascular problems has increasingly risen i.e. from 2,730 in 1975 to 6,352 and 7,213 cases in 1993 and 1995 respectively, while a total of 10,759 cases is expected by the year 2000.

TABLE 10: NUMBER OF ADMITTANCE AND DEATH CASES CAUSED BY CARDIOVASCULAR DISEASES 1975-2000

Year	No. of Admittance	No. of Death Cases
1975	16,347	2,730
1980	19,472	2,523
1990	66,530	5,459
1991	68,584	5,383
1992	69,284	5,487
1993	83,858	6,352
1994	89,119	7,118
1995	115,981	7,213
2000e	268,985	10,759

Note: e = Estimate
Source: Ministry of Health, *Annual Reports* (various issues), Kuala Lumpur

The increase in the modern diseases is illustrated in the number of neoplasm malignant or cancer-related diseases. In the early years of Independence, this type of disease had not been a major threat to the health of the population. However, the situation has changed considerably in 1980s and 1990s. For example, a total of 24,472 cases admitted to the hospital were caused by cancer related diseases. The number has risen to 29,295 and 32,752 cases in 1993 and 1995 respectively. In terms of the number of patients passed away due to this type of disease has also increased from 2,003 in 1987 to 2,224 in 1990 and 2,981 cases in 1995, (see Table 11). All these numbers have not yet included those who were admitted and passed away in the private hospitals in the country. Moreover, HIV carriers and AIDS disease are also increasing.

Data from the Ministry indicate that there were three cases of HIV carriers and a case of AIDS which were identified in 1986 with no death case caused by them, as yet.

TABLE 11: NUMBER OF ADMITTED AND DEATH CASES CAUSED BY MALIGNANT NEOPLASM IN THE GOVERNMENT HOSPITALS 1987-1995

Year	No. of Admitted	No. of Death
1987	24,472	2,003
1988	25,169	2,208
1989	27,841	2,214
1990	26,845	2,224
1991	26,054	2,186
1992	27,570	2,341
1993	29,295	2,234
1994	32,117	2,387
1995	33,189	2,763

Source: Ministry of Health, *Annual Report*, Kuala Lumpur

Nonetheless, the figure increased to 3,376 HIV carriers and 72 AIDS cases in 1994. There were two death cases caused by AIDS in 1987 and the number increased to 58 cases in 1994 (see Table 12).

TABLE 12: NUMBER OF HIV CARRIER AND AIDS CASES IN MALAYSIA 1985-1994

Year	HIV Carrier	AIDS Cases	No. of Death Cases
1985	-	-	-
1986	3	1	1
1987	4	1	2
1988	19	4	3
1989	177	6	3
1990	650	12	8
1991	1,672	14	14
1992	2,377	10	19
1993	2,498	18	14
1994	3,376	72	58
TOTAL	10,776	138	121

Source: Ministry of Health, *Annual Reports* (various issues), Kuala Lumpur.

THE PROVISION OF HEALTH CARE IN MALAYSIA

The World Bank estimated that in 1990, the world spent less than US$1,700 billion on health and the comprised of 8% of global income. The total amount of spending on health in the developing countries of Asia, Africa and Latin America totaled to about US$170billion. It was also recorded that the total annual health spending varies from less than US$10 per person in several African and Asian countries to more than US$2,700 in the United States. There was also considerable variations within regions. For instance, in Africa, Tanziana spent only US$4 per capita for health, while Zimbabwe spent US$42 per person each year.

In Malaysia, the government has been historically responsible for the provision of health care services. Since Independence, various health programmes and health care services through community development have been introduced and implemented throughout the country, in the urban as well as rural areas. Development in the health care have generally been focused on health care programmes for mother and child, family planning, the improvement in environmental sanitation and the improvement of diet practises amongst population. Other programmes have also been introduced specifically to reduce the gap between the basic health care provision and facilities within the urban and the rural areas. These are done mainly through the establishment of health centres and small clinics (or popularly known as rural clinics) in rural areas. All these can be seen through the budget of the Ministry of Health whereby, Malaysia has experienced an increase in real terms although the allocation remains more or less constant at about 5% of the National Budget. In 1965, a total of RM142.7 million was budgeted for health care programmes and this figure had increased to RM895.6 million in 1980. In 1995, the government allocated RM2.5billion for physical development and operating budget of the health care programmes in the country and this comprisied 5.31% of the national budget and 2.28% of the GNP(See Table 13). It was recorded that 76% of the total health expenditure is borne by the Government.

TABLE 13: ANNUAL BUDGET OF THE MINISTRY OF HEALTH IN MALAYSIA 1965-1995

Year	Annual Budget (RM)		Total	% of National Budget	% of GNP	Percapital Allocation
	Development	Operating	Total	Budget		Fill
1965	27,298,585	115,362,353	142,660,938	-	-	-
1970	26,000,000	157,033,101	183,033,101	-	-	-
1980	136,272,457	759,307,400	895,579,857	-	-	-
1986	159,277,400	1,174,345,000	133,622,440	4.33	2.46	83
1987	93,090,400	1,081,695,700	1,174,786,100	4.29	2.07	71
1988	121,987,800	1,117,411,900	1,239,399,700	4.41	2.04	73
1989	206,311,950	1,221,630,600	1,427,942,550	4.73	2.19	82
1990	345,716,280	1,278,135,500	1,623,851,780	4.86	2.14	91
1991	594,622,000	1,446,500,400	2,014,162,400	5.31	2.50	112
1992	689,416,200	1,663,262,400	2,352,678,600	5.18	2.68	126
1993	549,473,910	1,932,917,800	2,482,391,710	5.62	2.60	131
1994	337,082,800	2,053,422,100	2,390,504,900	4.07	2.30	121
1995	427,966,000	2,165,265,000	2,593,231,000	5.31	2.28	129

Source: Ministry of Health, *Finance Division* (various years), Kuala Lumpur.

Therefore, the majority of health and health-related facilities in the country belongs to the public sector funded through general taxation. The financing of these facilities come mainly from the public revenues. It is also recorded that the fees collected in the government hospitals contribute only about 5% of the total Ministry of Health's expenditure. In 1993, for example, the *Ministry of Health* operated 16 general hospitals and 85 district hospitals. These provided some 26,106 beds, while there were seven special medical institutions which provided 7,077 beds for the treatment of mental illness, leprosy and tuberculosis. Moreover, there were about six government hospitals operated by other ministries provided special services such as university teaching and research as well as medical services to populations, including members of the armed forces and the aborigines.

It is noted that the private sector provided about 24% of the total health expenditure in various forms. The existing private hospitals and clinics in Malaysia come along with history. In the late colonial period and early years of Independence, private hospitals were either church or community-based charitable institutions. Private hospitals also were established in order to provide rudimentary services which plantation companies were obliged to give for the employees under the labor legislation. In addition, a number of smaller nursing and maternity house were operated by private entrepreneurs(mainly doctors in partnership with family members or local business figures). In 1993, for instance, there were 180 hospitals and nursing homes established by the private sector and they supplied about 5,799 beds for the targeted population.

In Malaysia, there are a few other agencies, organizations or schemes which provide certain benefits to their respectives individuals or employees or communities. The **Social Security Organization (SOCSO)** for instance, implements a shceme for the provision of some benefits (compensations) to employees with respect to injury, invalidity or disease related to occupation. The scheme however, covers only those earning less than RM2,000.00 per month in the private sector. The **Employment Provident Fund (EPF)** also allows members to withdraw some of their saving for medical expenses. Other than this, the private health insurance which also provides a number of schemes in Malaysia, are found throughout the country, although they have not been generally well developed. Currently, many of the health insurance coverage are provided in the form of a package offered by the employers rather than through

the initiative of the employees. It was estimated that only about 250,000
persons were covered by private health insurance in 1983. By 1995, however,
the estimated insured population (life/health) was 15% and is projected to be
50% in the year 2000.

It is believed that a significant number of the population in urban and town
areas visit private clinics and hospitals where services provided are paid
through fee-for-service either by them or their private employers. Some
important proportion of the population also seek treatment from practitioners of
traditional medicine on the same mode of payment, although the number is
declining presently. For some bigger firms, they provide medical reimbursement
schemes to their employees and family members. The facilities and benefits
vary accordingly. A survey conducted recently found that nearly two-thirds of
the companies have some kind of medical reimbursement scheme for their
workers. The estimated amount of benefit payment consists of between 2% and
3% of the total employees' wages. The provision of health care is also available
through community-initiated and sponsored activities, thus they are poorly
organized and short-lived. At present, those who are relatively active
concentrate on urban and town-based and administrated by non-government
organizations (NGOs). Whereas in the rural areas, community-based health
care programmes have been implemented and coordinated by the government
under the implementation strategy of the primary health care level

THE PROCESS OF CHANGE IN THE HEALTH CARE SYSTEM

Malaysia, generally has been able to provide good quality health care in an
equitable manner. By utilizing only three percent of the nations' Gross
Domestic Product (GDP), the health services are available to almost all sorts of
community in the country in 1990. This was considerably lower than the health
expenditure of other developing countries as shown in Table 14. The relatively
smaller percentage of the health expenditure for the country is attributed to the
emphasis given to setting up of rural health infrastructure and the
implementation of promotive and preventive health care programmes which are
basically low-cost. The result in terms of health status in Malaysia however, is
far higher as compared to other developing countries as shown earlier in Table

14. Moreover, if compared to the USA where health care costs are about 12% of GDP (see Table 14), and yet 50 million of its population remain less or unaccessible to health care, it truly reflects that Malaysia need to study thoroughly the experience of the developed countries to suit our own health provision and financing system. All these indicate that there is an increasing interest in the way how health services should be funded both in developed and developing countries alike. It is also a reflection of financial pressures and financing mechanism in providing the accessible service throughout the community.

TABLE 14: HEALTH EXPENDITURE AS A PERCENTAGE OF GROSS DOMESTIC PRODUCT FOR SELECTED COUNTRIES IN 1990

Country	Percentage of GDP
Malaysia	3.0
Papua New Guinea	4.4
Thailand	5.0
China	3.5
Sri Lanka	3.7
Hong Kong	5.7
Korea	6.6
USA	12

Source: World Bank 1993 *World Development Report*, World Bank: Washington D.C.

In Malaysia, there are a number of situational pressures determining the recommendation towards corporatization of health care system. Like many other countries, health care cost is demonstrably escalating. More importantly, the issue of escalating health care costs and the need to search for the most appropriate and acceptable health care financing model has been identified as a serious emerging issue for the country. The issue will become even more critical in the coming decades when market forces and other less predictable factors will greatly influence the health care system. Meanwhile, the government is seen quite reluctant to increase the subsidy of the public health care delivery system. In addition, demographic changes have also dictated the pressure when variations in the size of the population, the composition of the population, differences in income levels affect and influence the health care needs and provisions as well as financing. Rising expectation from the middle classes also added to the pressure as reflected in the demand for high-technology (often followed by higher cost) medical care. Moreover, as income levels rise, and basic health problems associated with absolute poverty become less significant, they give rise to changes in the patterns of diseases. As standard of living improves and morbidity patterns changes, they have an impact on health care cost. As discussed previously, communicable diseases are gradually overtaken by diseases of the affluence.

Meanwhile, the unprecedented growth of the private medical hospitals or clinics presently has give a twist towards privatisation or corporatization. The increase in the number of private hospital and private clinics, has wide-ranging implications on the public sector and overall health care cost. Much of this increase has been due to major commercial investment. Table 15 indicates the growth of private hospitals, nursing homes and maternity homes in Malaysia.

TABLE 15: THE NUMBER OF PRIVATE HOSPITALS, NURSING HOMES AND MATERNITY HOMES IN MALAYSIA 1980-1995

Description	1980	1985	1990	1995
No. of Institutions	50	133	174	197
No. of Beds	1,171	3,666	4,675	7,511

Source: Ministry of Health, *Annual Reports*, (various issues): Government Printer: K.L.

The main feature of private hospital investments often comprises consortium involving corporations specialising in urban development and construction and local medical entrepreneurs. In addition, there is also a trend where state economic development corporations have also been active in private hospital investment. This is normally done through the formation of a consortium, such as the Johor State Development Corporation which has developed a number of hospitals in its own right through its health care subsidiary. Examples can easily be presented here. When one look at one of the Malaysia's biggest and most sophisticated hospital, the Subang Jaya Medical Centre. It is controlled by Malaysia's largest company, Sime Darby Berhad. The Berjaya Group, another example, through its subsidiary Berjaya Leisure, has acquired almost 89% of Hospital Pantai Berhad, while another example of conglomerate involvement in the private hospital sector is that of the Lion Group which owned about 70% of the Mahkota Medical Centre in the state of Malacca.

With the private medical services being mostly concentrated in high income areas, the distribution of equitable medical and health resources is thus made difficult. With the higher incomes, expectations and demands for health care, the cost of facilities and treatment also rise. Therefore, these existing opportunities taken by most private health sector and by being lucrative, are also able to attract more doctors, especially specialists from the public sector resulting in the public medical sector facing an acute shortage of staff. All these have added to the pressure towards privatisation or corporatization of the health care system in Malaysia. Originally, privatisation of the welfare state was launched by the government through the *Privatisation Policy in 1983* and the health care services are among the social services to be privatised under the *Privatisation Master Plan.*

In this relation, privatisation means the transfer of dominant responsibility from the government to the private sector's firms or agencies. This transfer may include the financing of health care itself as well as the supply of goods and services in terms of production and/or distribution either for both or each of them. Hence, there are two modes in which privatisation of health care should take place. One mode is that privatisation is viewed as a way of reducing Government's financial commitment to the provision production and distribution of goods such as health care. In this respect, the health care system will be relying more heavily on user fees and private health insurance. The other mode is seen as the government relinquishing its responsibility for the direct provision, production and distribution of selected health care services to the private firms or agencies.

Some changes on government policy towards private hospitals reflect strong official encouragement for its expansion and a series of incremental policy decisions supportive of the private sector. For instance, the Second

Outline Prospective Plan (1991-2000) singed the governments intention to foster the private sector as well as recognized the need for public policy to deal with the issues of quality care and accessibility (Malaysia 1991:150). Meanwhile in the Mid-term Review of the Sixth Malaysia Plan (1991-1995), the principal statement is that there is a need for the Ministry of Health to ensure that the distribution of man-power between the public and private sectors was equitable . Therefore, the expanded role of the private hospital sector is regarded as parallel to the long-standing policy of the government's intention to foster public-private sector cooperation and minimize competition between the sectors. The issue of health care is also included in the overall concept of a Caring Society in the national *Vision 2020*, i.e the government's articulation of its vision of a fully developed nation by the year 2020. In this view, social welfare policy has also demanded a greater role from the private health sector. All together, there are nine central strategic challenges laid out by the Vision 2020, and among the challenges which have more direct reference to health care are access to health facilities, quality and a caring culture and ethical society.

FROM PRIVATIZATION TO CORPORATIZATION: THE CHANGING PRESSURE ON HEALTH CARE REFORM

It is important to note that the call for a study of ways in which the health services delivery system could be made more efficient and equitable was made in the Mid-term Review of the Fourth Malaysia Plan (1981-1985). This concern specifically touches on the possibility of developing an alternative way of the provision of the delivery in the health services in Malaysia, inter alia, include: implications of increasing health care cost to the government; inequitable distribution of health care resources between urban and rural areas; over-dependence on services provides by the government; people's expectation on sharing the burden of health care cost. Following this concern, a number of studies were under taken by various quarters. These include the National Health Financing Study, National Health Security Fund, National Health Plan Study and the study on Corporatization of 14 General Hospitals. The first two studies which were conducted in 1984/85 and 1987/88 have made a number of recommendations in order to improve the present health care system.

These recommendations refer to some reformations which should be incorporated through increasing expenditure on health, improved efficiency through corporatization, the need to address manpower issues and regulate the growth of the private health sector. It was also recommended that the proposed reform should be gradual involving three main steps. Firstly, it is essential to have a proper database and control processes in order to make sure that the future national health care provisional strategy is acceptable, affordable, efficient and equitable. Secondly, it is essential to educate the public about options for health care financing within the wider framework of a national health plan. Lastly, it is essential to implement one or two national demonstration on health financing projects to ensure a relatively proper introduction of the new proposed system.

Another study on the National Health Plan was carried out in 1990/1992 with the purpose to recommend and integrating the health care delivery system through the involvement of the public, private and NGOs. The end product of the study is to develop a common planning methodology in order to produce a balanced health plan for the country. In line with this objective, the final report of the study emphasises on a number of recommendations including decentralization of the public health care system; reorganizing the health planning processes which would reassure a change in the role of the main players, medical community or general public; in this relation, the report stresses on a clear policy decision needed for this; the focus of planning should be on programme and organisational planning; an exercise on assessing disease burden should be conducted; and regulating private sector through direct control measures. As a follow-up of the Health Financing Studies' recommendations and in line with the Government's Privatization Policy, the government is now seriously considering the corpora-tization of public hospitals. In 1992, for instance, the *National Heart Institute* was the first public hospital to be corporatized. A study on corporatization of 14 General Hospitals was also commissioned in view of this consideration which was completed in 1995. The government is now considering the implementation of the study recommendations in the Seventh Malaysia Plan (1995-2000).

CORPORATIZATION OF HEALTH CARE SYSTEM: ISSUES AND CHALLENGES

There have been ranges of pros and cons issues in the corporatization of health care system in Malaysia, all of which will provide greater challenges for the government to start with. Corporatization and expansion of private hospital in the country will enable large amount of capital to be injected into the health care system. In this relation, it will undoubtedly enhance substantial infrastructure development to take place and relieve some of the pressure from the overburdened public health care system. More significantly, this rapid health infrastructural development which will take place in view of corporatization occurs without increased public expenditure. Apparently this would further assist the Malaysian economy to remain internationally competitive despite undergoing a period of difficulties arising out of the financial turmoil and economic recession by holding or reducing levels of domestic taxation. The purpose of corporatization of 14 hospitals across the country would also be to expand the plurality in the Malaysian health care system (i.e. corporatized hospitals, public hospitals other than the existing private health care) giving consumers more choices and this may contribute to greater efficiency, self-reliance rather than dependence upon the provision of inefficient health care as has been heavily subsidized by the government. The corporatization of public hospitals and health care system will enhance competition for clients into the Malaysian hospital system, since consumers will be able to compare costs and standards of services between the existing facilities available to them.

Corporatization will also provide an alternative management system and greater flexibility in recruitment and remuneration of hospital staffs. This will be highly essential in view of the existing hierarchical and bureaucratic approach of the civil service. Moreover, corporatization and the growth of private commercial hospitals here will encourage the promotion of higher standard of Malaysia's health care system internationally. Technology transfer will be facilitated through the participation of Multinational Corporations (MNCs) in management and capital investment as well as research and development. All these will further stimulate Malaysian health care corporatizations to start investing in neighbouring countries because health care system will become the future export commodity of the country even though the proportion, amount and value may be small. The corporatization of the public hospital will further promote a number of complementary areas where the private, the corporations and the public hospital will play their parts. At present, it is observed that public patients have occasionally been sent to private hospitals for certain specialist diagnosis and treatment. The government is also presently considering contracting private hospitals to treat public patients on a regular basis. At the same time, several private hospitals have provided training for medical personnel through the establishment of private colleges. All these will make a further smooth transition to corporatization process of public hospitals in the country.

The proposed corporatization will direct or indirectly lead to the rapid growth of corporate investment in hospitals as it is happening in the private hospitals. This will raise criticisms among those who are concerned with the interests of consumers in a number of aspects including societal values, equity, cost and quality. The corporatizations of public hospitals like the existing private health care, will make the services and facilities available only to those who are able to pay, those with private insurance or with employers', health care benefits. This reflects not only the concern of limited accessibility to the health care services, but also highlights concerns about equity. There will be several Malaysian leading corporate hospitals which offer the latest diagnostic and curative techniques and equipments, and high standards of accommodation, while at the same time the remaining public hospitals do not improve significantly from their present conditions. In view of equity issues, the geographical location of the 14 proposed corporatized hospitals and the existing major private hospitals in the country are mostly concentrated in urban areas with the highest concentration to be in Kuala Lumpur and Klang Valley. If this be the trend, it would further reflect the uneven distribution of health care services and facilities between the urban and the rural areas. This is particularly true when the poorest groups amongst the rural population and workers in rubber and palm oil estates have been provided with inadequate and little treatment yet very basic and minor first-aids. In the case of workers in the estates, for example, a study by the Malaysia Medical Association in 1988 found that only one full-time doctor is working in the plantation sector, and not a single dental officer, nurse or public health inspector exists. (see Rampal, Othman and Nagaraj 1988). While a follow-up study in 1994 indicated that no significant improvements had occurred after the six-year period (see MMA 1995). Despite the fact that small hospitals and health centres have been opened in regional areas, their services, standards of specilists and personnels available are unlikely to be similar to those in the urban areas.

High costs of the would be corporatized hospitals and commercial private hospitals to the majority of population also become concerns of many observers and raise the question of limited accessibility. For example, the Health Ministry has even raised this concern to private hospital in 1993 to lower their fees to accommodate middle and lower-income patients (NST 1993), while in 1995 the Ministry proposed the private hospital to allocate 10% of their profit to a welfare fund for charitable purposes in the health sector (NST 1995). The high cost of medical treatments in the private hospital was clearly rampant when even the Deputy Domestic Trade and Consumer Affairs Minister had described some of the existing private hospital fees as exorbitant, their profit very high. In view of this too, the Minister encouraged private hospitals to treat large number of patients at a lower margin of profits. Considering that the question of accessibility is raised in the existing private hospitals, there will be an identical issues which would be stipulated in the corporatization of the public hospitals. Moreover, experience in corporatization of several government agencies and projects such as North-South Highway, Indah Water etc has shown how difficult they have been in determining rate and costs which should be set for the consumers. It seems that the profit motive alone does not appear to have resulted in healthy and vigorous competition and improvements in the quality of services provided. Therefore, there is the issue of accreditation system which would have to be developed and that its standard guidelines would be compulsory for all the corporatized and private hospitals.

The privatization and corporatization of hospitals would also raise the issue of outflow of medical staffs and experts to the privatized and corporatized hospitals and hence leaving public hospitals into a chronic shortage of labour. This would lead to a stiff competition not merely within the privatized and corporatized hospitals, but also between them and the public hospitals. This issue has become highly critical since the time many medical staff, specialists and nursing staff left the public sector to take advantage of what they believe to be better pay, work conditions and career prospects. For example, in 1994 a total of 838 medical posts (almost one in four) were vacant in Malaysian public hospitals (NST 1994), leaving an issue for Malaysian health planners to ponder over. It was also recorded that in mid-1995, the public hospitals were still short of 1,638 nurses or 11% of its requirements despite the recruitment of foreign nurses, the easing of retirement regulations and financial incentives (The Sun 1995). If the outflow of specialists, medical experts and nursing staff continues especially before their period of compulsory services has expired in the era of corporatization, the government would loose the substantial amount of bond and capital cost expenditure.

It seems that the proposed corporatization of public hospitals and the expansion of private hospitals would also contradict the government's recent emphasis on the development of health promotion and prevention and reduce the need for institutionalized care through early outpatient diagnosis and treatment (see Ministry of Health 1990 and Mahathir 1993). Since the prime rationale for *"commercial hospitals"* would be to market their services for profit, this emphasis would is likely to be irrelevant. Moreover, the proposed corporatization and expansion of private hospitals is also viewed as vulnerable in an economic downturn nowadays. Before the crisis, a growing demand for exclusive and private health care guaranteed the continuing economic propriety and future sustainability of commercialised hospitals. Nonetheless, a recession now might have serious implications on the proposal since many of the would be commercialised hospitals would rely on out-of-pockets payments by middle-upper class Malaysians. This class people would return to the public health care and hence raising the issues on the increasing of public hospitals.

It is also important to note that the growth of commercial hospital with a proposed corporatization of health services raises universal issues on ethical and community values. The proposed health care system poses concerns that commercial hospitals may undermine some of the principles of the "caring society" that are clearly envisaged in the "Vision 2020". It has been the practise of many hospitals to cross-subsidize the treatment of poor patients by charging a premium on those who are better off. How far this aspect is being taken into consideration in the case of corporatized hospitals is hard to be certain.

Concluding Remarks

Health care system in Malaysia has been the subject of considerable focus in studies and discussions and from it various issues and challenges have been generated for the public, private, policy-makers, academicians and the government to consider. In many cases, greater attention given to the country's health care system is highly correlated to the continued economic growth, the development of existing and new urban areas, an enlarged middle class, increased in the standard of living among the population, inclusion of hospital insurance in salary package and a growing demand for a high quality of health care system. The growing commercialization of the public hospitals and efforts from the government to upgrade the existing general hospitals through privatization strategies and then its intention to corporatize them are among the obvious issues. These have rapidly changed the health care system, perception and expectation of the public, health care provision and financing, and hence has a considerable impacts on the issues and challenges for the future health care system in Malaysia.

The privatization efforts and strategies, and the intention to corporatize the public hospitals, other than expansion of private hospitals through corporate business ventures have indeed provided greater alternatives to the public for hospital care services. The initiative towards this plurality and diversity is seen as a way of developing the hospital system. It will undoubtedly enhance substantial infrastructure development to take place without the need for increased public expenditure and thus relieve some financial burden for the government. It also means assisting the health care services to be more internationally competitive. Greater efficiency and flexibility in the management of health care services such as recruitment and remuneration of hospital staffs are also seen to take place. Furthermore, the involvement of big companies and multi-national corporations (MNCs) in lucratively private investment will further enhance the promotion of higher standard of commercial hospitals and further facilitate the transfer of advanced technology to the locals.

Nonetheless the privatization and intention to corporatize public hospitals will raise a number of issues such as societal values, equity, pinching staffs, high cost and low quality. In addition, the existence of regional dualism vis-a-vis. rural versus urban settings will create serious and crucial problems with respect to the affordability of both the rural and urban poor of the country to finance their health care cost. All these have resulted in greater challenges in the balance of future health care system and health care financing in the country. At present, some privatization programmes in some parts of the public hospital services has relatively served the people well and have reduced the governments' financial burdens. There are strong indications now that the cost of health care services is exceeding the capacity and affordability of the government to fund it. In view of this, consistent studies and reviews of the fee structure for the government hospitals are frequently made to find a solution of the possible problems in the national health financing scheme through corporatization strategies. It is now realized that there is no single perfect mechanism of health care provision since each system has its strengths and weaknesses. Past experiences from the United States and some other European countries should provide a good lesson to the government to remain selective and careful in adopting any scheme or system. It seems that the intention on corporatization of public hospitals is more appropriate as a complement to the introduction and the establishment of a health care financing scheme. This is because some of the criticisms on societal values, equity, cost and quality will be well answered. Moreover, it will be more effective than any form of government direct intervention, rules or regulations to control the health care market.

REFERENCES

Abu Bakar Suleiman 1993, "The View of the Ministry of Health on the Role of the Private Sector, the National Health Conference", 13-14 May, Kuala Lumpur.

Abu Bakar Suleiman 1996, "Health Care Financing in Malaysia: Future Strategies" the First Joint Ministry of Health-Academy of Medicine Scientific Meeting, 1 November, Kuala Lumpur.

Barraclough S. 1997, "The Growth of Corporate Private Hospitals in Malaysia: Policy Contradictions in Health System Pluralism" International Journal of Health Services, Vol. 27, No. 4, (643 - 659).

Chee H.L. 1990, Health and Health Care in Malaysia, Present Trends and Implications for the Future, Institut Pengajian Tinggi, Universiti Malaya; Kuala Lumpur.

Jabatan Penerangan Malaysia 1991, Obstetrik dan Ginekologi: Asas Kesihatan dan Pembangunan; JPM: Kuala Lumpur.

Malaysian Medical Association 1995, Survey on the Health Care Delivery System in the Plantation Sector in Peninsular Malaysia, MMA: Kuala Lumpur.

Ministry of Finance, Annual Reports (various issues) Government Printer: Kuala Lumpur.

Ministry of Health, Annual Budgets, (various issues), Finance Division: Kuala Lumpur.

Ministry of Health, Annual Economic Report, (various issues), Government Printer: Kuala Lumpur.

Moha Asri Abdullah 1996, "Reformasi Perkhidmatan Kesihatan: Sejauhmanakah ia perlu". Dewan Ekonomi, Disember, Kuala Lumpur.

Moha Asri Abdullah 1997, Pembangunan Perindustrian di Malaysia, Fajar Bakti, Shah Alam.

Osman Ali 1995, "Menangani Peralihan Epidemiology Akibat Permodenan dan Perindustrian", Simposium Kebudayaan Indonesia-Malaysia Ke VI, 22 - 23 November, Kuala Lumpur.

Rampat L., Othman P., and Nagaraj S, 1990, A Study on the Health Care Delivery System in Plantation Sector in Malaysia, Malaysian Medical Association: Kuala Lumpur.

World Bank, 1993. World Development Report, World Bank: Washington D.C.

World Bank, 1996. World Development Report, World Bank: Washington D.C.

Newpapers

New Straits Times, July 23, 1993.
New Straits Times, May 16, 1994.
New Straits Times, December 5, 1994.
The Sun, July 25, 1995.
New Straits Times, November 7, 1995.
New Straits Times, January 18, 1996.
New Straits Times, April 23, 1996.
The Star, June 11, 1996.

Chapter 6

POLITICS OF PRIVATISATION: THE CASE OF MALAYSIA'S TELECOMMUNICATION

Richard Allen Drake & Mohamad Md. Yusoff

INTRODUCTION

The recent explosive growth of information technologies has dramatically affected the place of telecommunications in the life of nations. It now occupies pride of place among the infrastructural means of economic activity. This development has been likened to such other revolutionary changes as the railroads, the automobile, and even the printing press. It is asserted that any nation state whose legitimacy depends upon economic prosperity, or the promise thereof, has no recourse but to make provisions for this new component of economic infrastructure. For most countries, the capital for this infrastructural development is typically beyond the governments resources and they have found it necessary to enlist private capital (Roche and Blaine 1996: 12ff).

Since the late 1970s, the worldwide telecommunications industry has been undergoing tremendous change as a result of several factors: the emergence of new communications technologies, the globalization of communications, and the increasing importance attributed to information-based activities in national economies. These changing conditions have sparked a debate among policy-makers over the appropriate response of governments to the changing telecommunications environment. A recurring theme of this debate is whether governments should seek to minimize their presence in the industry, both as service providers --- through privatization and liberalization --- and as regulators.

This paper takes as its springboard a specific aspect of this question: whether the same benefits anticipated by proponents, who base their expectations on conditions in the advanced economies of Japan and the West, will accrue in developing nations as well. The first section of the paper considers this question, finding that the potential gains provided by liberalization and privatization are sufficiently uncertain to raise questions over why developing countries are pressing forward with the policies. In an effort to understand the origins and anticipated outcomes of these policies, the subsequent sections examine the recent policy history of Malaysia's Telecoms Department which, since the early 1970s, has been expanding competition in the market and was itself privatized in 1987. Among the conclusions reached by this analysis are that, whatever the stated objectives pertaining to economic efficiency, increased competition, and the easing of the government's burden, liberalization and privatization are functioning primarily to channel wealth and power into the hands of a favored elite. (Kennedy, L.B. 1990, 91)

THE PROBLEM OF PRIVATIZATION

One of the most striking aspects of the privatization debate is the lightening speed with which privatization and liberalization have moved to the top of the policy agenda and the list of policy options in many countries. As David Heald, a critic of privatization policy points out, "privatization" is a word that had scarcely been heard before 1979 (1984: 36). Indeed, much of the privatization-related literature to date has been encumbered by the need to give lengthy definitions of privatization and its possible permutations.

The willingness of people to so readily and quickly accept the policies of privatization and liberalization is surprising because they are fairly contentious issues. There are, of course, disputes between those who see the issues entirely in terms of economic efficiency and those who adhere to the liberal tradition of state guardianship of social welfare. But even among those who have found common ground on which to consider the issues, there are differences of opinion: whether the relief brought to national budgets through privatization is a long-term gain or a short-term fix; whether denationalization promotes or hinders increased competition; even whether natural monopolies still exist in fields such as telecommunications. These become protracted arguments when a lack of experience produces uncertainty and risk.

Despite these concerns, privatization has proceeded apace, in fields as disparate as public transportation, garbage collection and medical services, and in countries as dissimilar as Great Britain, Chile, Mali, and Japan. In practical terms, the debate becomes not one of whether, but how, in an almost cookbook fashion, to go about the business of privatizing and liberalizing.

In telecommunications, these twin policies have dramatically changed the familiar landscape of the industry. Throughout the world, there is a tradition of state-operated telecommunications systems which is as old as the provision of the service itself. Today however, there is no longer a single member of the OECD which has not liberalized at least the provision of terminal equipment, while others have begun to open their basic services networks and international services to competition. Japan and Britain have completely privatized their systems.

Increasingly, we are seeing these same policies emerging in developing countries where state operation has also been the tradition. Malaysia, Botswana, Thailand, Zaire, and Argentina are among those which are reported to be considering or actively implementing policies of privatization and liberalization. But if there are uncertainties over these policies' merits when applied in industrialized states, the questions are thornier still when the somewhat different circumstances of developing countries are considered.

Among the benefits that proponents of privatization envision are the diversification of telecommunications service offerings, the widening of opportunities accruing from research and development efforts, and the expansion of innovation considered crucial to gaining a share of the international market for information goods and services. (H. Ergas & Okayama 1984) Such benefits may, in fact, be obtained, although all of these appear, on the face of it, to be dependent on a well-developed national telecommunications sector. Although there are exceptions, most developing countries are not characterized by such advanced systems, suffering as they do from the constraints of a limited national research and development capability and capital pools already too overextended to finance the huge investments required to modernize their systems, let alone underwrite innovation. Other issues include the comparative costs of running the system versus creating effective regulatory machinery, and whether federal coffers ultimately gain or lose if new competitors or operators are profit-repatriating, foreign-owned firms.

Such concerns as these have made skeptics of some observers. As Heald notes, "Just as the developing countries have gone through stages when state direction and ownership were seen as the dominant requirement for economic development, privatization seems to be emerging as a panacea" (1988: 70). If this is so, two questions naturally follow: who is offering this "panacea," and, under what conditions is it being accepted? With regard to the first question, the answer seems fairly clear: The enhancement of competition, particularly through privatization and liberalization, has been a cornerstone of the free-market policies of the Reagan and Thatcher administrations, and it has emerged as an objective for those governments' international agencies. Policies geared to the reduction of the size of the state and promotion of private competition have also become common features of IMF stabilization programs and, on occasion, as conditions for multilateral loans. (Cook and Kirkpatrick 1988)

To say that the pro-competitive policies of privatization and liberalization are closely tied to bilateral and multilateral assistance, however, is to suggest, as Cook and Kirkpatrick do, that privatization "may simply reflect the policy-maker's judgment as to the token measure needed to secure the continued inflow of foreign assistance" (1988: 30). Yet, while it is, as they claim, "rare for liberalization to follow some intellectual conversion of policy-makers" (Ibid), there remains ample distance between pandering to international agencies and intellectual conviction to explain a developing country's decision to implement these policies.

In Malaysia, whose experience is considered in more detail throughout the remainder of this paper, there is some evidence that the World Bank urged privatization. (Chanda, N. 1986) But what the policy history of the Telecoms Department suggests--and it is the task of this paper to show---is that liberalization and privatization were less policy innovations introduced by exogenous forces than they were tools (albeit, very fashionable ones) taken up by political elites to further and legitimize the historical process of wealth redistribution from the state to members of the elite.

In order to assess the actual role of the recent policy changes in Malaysia, it is necessary to place them within their historical context. The use of privatization, in fact, dates to the early 1970s, when Malaysia's New Economic Policy (NFP) encouraged the expansion of private enterprise opportunities for ethnic Malays. Working towards achievement of that goal, the Malaysian Telecoms Department established several methods of channeling lucrative contracts to Malaysian entrepreneurs. By the end of the decade a fairly healthy private telecoms industry had been fostered in which Malays predominated. Its constituents had also begun, however, to cultivate political connections which served them well under the Mahathir administration. By the mid-1980s, all but nominal authority for dispensing contracts had been removed from the Telecoms Department, which was dominated by engineers, and assumed by the politicians at higher levels of government. With liberalization, the spoils to be distributed were ftuther expanded. In this context, the implementation of privatization was little more than the conclusion to a long process of directing wealth and power to a favored few. (Kennedy, L.B. 1990)

The information reported here reviews telecommunications policy in Malaysia starting in 1972, shortly after the New Economic Policy was adopted. Sources of the information presented include interviews with current and former employees of the Malaysian telecoms system, government officials, and industry representatives; reports from the Malaysian press for the period 1970-1997; and Malaysian govennnent documents. Because several of those who were interviewed requested anonymity, we have chosen to not cite interviews.

TELECOMMUNICATIONS POLICY IN MALAYSIA: 1972-1980

The years 1969-1970 were a turning point in Malaysia's history. The country has a multi-ethnic population, dominated numerically by ethnic Malays, but in commerce by Chinese Malaysians. In 1969, interracial tensions reached fever pitch and bloody riots broke out in the major urban areas. In the aftermath of the riots, the New Economic Policy was implemented, having two goals: to eradicate poverty and restructure the society towards a more equitable distribution of wealth and opportunity.

The NEP, which expired in 1990, took as its task the equalization of economic opportunity for all citizens by seeking to eliminate the identification of economic function with race. (Third Malaysia Plan 1976) In practice this has meant that the policy provides the mechanisms for improving the lot of Bumiputeras, or ethnic Malays; among these are "state subsidies, favorable treatment under licensing and franchising regulations, quotas in jobs and university places, concessional loans and grants to enter industry and trade, and privileged access to capital markets" (Mehmet: 1986). The NEP also reaffirmed the role of the state as the protector of the Malay people, thereby creating a rationale for a burgeoning government bureaucracy to oversee and promote the process of restructuring. As Ozay Mehmet notes, between 1970 and 1983, there was a nearly fourfold increase in the federal public service, reflecting the expansion of such existing services as health and education, but also the establishment of statutory bodies to carry out the mandates of the NEP. (1986:8)

One aspect of the implementation of the NEP which has received some critical discussion by scholars is the extent to which the riots and subsequent policy changes were the result of Malay impoverishment. Although there can be no doubt that enormous economic disparities existed between Malays and Chinese, it is also clear that there was a growing middle-class of educated and well-employed Malays, who, from the early 1960s, had sought an expanded role for the state in improving the economic status of Malays. For this group, the riots provided unarguable evidence in support of their position, and in short order the 20-year, comprehensive policy for rearranging the entire structure of social relations was produced. Members of this class would emerge as key players in the telecommunications industry, as we shall see. (Kennedy, L.B. 1990)

In that industry, the year 1972 marked a turning point. During the 1960s, the National Telecoms Department, Jabatan Telecom Malaysia (JTM), had maintained a fairly positive reputation for its service. Indeed, in the mid-1960s, the World Bank had pointed to the Department as a model for other developing countries to emulate. But as the country developed according to orthodox principles of modernization through urbanization, the Department was unable to meet the increased demand. Demand had always outpaced supply: At independence in 1957, roughly 2,000 applications for telephone service remained unfilled, and this number increased persistently during the 1960s to about 10,000 in 1966, where it held steady until the early 1970s. But after 1972, growth in demand took off, and despite the Department's continued expansion of the network, the number of unfilled orders increased dramatically, reaching 133,606 in 1980, nearly ten times the 1972 figure. (JTM Annual Reports 1990)

The size of JTM's staff also began to grow after 1972, having held to between 8,000 and 10,000 since 1967. From 9,600 employees in 197 1, there was a jump to 14,000 in 1972, and by 1980, JTM had over 25,000 employees (JTM Annual Report, 1993). However, the increases in staff had less to do with trying to improve the operations of the Department that it did with efforts to provide jobs to the underemployed Malay population. Hence, training was underemphasized, and JTM became something of a repository for the unskilled. The enormous size of the staff, its inability to function efficiently (let alone meet demand), and the inevitable corruption that accompany these conditions, in combination rendered JTM one of the most despised symbols of government bureaucracy by the late 1970s. (Kennedy, L.B. 1990)

Finally, the year 1972 was significant as the year in which JTM turned to an outside contractor to take over a failing part of its business - an act of privatization that predated the term. Although in itself the action appeared minor, affecting only the operation of pay telephones in one urban area, it signaled a new direction in policy, which ultimately resulted in the creation of a Bumiputera-dominated private telecoms industry. The four firms which emerged as leaders of this industry, Sapura Holdings, Binafon, Electroscon, and SriComm, are all owned by former Telecoms employees who recognized the favorable environment that was being fostered by JTM policies.

During the late 1960s and early 1970s JTM had been plagued by operational problems with public coin-collecting call boxes (CCBS) due to vandalism, a slow collections system, and insufficient resources for maintenance. The press occasionally featured photographs of boxes wrenched apart by vandals and letters to the editor complaining about the small number, poor placement and unreliable service of public phones. In 1972, the Managing Director of United Motor Works (UMW), a private firm, proposed to JTM that the installation, collection and maintenance of CCBs be franchised to a subsidiary of UMW. A profit-sharing arrangement was struck and a new firm, Uniphone Sdn. Bhd., was established.

The Managing Director of UMW who proposed and later oversaw the new enterprise was Shamsuddin Kadir, a Malay, who had joined UMW only about a year before, after working at JTM for over a decade. At the time of his resignation from the Telecoms Department, he held the post of Acting Director of Telecoms and thus was equal in rank to Buyong Abdullah, another Malay who became Director General of JTM in 1972. Shamsuddin left JTM for UMW, giving up the security of a government service post (something rarely done), because he saw greater opportunities in the post-1970s private business environment. His stay at UMW was short, however. With the success he was able to make of the CCB venture, he bought Uniphone from UMW and began to expand in the telecommunications business.

Shamsuddin's convictions about the greener pastures of the private sector were shared by another former Telecoms employee, Abdul Karim Ikram. Also a Malay, Karim had tired of the bureaucracy, poor salary, and limited opportunities of his administrative post at JTM. After gaining some experience in the private sector, Karim put his insider's knowledge of Telecoms to work. Aware of a cost inefficiency associated with the junction cabinets imported by JTM, he established Zal Fnterprises to manufacture the equipment locally and became a key supplier to JTM. (Kennedy, L.B. 1990)

While the security of government jobs has usually been more valued in Malaysia than the potentially higher wages that might be earned in private enterprise, the risks of abandoning that security have not been as great as they might have appeared to others. First, it was clear to both Shamsuddin and Karim that telecommunications was a growing and under-served market. More importantly, however, the specifications of the NEP made the private telecoms industry an unusually attractive alternative to government service. JTM had traditionally been supplied entirely by foreign vendors; initially from Great Britain, then other European countries, and, even later, Japan as well. These firms were anxious to participate in Malaysia!s surging telecommunications market. Under the terms of the NEP, however, foreign as well as Chinese involvement in the economy was to be reduced, while Burniputera entrepreneurs were to expand their role---either through individual enterprise or joint ventures. Partnerships in the industry held obvious promise to both sides: the Bumiputera businessmen provided an entry to the market, while the foreign firms supplied the technical knowledge, institutional support, and financial strength. Thus, by the mid- 1970s, Sapura Holdings had joined forces with Siemans of West Germany, and Binafon had entered a partnership with NKF Kabel, a Dutch firm backed by Phillips. (Kennedy, L.B. 1990).

The opportunities that existed were apparent to others as well. In 1975, JTM's Director General, Buyong Abdullah, turned 55 and retired from the Civil Service after 22 years of service. One of Buyong's final acts as Director General was to further expand the role of private contractors for telecommunications services, and then became a contractor himself. Telecoms, like the National Electricity Board and others, had for some time been using private contractors for civil service jobs such as digging trenches for cables. These jobs had been tendered to private engineering firms, often Chinese-owned. Under Buyong's policy, civil service contracts would now be let on a "round- robin" basis to registered Jadual Kadar Harga (JKH, Schedule of Rates and Prices) Contractors. Virtually guaranteed of non-tendered contracts once registered, a number of former JTM employees established contracting businesses or directed their energies in this direction. The first round of registrations was held in 1975, and among those who registered were the firms run by Shamsuddin, Karim, and another longtime Telecoms employee, Mohktar Mohiddin. Also registered shortly thereafter were the firms owned by the freshly-retired Buyong and another recent JTM retiree, Zahari Hassan. (Kennedy, L.B. 1990)

The JKH contracting system seemed to work quite well, although JTM was still falling far short of meeting the demand for telephone lines. In 1979 JTM's new Director General, Hassan Wahab, modified the policy in two important ways which he believed would promote the goals of the NEP. First, works that could be contracted were to include not just civil works, but also the laying of cable, a job formerly handled only by Telecoms engineers. Further, the registration system became more complex, recognizing Bumiputera contractors as such. Under the new JKH system, the Ministry of Finance would review each firm's equity and staff structure, while JTM would assess its technical expertise. On the basis of these evaluations firms would be placed into classes. Class A included contractors who could lay the large capacity main and junction cables and take on contracts valued at over $1 million. Class B companies could lay main and junction cables in jobs valued up to $1 million. Class C firms hung the overhead lines, which required less expertise, and took jobs valued at no more than $500 thousand. In the first round of evaluations, the firms owned by Shamsuddin, Karim, and Mohktar emerged as Class A firms. After two subsequent rounds, there were some 25 companies registered, although only the three previously mentioned had obtained Class A status. (Kennedy, L.B. 1990)

The significance of the new JKH system cannot be underestimated. First, the use of the JKH contracting system effectively undercut the use of competitive bidding, placing in bureaucrats' hands the task of allocating contracts---decisions which could scarcely be questioned. Second, the new system changed the fortunes, both literally and figuratively, of the participating firms. The new system was tremendously lucrative: One of the contractors estimated his firm's annual earnings between 1976 and 1980 at $2-3 million. Further, the contracts allowed the firms to build up a workforce, a vehicle fleet, a core of trained technicians, and a reputation.

Fueled by the assurance of future, contracts and encouraged by the government's efforts to ease their expansion, many of the firms also branched into new areas of telecommunications. Sapura Holdings, for example, whose subsidiaries included a Class A contractor and the holder of the coin-collecting box contract, began to manufacture telephones, becoming the primary supplier to Telecoms.

Thus the JKH system changed the face of the Malaysian telecoms industry. Once dominated by foreign firms, the industry was increasingly localized, even if the more sophisticated products were foreign-trademarked goods produced through licensing agreements. Contractors also found viable avenues for expansion into the manufacture of entirely domestically-produced goods such as telephone poles, distribution boxes, and manhole covers. JTM administrators, mindful of the NEP, continued to direct contracts for equipment and services to these firms. By the end of the decade, there were enough private firms doing business in teleconununications to comprise a significant, young, domestic telecoms industry. A number of Bumiputera telecoms companies were well established, having essentially taken over the civil works and cabling markets. The four largest of these were major cabling contractors who had expanded into other related areas, such as the manufacture and/or installation of equipment. The local cable manufacturing industry, still notably dominated by foreign and Chinese firms, was thriving, with local firms being given an advantage over foreign in bidding, and supply contracts lasting three years. The extent to which the industry had developed was perhaps evident as well in the formation of two lobbying organizations, one established by cabling contractors and the other by the major cable manufacturers.

If the private telecoms industry was flourishing as a result of government policies, however, JTM was floundering. Efforts to overcome the shortages of telephone lines were stymied by the government's persistent refusal to allocate the funds requested by the Department. According to a highly-placed government official, during the first three Malaysia Plans (covering the period 1966- 1980), the Department never received more than 50 percent of its original requests. Further, the constraints imposed by the government's budgeting system, which involved numerous rounds of proposals, cuts, and revised proposals, made network growth planning almost impossible. At the same time, pressure to increase employment continued to swell JTM's workforce, resulting in a single year in the doubling of the lowest rank of workers (JTM Annual Report, 1990).

By the end of the 1970s, then, there appeared ample cause for assessing the capability of JTM as a government department to correct its operating and servicing problems. There also existed, largely as a result of Telecoms' policies, a private sector representation that established and was nurturing key political affiliations. Increasingly influential in the Ministry and above (terms used to describe these relationships included "close affinity" and "close rapport"), members of the industry had their own agenda and set of solutions to JTM's problems, for which they actively lobbied. (Kennedy, L.B. 1990)

TELECOMS POLICY 1980-1987

In 1980 the Fourth Malay Plan was announced for the period 1981-1986, and included in its budget was an allocation of M$1,399 million, the full amount sought by JTM (Midterm Review, p. 84). Along with the allocation came the expectation that JTM would completely revitalize its system. Despite urgings from JTM officials that "if you get married and you don't have any children in the first three years, you can't expect in the fourth year suddenly to have four children," the government pressed for the immediate modernization of the entire system, including the installation of 1.2 million lines.

In July of 1981, the course of national politics took a turn. After a period of ill health, Malaysia's Prime Minister, Tun Hussein Onn, resigned his post to the Deputy Prime Minister, Dr. Mahathir Mohamed. Mahathir had fairly radical ideas about how to promote Malaysia's development, and he began to pursue his ambitions as a managerialist and a technocrat.

Fundamental to Mahathir's vision was the inculcation of discipline and efficiency, and the emulation of Japanese and Korean standards of personal behavior. It appears that Mahathir found in JTM, with its bloated staff and reputation for corruption, an example of the very wastefulness and inefficiency he loathed, while in men like Shamsuddin Kadir, with whom he had formed an acquaintanceship, he found paragons of enterprise.

By late 1981, there was clear evidence of Mahathir's doubts about the ability of JTM to carry out the modernization plan and also his intentions for resolving the issue. In November, Mahathir's Deputy Prime Minister visited JTM headquarters and publicly reprimanded the Department for its inefficiency, ordering its administrators to begin using private firms as turnkey contractors in project implementation. Several months later Telecoms was ordered to make no further purchases of stocks until notified, pending the signing of turnkey contracts for the expansion of the network. (Kennedy, L.B. 1990)

The concept of turnkey contracting was not new to either JTM or to members of the private telecoms industry. In 1981, Karim Ikram, now a Class A contractor, had proposed the use of turnkey cabling contracts to JTM, his former employer and now his customer for equipment and cabling work. At his side as he made the proposal was a new business partner, NKF Kabel, which had designed a computer protocol for costing the component jobs of a turnkey contract in a previous Saudi Arabian contract. Having developed the protocol, NKF was anxious for new markets in which to put it to use. The proposal had fallen flat at JTM, however, for the Director General, Nadzim Abdul Hamid, had consulted on the Saudi project and reportedly found the method effective but unnecessarily costly. For JTM, given its huge workforce, turnkey contracting would make its staff redundant. Further, he and others balked at the notion of relinquishing the task of planning the network to private firms.

Within a short time, however, the resistance of JTM was overridden by higher officials. The government had been clearly convinced of the merits of turnkey contracting, and merely needed to decide at the Ministry level to whom the network expansion contract would be given. Although several possibilities were raised, in the end it appeared that only one had been seriously considered: each of the four Class A firms was awarded, without tender, one-fourth of the total contract. For these firms, which had handled jobs valued at M$1-5 million as the largest JKH contractors, the turnkey contracts were worth M$636 million apiece. (Kennedy, L.B. 1990)

The turnkey contracts had an immediate and devastating impact on many in the nascent domestic telecoms industry. Although the contracts were written in such a way as to mandate the use of local subcontractors and suppliers, the Class A firms nonetheless established subsidiaries from which they sourced materials and labor, effectively eliminating the business which had kept afloat the smaller firms. Additionally, all four of the major contractors entered into partnerships (in one case at the apparent insistence of the government) with foreign firms, which again pulled the market out from under the small local firms; particularly the cable manufacturers. By losing the direct line to JTM for contracts, the smaller Class B and C firms lost both their cabling contracts and also the manufacturing sidelines which they had developed, while the cable manufacturers watched their market evaporate. By 1987, it was estimated that only six to eight of the small contractors still maintained offices, down from some 38 in the early 1980s, and the remaining cable companies were undergoing restructuring. (Business Times 1987)

By the end of 1985, when some 70 percent of the 1.6 million (Mid-term Review - Fourth Malaysian Plan 1984) new lines were to be installed under the contracts terms, only 46 percent had actually been implemented and approved, and JTM was embroiled in continuing battles with the contractors over the procedures for handing over lines, the quality of workmanship, and the scope of the contracts. Objections were raised by JTM's management as well as by some of the smaller members of the rapidly disintegrating local telecoms industry. Even Ministry officials objected to the lack of progress of the contracts. But these objections were to no avail. It soon became clear that the contracts had support at the highest levels of government and that unduly strenuous protests could sharply delimit one's career options. In sum and substance, JIMs authority to operate the national telecommunications system had been severely restricted. The locus of power had shifted decisively upward.

With the Telecoms Department out of the business of network planning and development, its responsibilities were now limited to the operation of the network, supply of terminal equipment to customers, and the provision of VANS, such as radio paging, cellular telephones, satellite data transmission and PABXs. But the last two had also caught the attention of the private telecoms industry and liberalization was placed on the policy agenda. The route by which liberalization of the VANs was achieved is instructive of how influence was being wielded.

The liberalization of VANS appears to have been a by-product, although not necessarily accidental, of the machinations that had led to JTM's privatization. According to the director of a leading telecoms firm, Shamsuddin Kadir of Sapura Holdings was approached personally by Mahathir to take over the helm of a privatized JTM. Shamsuddin declined. As the major supplier of telephone instruments to JTM and a Class A turnkey contractor he was reportedly skeptical that he could avoid charges of conflict of interest, no matter how he distanced himself from his own company. He did, however, offer to commission a study into the feasibility of privatization. The study was authored by the Arthur D. Little Company and presented late in 1983. (Kennedy, L.B. 1990)

In addition to recommending the privatization of JTM, the study broached the issue of liberalization. While calling for prudent regulation, the study urged immediate liberalization of the VANS market. In particular the argument was made that JTM was so busy with the modernization program that it could not effectively meet the needs of business customers to the detriment of Malaysian commerce. (Arthur D. Little 1983)

Both the terminal equipment and VANS markets have now been opened to private suppliers licensed by the Ministry. One need not look hard to see who the main beneficiaries of the liberalization policy have been. Shamsuddin's Sapura Holdings, the parent company of Uniphone and a turnkey contract holder, no longer constrained by JTM's conservatism in ordering, now holds a panoply of manufacturing licenses from foreign firms. Another subsidiary of

Sapura - Komtel - shares the most lucrative radio-paging market with Kilatcom, a subsidiary of a second turnkey contractor. A third holder of a turnkey contract, Electroscon, is a major distributor of terminal equipment, as is Electronic Systems, a recently-incorporated firm which has ties to the Fleet Group, the investment holdings company associated with Mahathir's political party. In short, the licenses for the most lucrative services have gone to the political heavyweights, leaving the lesser spoils for the less influential.

These consequences of the liberalization policy provide a framework for understanding the privatization of JTM. There are two stages to the privatization of the Telecoms Department, only one of which, tellingly, has been implemented to date. First, the Department was removed from being a government department, reestablished as Syarikat Telecoms Malaysia (STM) and licensed by the Ministry. The separation from the government is only nominal, however, since the Minister of Energy, Telecoms and Posts, a Cabinet official, holds rate-making authority, decides who will sit on the Board of Directors, and can change at will the terms of the operating license. Although at some future date shares of the company will be sold on the Kuala Lumpur Stock Exchange---the second stage of privatization---it is unclear when that will happen and whether it will bring a greater degree of autonomy to the company.

In the meantime, that very lack of autonomy has had profound implications. As was encouraged in the Sapura-commissioned feasibility study, there has been a reshuffling of top administrators and the addition of several layers of Ministry-appointed management from outside JTM, further reducing the already-limited authority of former top management. This move was predicated on the purportedly immutable "civil service mentality" of JTM's former administrators and on their lack of training in the entrepreneurial ways of the private sector. This rationale has also served to justify the close monitoring, even surrogate management, of STM by the Ministry.

At the same time, pieces of STM's business are being parcelled out as a continuation of the privatization policy, which is now operating on a "first-come, first-served" basis. The operation of coin-collecting call boxes, over which STM had hoped to reassert control, was licensed in 1988 to a subsidiary of Sapura Holdings as a non-tendered, 15-year national monopoly. In cellular radio, one of its most lucrative services, STM is reportedly being pressed into a joint venture with the Fleet Group, the holding company associated with the ruling party. Far from having any incumbent's advantage in seeking licenses for telecommunications services, STM is forced to relinquish critical segments of service to its rivals. And those rivals are selected through a non-competitive process in a fledgling regulatory body in a highly politicized bureaucracy. Should it continue to pillage STM of its service offerings, the government may find that it has scored points with a political elite, but in the process has so weakened STM that re-nationalization is required. (Kennedy, L.B. 1990)

DISCUSSION AND CONCLUSIONS

Although there are a variety of obstacles identified as preventing full-scale privatization--- which ironically include the firm's overly large staff and its indebtedness following the turnkey contract---these serve more to underscore the speed with which the first stage of privatization was undertaken. The review of policy antecedents to privatization suggests some reasons for this. Having created an elite within the telecoms industry, first by limiting the field of players to Bumiputeras and then separating the greater from the lesser through the turnkey contracts, the government was faced with increasing pressures to accelerate the flow of resources to that elite. Privatization, in conjunction with the market-entry restrictions provided by the new regulatory bureaucracy, essentially created a legitimized mechanism for dividing the spoils between the key players. Further, any argument that privatization is promoting the goals of the NEP must reckon with the discriminatory nature of the results, which clearly benefit certain Bumiputeras over others.

Privatization has been touted by many in recent years as the solution to the problems of developing counties' stagnant economies, resulting in pressure being applied to reduce the role of the state. This examination of the Malaysian case has sought to show that if the privatization policy appeased external voices it was a happy coincidence for, far from a policy innovation, privatization was a natural conclusion to the long-term process of channeling wealth and power to a select few. Further, given the increasing use of non-tendered contracts and the gaining of licenses on a first- come-first-served basis, if the privatization policy has satisfied those who advocate competitive markets, it has been through the trappings rather than the substance of competition. (Kennedy, L.B. 1990)

MALAYSIAN TELECOMMUNICATIONS IN THE COMING INFORMATION AGE

A study of the Malaysian Telecommunications Department provokes much larger questions than merely the politics of political favoritism among the governing elites in the trend toward privatization, deregulation, and expansion of the industry. Telecommunications involves not only telephones, cellular telephones, paging, voice mail, etc., but also broadcasting, data transmission and computer networking. To expand these services, two satellites have been launched and very ambitious plans for their use have been drafted. Indeed, Malaysia is moving to be in the forefront of the "information revolution." In a January 16, 1997, speech at UCLA, after conferring with the major players in Silicon Valley, Prime Minister Dr. Mahathir made Malaysia's plans for a "Multimedia Super Corridor" (MSC), stretching from the new international airport into the capital city of Kuala Lumpur, the cornerstone of the country's strategy for becoming a developed nation by 2020 (Far Eastern Economic Review, Feb. 27, 1997). The speech was an appeal to multinational corporations to set up shop for their information services in this MSC, which will offer an ideal location for the articulation of their various entrepreneurial ventures in Asia. Featured in the speech were all the facilitative arrangements and laissez-faire encouragements that multinationals like to hear from governments, continuing the trend in privatization, deregulation and expansion of media, characterizing the spread of neoclassical economics in development theorizing that is the focus of this paper (Star Online, Jan. 17, 1997).

Obviously, such dramatic technological changes are likely to have large-scale sociocultural consequences as well. Many difficult issues facing Malaysia at this juncture in its rush toward developed-nation status are uncomfortable dilemmas and contradictions that will inevitably be affected. Among these issues are democratic political form in the context of authoritarian political process, industrialization in the context of a labor shortage, balancing privatization of state enterprises with state regulation, "looking East while wooing the capital of the West," developing materially without suffering from the ills of modernity, Malay political dominance (and their claim to cultural dominance) in the context of three other ethnic groups too large to ignore, and the social stability necessitating religious tolerance in the context of rising fundamentalist Islamic intolerance (Kahn and Wah 1992).

Malaysia's development strategy has clearly embraced the econophoria of capitalist economic globalization. Such favorable economic context is thought to require political stability and this has been achieved by, what by regional standards is, a merely semi-authoritarian government. However, transformation into the information society of the next millennium will surely have significant consequences for the struggle over authoritarian political control.

If we take as a model the experiences of Western cultures, the spread of television broadcasting into the hinterlands and the multiplication of programming channels presents several possible concerns: the "cultural imperialism of the West" (Schiller, 1976), the construction of a "consumer culture" and its exacerbation of conflict between the "haves" and "have-nots," hyperconsumption and lifestyles-advertising targeting which can threaten traditional values (Gerbner et al. 1996; Andersen 1995). On the other hand, TV, along with film, has also been characterized as mollifying social tensions in a sort of "safety valve" effect (Kunczik, 1984: 170ff). The construction of a lowest-common-denominator pop culture tends to replace traditional, local cultural expression for younger people. The proliferation of media images and lifestyles can be fashioned into counter-images and articulated with social grievances to organize social and political resistance. The present state of government control of the mass media (four TV channels and the major newspapers) would likely be much diminished, and likewise its capacity for authoritarian political control. As Edwin Parker has put it, telecommunications and information technology can serve criminals, terrorists and revolutionaries as surely as it can serve oppressive governments (1992: 148). At this point the government's position is that it can favorably control mass media content by denying access to Western, particularly U. S. sources (Star Online, March 16, 1997). However, expansion will necessitate commercialization and commercial mass media tends not to thrive on wholesome programming. The economic pressure will be toward those aspects of drama with universal appeal: crime, violence, sex, etc.

With respect to the spread of telecommunications capabilities and information processing technologies, the social and political consequences are futuristic, if nonetheless, momentous. The greater capacity for government surveillance has long been appreciated. Malaysia's rush to "smart government," "smart cards" carried by all citizens, and "total policeman" sporting hand-held computers to access government databases (Star Online, March 16, 1997) could give a chill to civil libertarians. Clearly such capabilities are more likely to serve the "politically active." "Modernizing elites" are legitimated by their mastery of the advanced technologies. Information technology has the potential to further exacerbate social divisions and inequalities. With the expansion of high-tech job opportunities simultaneously comes the possibility of "sweated labor in so-called telecottages, exploited by employers and denied the benefits of employee protection and full time contracts" (Martin 1995: 9).

In fact, industrialization in the context of a labor shortage has been a major contradiction for Malaysia. Multinational corporations seek a low-wage environment, and the labor-shortage pressure for higher wages has been dealt with, to this point, through the "cat-and-mouse game" of illegal immigration of workers from Indonesia, Philippines, Thailand, Bangladesh, etc. It is particularly in this respect that the rush into the information age is so attractive to Malaysia. Information technology offers the opportunity, to emphasize capital-intensive enterprise over labor- intensive industries, a major caveat being the high-level skills involved. Of course, the MSC project is the centerpiece of this strategy. It will favor investment in which information input is more significant than cheap labor. Furthermore, it would seem to present possibilities for avoiding environmentally devastating trade-offs in pollution and resource-exhaustion bargaining typically associated with attracting heavy industries.

Can Malaysia leapfrog over industrialization into a post-industrial economy? Leery of "modernity" for its accompanying ills of Western culture, can Malaysia fast-forward to "postmodemity?" Such is the tone of the Far Eastern Economic Review coverage of this development (February 27, 1997). And, if it can, what are the prospects for the other related sociocultural dilemmas? We must be equivocal here as Malaysia's planned development into the information age is indeed to participate in a development that is without precedent (Estabrooks 1995).

It is impossible to know how much Dr. Mahathir's vision for Malaysia's future is informed by postinodemist theorizing. However that may be, it is interesting to note that this culture of "late capitalism," as sketched out by various theorists (Featherstone 1991), would seem to lessen the strain of several of the major contradictions of Malaysia's nation-building efforts.

As capitalist economic order spreads via multinational corporations, nation-state boundaries become highly permeable. Not only finance and technology, but also people and cultures, have unprecedented freedom of communication (Appadurai 1990). The role of the state in the centralized, bureaucratic organization of economic development is lessened in favor of private enterprise responding to the opportunities of the global market. This lessened role of the state makes "nation-building" from a complex of ethnic group interests less pressing, as a culturally homogeneous nation is no longer legitimized by the need for cultural integration to lessen cultural barriers to economic participation. Economic efficiency and instrumental rationality provide the ordering principles.

If cultural difference is less problematic, and the various cultures can have access to the media, then the stultifying homogenization of culture that typifies the Western mass communications industry need not result (Browne 1996). In fact Malaysia has a respectable record in this regard, as its various ethnic groups have long had access to radio and TV programming. It will be primarily with respect to the religious expressions in media that difficulties are anticipated. To this point only Islamic religious content is permitted on TV, but other religions are pushing for deregulation in this regard (Star Online, March 9, 1997).

Mass media broadcasting and telecommunications proliferation offer new opportunities for local cultures to "reinvent traditions" from the plethora of motivating images, and to have their voices heard (Kahn 1995). Rather than a homogenized national culture, a pastiche of traditional cultures can be celebrated as a strength. In this latest version of the divide-and-conquer strategy, economic prosperity triumphs over intolerance because of its demand for social stability.

If economic globalization by means of information technology in accordance with neoclassical economic principles is the context in which developing nations must organize economic development, as is the consensus these days, then Malaysia's MSC project is not only breath-taking in ambition but also necessary. No one can say at this point whether it will succeed or fail, but its perspicacious grasp of this moment of opportunity is admirable. Certainly the developing countries that fail to participate in the telecommunications and information technology revolution are going to have one more major development barrier with which to struggle (Roche and Blaine 1996: 2ff).

REFERENCES

Ahmad Zakaria, Haji (editor) (1987). *Government and Politics of Malaysia.* Singapore: Oxford University Press.

Andersen, Robin (1995). *Consumer Culture and TV Programming.* Boulder, CO: Westview Press.

Appadurai, Mun (1990). Disjuncture and Difference in the Global Cultural Economy. *Public Culture,* 2(2, Spring): 1-23.

Arthur D. Little Company (1983). *The Advantages and Disadvantages of Privatizing Jabatan Telekom Malaysia.*

Bjorn, Welienius and Peter A. Stern (1994). *Implementing Reforms in the Telecom Sector.* Washington, DC: World Bank.

Browne, Donald P,- (1996). *Electronic Media and Indigenous Peoples: A Voice of Our Own?* Ames, IA: Iowa State University.

Carnoy, Martin, Manual Castells, Stephen S. Cohen, and Fernando Henrique Cardoso (1993). *The Global Economy in the Information Age.* University Park, PA: The Pennsylvania State University Press.

Crouch, Harold (1992). Authoritarian Trends, the UMNO Split and the Limits to State Power. In *Fragmented Vision: Culture and Politics in Contemporary Malaysia* (Joel S. Kahn and Francis Loh Kok Wah, editors). Honolulu: University of Hawaii Press.

Duch, Raymond M. (1991). *Privatizing the Economy: Telecommunications Policy in Comparative Perspective.* Ann Arbor: The University of Michigan Press.

Estabrooks, Maurice (1995). *Electronic Technology, Corporate Strategy and World Transformation.* Westport, CT: Quonun Books.

Far Eastern Economic Review. February 27,1997: 44-50.

Featherstone, Mike (1991). *Consumer Culture and Postmodemism.* London: Sage Publications.

Gerbner, George, Hamid Mowlana, and Herbert I. Schiller (eds.) (1996). *Invisible Crises: What Conglomerate Control of Media Means for America and the World.* Boulder, CO: Westview Press.

H. Ergas and J. Okayama. (1984). *Changing Market Structures in Telecommunications.* North Holland: Elsevier Science Publisher.

Heald, David (1988). The Relevance of UK Privatization for LDCS. In *Privatization in Less Developed Countries* (P. Cook and C. Kirkpatrick, editors). New York: St. Martin's Press.

Hobsbawm, E. and T. Ranger (eds.) (1983). *The Invention of Tradition.* New York: Columbia University Press.

Hukill, Mark A. and Meheroo Jussawalla (1989). Telecommunication Policies and Markets in the Asian Countries. *Columbia Journal of World Business* (Spring).

JTM Annual Reports. (1980-1990's).

Kahn, Joel S. (1995). *Culture, Multiculture, Postculture.* London: Sage Publications.

Kahn, Joel S. and Francis Loh Kok Wah (eds.) (1992*). Fragmented Vision: Culture and Politics in Contemporary Malaysia.* Honolulu: University of Hawaii Press.

Kennedy, L.B. (1990). *Privatization and It's Policy Antecedents in Malaysian Telecommunications.* Unpublished Ph.D. Dissertation, Ohio University.

Kunczik, Michael (1984). *Communication and Social Change: A Summary of Theories, Policies and Experiences for Media Practitioners in the Third World.* Bonn: Allan and Lieselotte Yahraes.

Leong, Choon Heng (1991). *Late Industrialization Along with Democratic Politics in Malaysia*. Unpublished Ph.D. Dissertation. Harvard University.

Martin, Williazn J. (1995). *The Global Information Society.* Hampshire, England: Aslib Gower.

Mosco, Vincent (1988). Toward a Theory of the State and Telecommunication Policy. *Journal of Communication,* 3 8(1): 107-124.

Nayan Chanda. (1986). High Cost of Equity. *Far Eastern Economic Review* (August 7).

Ohmae, Kenichi (1991). *The Borderless World: Power and Strategy in the Interlinked Economy.* New York: Harper.

Onn, Fong Chan (1989). The Malaysian Telecommunications Services Industry: Development, Perspectives and Prospects. *Columbia Journal of World Business.*

Ozay, Mehmet (1986). *Development in Malaysia.* Kent: Croom Helm.

P.Cook and C.Kirkpatrick.(1988). Privatization in Less Developed Countries: An Overview. New York: St. Marfin's Press.

Parker, Edwin B. (1992). Developing Third World Communications Markets. *The Information Society,* 8:147-167.

Rahim, Syed A. and Anthony J. Pennings (1987). *Computerization and Development in South East Asia.* Singapore: Amic.

Roche, Edward Mozley and Michael James Blaine (eds.) (1996). *Information Technology, Development and Policy: Theoretical Perspectives and Practical Challenges.* Brookfield: Avebury.

Schiller, Herbert 1. (1976). *Communication and Cultural Domination.* White Plains, NY: International Arts and Sciences Press, Inc.

Star Online.: www.jaring.my/~star/

Sussman, G. (1988). Information Technologies for the Asian Region: the Political Economy of Privatization. In *The Political Economy of Information* (Vincent Mosco and Janet Wasko, editors). Madison, WI: University of Wisconsin Press.

Third- Fourth and Fifth Malaysia Plan, 1976-1980, 1981-1986, and 1987-1990. Kuala Lumpur: Government Printers, 1976, 1984, 1987.

Ure, John (1993). Corporization and Privatization of Telecom in Asian Countries. *Pacific Telecommunication Review,* 15(l):3-15.

Chapter 7

PRIVATISATION OF SOCIAL REPRODUCTION: A CASE STUDY

B.N. Ghosh

INTRODUCTION

Privatisation of social reproduction like education and public health services (PHS) has become an important issue in recent years in Malaysia. The issue is critical in the sense that it is a reflection on the legitimacy of the government as a social welfare maximising agent and also on its ability to provide goods for social reproduction. The present article will consider the privatisation problems of PHS in Malaysia. The first part of the discussion will concentrate on the salient features of PHS followed by an analysis of the determinants of resource allocation of PHS. The third part will discuss problems relating to health care products, followed by an analysis of privatisation and allocative inefficiency. The next section will give an idea about the problematics of PHS, and the last section will make some concluding observations.

SALIENT FEATURES OF PUBLIC HEALTH SERVICES (PHS) IN MALAYSIA

Malaysia is said to be a country of efficient and comprehensive health care system. Jacob Meerman found that in the seventies, Malaysian public health system was not only egalitarian but also better compared to many other countries with the same level of per capita income (Meerman, 1979, p. 1). The statement seems to be valid even today. An examination of some critical indicators like people per doctor, infant mortality rate, and life expectancy will show that over the years, Malaysia's performance in the field of health care system has become satisfactory compared to LDCs which are similar in terms of per capita income (Table 1). All these achievements have been made possible by proper health care management and increasing per capita income.

If one considers three very important indicators of PHS, such as, life expectancy, infant mortality rate, and people per doctor, one can find an unmistakable relationship between each one of these variables and per capita GDP (Table 1).

TABLE 1 - PER CAPITA GDP, LIFE EXPECTANCY, MORTALITY RATE AND PEOPLE PER DOCTOR

Country	GDP per capita (PPP)	Life Expectancy	Infant Mortality Rate	People per doctor
US	28,515	77	8	387
Germany	20,864	76	6	333
Japan	23,440	80	4	545
France	21,860	77	6	320
Britain	20,170	76	6	581
Italy	20,545	78	7	195
Canada	21,800	78	6	446
Hong Kong	24,085	79	4	772
Singapore	24,610	77	4	667
Taiwan	15,370	75	4	903
Vietnam	1,430	67	34	2,298
Bangladesh	1,450	57	85	12,500
Myanmar	753	59	79	12,500
Switzerland	26,315	78	6	585
Malaysia	9,835	72	10	2,063
Australia	19,960	78	7	400
Indonesia	4,140	63	50	6,786
India	1,500	61	75	2,165
South Africa	4,215	64	51	1,750
Philippines	3,020	67	40	1,016
New Zealand	18,250	77	7	321
Nigeria	1,345	53	84	5,882
Pakistan	2,410	62	88	2,000
Sri Lanka	3,415	72	14	5,888
Brunei	19,500	75	8	1,133
Thailand	8,165	69	26	4,361

Source: Data collated from *Asia Week* 16 January 1998, p. 51

From Table 2, the following three types of correlation become very clear.

	Correlation	Nature and Magnitude
1.	Per capita GDP and Life Expectancy	+0.89
2.	Per capita GDP and People Per Doctor	-0.83
3.	Per capita GDP and Infant Mortality	-0.66

The correlations are found to be high and statistically significant at one per cent level in each case. These correlations are true not only among the developed but also among the developing countries. As a matter of fact, Malaysia's achievement in life expectancy, population per doctor and infant mortality rate is much better compared to other developing countries with more or less the same per capita GDP. All these three health variables have been found to be well-correlated to health expenditure. For instance, the correlation value between infant mortality and public health expenditure in Malaysia is found to be fairly high (-0.72).

The inter-temporal changes in some of the health indicators can now be stated with the help of some data (Govt. of Malaysia, 1996, p. 539). The infant mortality which was 40.8 in 1970, came down to 33 in 1975, 24 in 1980, 17 in 1985, 13 in 1990 and 10.5 in 1995. Life expectancy at birth for males went up from 66.7 in 1980 to 69 in 1990 and 69.3 in 1995. The corresponding figures for females were 71.6 (1980). 73.5 (1990) and 74.0 (1995). Crude death rate per thousand people came down from 5.3 in 1980 t0 4.7 in 1990 and 4.5 in 1995. Doctors per ten thousand population increased from 2.8 in 1980 to 3.9 in 1990 to 4.5 in 1995. The doctor population ratio which was 1: 2986 in 1986 improved to 1:2852 in 1987, 1:2700 in 1988, 1: 2638 in 1989, 1: 2533 in 1990, 1:2441 in 1991, 1:2411 in 1992, 1:2301 in 1993, and 1:2207 in 1994. In 1998, the doctor population ratio improved to 1:2063. The government has the target of 1:1,500 by the year 2000. All these have been made possible by positive government policy to give PHS the status of basic goods/services in the country and to effect their delivery through a large number of ancillary and paramedical forces.

In terms of absolute number, medical professionals and allied health professionals have shown quite satisfactory progress. For instance, the number of doctors increased from 7,000 in 1990 to 9,500 in 1995. The stock of dentists increased from 1,470 in 1990 to 1,790 in 1995. The number of pharmacists increased from 1,239 in 1990 to 1,620 in 1995. The number of allied health professionals including dental paramedics, medical assistants, laboratory technologists, nurses, occupational therapists, public health inspectors and radiographers also increased substantially between 1990 and 1995. All these figures are projected to be much higher in the initial years of the next millennium (vide the section on *problematics* , infra).

Medical expenditure is highly subsidised in Malaysia, and it is mildly progressive in character because larger number poor households are benefited by such expenditures (Griffin, 1992, p. 130). The cost of financing the health care system has considerably gone up in recent years. Health care cost for the government has risen significantly with 200 per cent increase in the operating budget alone from 1985 to 1995. However, government spending on health care as a percentage of GNP is constantly decreasing. For instance, public sector health expenditure which was 2.14 per cent in 1985 came down to 1.68 per cent in 1990 and 1.4 per cent in 1994 of GNP. This is too low for a rapidly developing country with a fairly high level of per capita income. The per capita public health expenditure increased from RM79.00 in 1986 to RM125.00 in 1994. As the economy develops, it is true that the share of health care as a percentage of GDP or GNP increases perceptibly. The United States of America allocates 14 per cent of the GDP to health care. The private insurance sector in Malaysia is not well developed to finance partly the health care system. Only 15 per cent of the country's population has either life or health insurance policy (Gomez, 1998, p. 2). If, however, extra resources are found out, the *allocative efficiency* may improve in the health care sector, and the burden of the government may be reduced to some extent.

The allocation of the government resources for the health care system is continuously increasing in the country. For instance, in the Sixth Plan, the government allocated RM2,498 million on account of patient care services, public health services and other components of health services. The allocation in the Seventh Plan has increased substantially to RM2,650 million. The allocation for the rural health services has always remained higher than the allocation in urban health services. However, the allocation have not been found to be sufficient for the growing demands for health services. On the basis of available data on per capita public health expenditure and per capita GDP for 1986 and 1994, it has been possible for the author to estimate the *income elasticity of demand* (ηYe) for health care in Malaysia. The result is given below:

$$(\eta Ye) = 0.78$$

The value being less than unity, it shows that health services are necessary goods and not luxury goods. As such, the demand for such goods is likely to increase as income increases even if the cost becomes higher. But since higher cost may not be justified on the ground of equity, *differential* cost structure of public services for the poor and the rich will be warranted in Malaysia. There are, of course, many alternative ways to cut public cost. These are self-medication programme for the public, payment of medical health services by the employers, privatisation and so on. However, it needs to be emphasised that the reduction in cost must not impinge on equity, effectiveness, efficiency, and empowerment. The participation by patients in the management of health care and also in the estimation of cost must be ensured for the sake of transparency and accountability. The government is, however, cutting down its allocations for health to reduce its financial burden but there is a limit as to how far such cuts should be made without causing undue hardship to the sick. There are many possibilities to reduce the cost to some extent by prescribing generic drugs, by reducing the use of unnecessary costly drugs, and also unnecessary clinical tests and so on. Some resources can be saved by reducing wastage and over-treatment.

DETERMINANTS OF RESOURCE ALLOCATION FOR PHS

Each year, the government of Malaysia allocates resources for the improvement of public health services. In order to know the significant determinants of resource allocation for PHS, the present study uses a multiple regression analysis. Based on *apriori* and *aposteriori* information obtained from published theoretical and empirical studies on the subject, one can identify five major factors which are phenomenologically related to the allocation of resources for public health services. The formal *ex-ante* relation is shown in the model that is presented below, and it will be tested by means of multiple regression analysis.

The model:

$$RAPH = f (BED, HOS, MED, POP, GDP)$$
$$RAPH = \beta_0 + \beta_1 BED + \beta_2 HOS + \beta_3 MED + \beta_4 POP + \beta_5 GDP + \mu_I$$

where

RAPH = *Resource Allocation for Public Health Services*
BED = **Number of Hospital Beds**
HOS = **Number of Hospitals**
MED = **Number of Medical Personnel**
POP = **Population (Number)**
GDP = **Gross Domestic Product (RM in Million)**
β_0 = **Intercept**
β_1........ β_5 = **Partial Regression Coefficients**
μ_1 = **Error Term**

The data for the analysis are collated from the publications of Ministry of Health, Government of Malaysia for the period 1986 - 1996.

The empirical results of the analysis can be gleaned from the following Table (Table 3).

TABLE 3 - REGRESSION RESULTS OF DETERMINANTS OF RESOURCE ALLOCATION

	Coefficients	T-values
Intercept	1397972	2.14*
BED	16292.6	0.70
HOS	-1383.4	-2.44**
MED	-86407.0	-1.91**
POP	34.3	1.64**
GDP	0.04	2.15*
F = 5.436*		
R^2=0.84		
N = 11		

Note: * Significant at 5% level
** Significant at 10% level

From the Table, it appears that our model can explain 84 per cent of the changes in the allocation of resources for public health services in Malaysia (R^2 = 0.84). The "F" value is significant at 5 per cent level. This implies that with 95 per cent level of confidence, it can be said that resource allocation for PHS in Malaysia is linearly related to all the independent variables used in the model. All independent variables, excepting one, are found to be statistically significant. While the influence of the number of hospital beds is found to be statistically insignificant, the impact of GDP is manifested to have high positive significance on resource allocation for public health services in Malaysia.

STRUCTURE OF PHS

The institutional structure of PHS in Malaysia consists of both rural and urban health care systems. The rural health care system consists of rural clinics, health centres, mobile units, health sub-centres, mid-wife clinic, and *desa* clinics. The urban system includes hospitals with out-patient and in-patient facilities, poly-clinics and so on. The rural health system is served by a large number of para-medical and ancillary personnel. However, many costly health services are not available in the rural areas compared to urban areas. The issue of rural-urban differentials will be taken up in the section on *problematics*. Many changes have been taking place in the area of health care services in Malaysia. These include introduction of telemedicine, policy of self-medication by the people and privatisation of some health care services which are still new in the area of public health care services.   The institutional structure also incorporates public and private health care services. In Malaysia, both public and private sectors provide substantial shares of total medical services. Nearly 50 per cent of the physicians who practise western medicine, and more than 40 per cent of hospitals are in the private sector. The share of private sector in the total health care supply is gradually going up.

Another important dimension of the structure of PHS relates to the dichotomisation of health care services into preventive and curative services. The preventive and promotive health care services include such programmes as health education, immunisation, control of communicable and non-communicable diseases, environmental health and sanitation, nutrition, occupational safety and health. The government has intensified health education programmes throughout the countries. The immunisaton programme covered 91 per cent of infants and more than 90 per cent of adults in 1995. The programme contributed significantly in improving infant and toddler mortality and the incidence of other diseases.   Under the *school health service programme*, nutrition has been included as a necessary part. This has benefitted over 600,000 pupils in schools in 1995. The food quality control programme contributed to a reduction in the incidence of food-borne diseases from 7,510 in 1992 about 3,390 in 1990 (Govt. of Malaysia, 1996, p. 536). The environmental and sanitation programme and occupational safety and health have been given priority in promotive and preventive health services in the country.

The curative health services include the expansion of curative health care facilities in hospitals and poly clinics. Between 1990 and 1995, many new hospitals were opened, and the number of beds were increased. These hospitals expanded specialist services and general outpatient services. Similarly, thirty new health centres and seven rural clinics were opened during the Sixth Plan period. The government undertook measures to ensure that the public had access to good quality, safe and efficacious pharmaceutical and health care products.. Apart from all these, the government has also significantly increased the output of health manpower and has also intensified medical research in the area of health care system in the country. All these facilities and services are going to be provided on continuous basis and on increasing scale in the new millennium.

HEALTH CARE PRODUCTS: DRUGS AND PHARMACEUTICALS

Malaysia's main concern in the area of PHS is to make essential drugs available to the public at reasonable cost and also to ensure the rational use of drugs. In other words, the national drug policy is to ensure the availability, accessibility, and affordability and proper use of drugs (Suleiman Abu Bakar, 1997, p. 13). In Malaysia, only those pharmaceuticals which meet the required standards of quality, safety and efficacy of the Drug Control Authority (DCA) are permitted to be sold in the country. The DCA has registered nearly 15,000 pharmaceuticals and health care products comprising nearly 4,500 over-the-counter drugs, over 7,000 prescription drugs, over 3,000 traditional medicines and nearly 350 cosmetic products. Malaysia has stringent control over the manufacture and circulation of drugs in the country. The producers, importers, wholesalers, and retailers have to conform to the established standards of the country. If the standards are not maintained, the drugs are recalled from the market. From January to June 1997, nearly 3.0 per cent drugs and medicines were recalled from the market. Post-marketing surveillance is regularly conducted with respect to drugs which are circulated in the market. The safety aspect of drugs marketed for the use of consumers is also monitored regularly by a committee. The Surveillance Committee started functioning since 1987.

Malaysia is still not self-sufficient in the production of drugs and medicines required in the country. In 1995, Malaysia produced drugs worth nearly RM1 billion, and 70 per cent of this was imported, and other health care products amounted to RM3 billion (Suleiman Abu Bakar, 1997, p. 13). The local products include traditional Malay, Chinese, and Indian medicines. The total value of these medicines amounted to nearly RM2 billion. There are in the country more than 80 licensed manufacturers, 160 licensed importers, and 600 licensed wholesalers, over 700 retailed pharmacies and about 3,000 retail outlets for different types of drugs and medicines. There are many distribution channels in which private medical practitioners control 45 per cent of the total annual value, followed by hospitals, drugs stores, pharmacies, and others. Alternative medicine, holistic medicine, and complementary medicines are regularly used in Malaysia. However, it is far behind many western countries regarding the acceptance and practice of alternative medicines. It is the indigenous mystic healers (*bomohs*) who are also consulted in cases of terminal illness, and major maladies. Herbal supplements are also given to patients in addition to prescription drugs. Thus, in Malaysia, there is side-by-side existence of western medicine and traditional medicine.

There is no stringent control on drug prices in Malaysia, and the yearly rate of increase of drug prices varies between 3 and 4 per cent annually. However, one interesting feature of drug price fluctuation is that some drug prices also plummet from time to time. The rate of price reduction was between 1 and 6 per cent during the period 1992 - 1995. The price decrease is mainly experienced in the case of very essential and commonly used drugs. Thus, on the whole, Malaysian generic market can be said to be competitive, and the prices in the drug market are more or less stable. The allocation for health is about 17.6 per cent of the total allocation for the social sector. In 1997, the Ministry of Health was allocated a total of RM 3.45 billion which was nearly 6 per cent of the total national budget and 2.6 per cent of the GNP. The allocation for drugs accounts for nearly 8.0 per cent of the health budget. The allocation for health is not really sufficient, and Malaysia's expenditure on health is indeed low as compared to other countries. As a matter of fact, the proportion of GNP spent on health went down 3.5 per cent in 1980 to 1.7 per cent in 1990. The allocation is indeed very low when compared to escalating drug prices since currency depreciation of 1997.

The Ministry of Health has formulated and implemented since 1983 a drug list comprising 730 active substances and 1,125 formulations for the use of the country. If any drug which is not mentioned in the list is to be used, prior permission from the Director General of Health is essential. The medicines used have both *generic* and *brand* names The list of drugs is revised from time to time in order to introduce new drugs or to replace old drugs. The public sector is very thorough and up-to-date in the method of drug formulation, drug listing, drug protocols, and therapeutic guidelines. However, the private health sector is not much concerned with all these mechanisms. It is urgently necessary to introduce a common national drug list for both the public and private health sectors. For the information of the consumers, it is also necessary to circulate guidelines and information leaflets. The government of Malaysia seems to be highly concerned with the increased cost of health care services, and has taken the following measures to keep the cost under control.

(i)   A national essential drug list consisting of 1,200 drugs have been prepared for the public health sector. Almost all the essential drugs that are commonly used can be prescribed from this list. The list ensures that patients are not prescribed more expensive drugs when less costly drugs are available in the country,

(ii)   In a rapidly developing country like Malaysia, people are generally interested in using the branded drugs which are more expensive but maybe of better quality. These drugs are mostly imported and are manufactured by Multinational Corporations (MNCs). The generic drugs are very cheap but sometimes the patients do not know the names of generic drugs, and medical practitioners do not generally prescribe generic drugs. The use of generic drugs can considerably reduce the cost of health care, and can also give impetus to the local pharmaceutical industry. Therefore, it is necessary to popularise the use of generic drugs rather than branded drugs. Simply by shifting to the use of generic drugs, health care cost can be reduced by at least 50 per cent in the country. The branded drugs produced by MNCs are extremely expensive compared to the generic drugs. For instance, the cost of branded anti-rheumatic drug like voltaren (Diclofenac Na) is RM0.27 per 25 mg. tablet which is 900 per cent higher than the generic equivalent which costs only RM0.03 per tablet of 25 mg. In the same way, the branded price for antibiotic Amoxcycillin Oral Suspension (125 mg/5ml) is RM11.90/60 ml which is 1,044 per cent higher compared to the generic product which costs only RM1.14/60 ml.

(iii)   There are in the country about 40 patent products out of 10,000 products registered with the Drug Control Authority of Malaysia. The patented drugs are marketed by MNCs. The prices of these drugs are not within the control of the Malaysian government, and are sometimes higher by 29,000 per cent compared to the alternative drugs with the same pharmacological classification. It would be necessary for the government to encourage the use of cheaper alternative drugs with same pharmacological components in private and government hospitals to reduce the health care costs drastically.

(iv)   In order to help the consumer to know the cost of treatment, it would be imperative to introduce itemised billing by the private hospitals and clinics. This practice may be made obligatory so that the consumers are not exploited. As a matter of fact, health care cost in the country can be substantially reduced if there is cooperation and collective efforts by manufacturers, traders, and prescribers of drugs and medicines. However, in order to ensure this, the intervention by the government is extremely essential.

The pharmaceutical industry in Malaysia is continuously growing and is well worth about RM1 billion, although many of those involved in the industry are importers and distributors. However, the investment in R&D is only 15 per cent of the total turnover. The percentage of investment devoted to R&D is very low in the drug industry. The MNCs do not have R&D departments in Malaysia. It can be said that no basic research is carried on in Malaysia regarding drugs and pharmaceuticals. One of the main reasons for low investment in R&D is the lack of skilled manpower. Malaysia has never encouraged the drug multinationals to operate in Malaysia in the same way as the MNCs in the industrial sector. Technology transfer is not taking place in the drug industry. Foreign experts are coming on short term basis, and they are not involved in fundamental research for the growth of drug industry in Malaysia.

PRIVATISATION AND ALLOCATIVE INEFFICIENCY

Privatisation of public health services in Malaysia can be looked upon as the manifestation of *government failure* in the provision of public health services. The idea to introduce privatisation in public health services (PHS) gained momentum in the late eighties basically as an offshoot of two impelling forces; *first,* privatisation is regarded as an essential strategy of capitalist development that had already been introduced in the services and the manufacturing sectors in the country with so-called high rate of success, and *second,* the cyclical downturn in the economy not only made the government poorer but it also reduced the productivity and efficiency in the public sector. Thus, after recession, restructuring was necessary to increase the efficiency in the government, and the introduction of privatisation was the natural choice because it was believed that the principle of marketism could bring more competition that will increase efficiency. The spirit of privatisation was in the air in the eighties and many industries and essential services were privatised. The privatisation of health services had the following objectives:

(i)   (i)To reduce the financial and administrative burden of the state.

(ii)   To use the resources in a more efficient manner so that allocative efficiency can be achieved.

(iii)   To introduce competition in the system so that general efficiency can increase.

(iv)   To increase efficiency so that consumers' surplus and satisfaction may increase, and there may be saving of time.

(v)   To release public resources to be diverted elsewhere to higher priority areas or for promotive and preventive health care development.

The basic rationale for the introduction of privatisation in the area of PHS was in line with World Bank's (1993) idea relating to investment in health (as referenced in *Medical Tribune* 1st May 1998, p. 15). Health care is regarded as a *private good* and the responsibility for the health care lies in private individuals. Thus considered, privatisation of health policy is based on two complementary principles: the reduction of state intervention and public responsibility, and the promotion of diversity and competition. The question of social welfare should be seen as the responsibility of the private domain, and the government should only intervene when the private sector will not or cannot respond. There are two other adjunct principles for the privatisation of health services. *First,* the public sector is generally inefficient and inequitable, whereas the private sector is more efficient and more equitable since it must conform to market dynamics of free-choice and competition. The limit of responsibility of the government in the case of privatisation is to look after those public activities which are targeted to the poor people.

It has been argued by Charles Griffin that interactions between public and private sectors can help target public subsidies better if the higher income groups use privatised medical facilities. Through the use of means test, user fees, and insurance coverage for the higher income group, sufficient resources can be accumulated to allow the government to target its health subsidies for hospital inpatient and outpatient services (Griffin, 1992, p. 130). It has been found from the experience in Malaysia that higher income households get themselves out of the public sector health care system in favour of privatised health system which is more efficient, time-saving, and comfortable. This can create a larger pool of resources which can be used for the poor patients. Thus, it was thought initially that privatisation of health services will create additional resources at the disposal of the government, which prompted the latter to introduce privatisation in the public health services in Malaysia.

Privatisation was regarded as an attempt to complement public sector in the provision of health care goods and services, and it was sought to be introduced in *supportive services* like catering services, hospital laundry services, disposal of clinical wastes and biomedical engineering. The form of privatisation introduced in Malaysia was *contracting out services*. However, gradually, institutions along with services were started to be privatised in public health sector. Thus, as an offshoot, the National Heart Institute was privatised in 1992.

It was thought that privatisation was to be done through gradualism because the time was not yet ripe to push the matter fully at one go. As a matter of fact, it was realised at the government quarters that per capita income in the country, around RM8,000, was not really enough to support full scale privatisation of health services. However, in the meanwhile, some of the hospital services have already been privatised on experimental basis and the agenda for future privatisation includes the following: (i)12 general hospitals are going to be privatised soon, (ii) clinical services are also in the agenda for privatisation, (iii) outpatient and emergency departments in government hospitals will charge extra fees after the office hours, and (iv) Kuala Lumpur maternity hospital is in the list of immediate privatisation. In future, the citizens will have to pay health insurance fees plus direct payment as user fees for using health services in Malaysia, when privatisation becomes fully operative.

Be that as it may, the concept of high *measured income* as the basis of privatisation is often misunderstood by many. It is not really the absolute income but the relative income as determined by income distribution pattern of the country which is a more important determinant of effective entitlement for health services (Sen, 1981). Even at the high level of absolute income, health care services may not be equally or fully accessible to the consumers. The best examples are United States and United Kingdom.

Privatisation is likely to create many adverse impacts , and some of these have already become apparent after the privatisation of the National Heart Institute (NHI) in Malaysia. The following are some of the major negative effects of privatisation of PHS.:

First, charges for medicine and services are generally higher in privatised hospitals which people in lower income group cannot afford, and as the case of NHI shows, 50 per cent of the patients are from low-income category.

Second, higher prices generally do not reduce the demand for essential medical care: *the income elasticity of demand for* PHS is less than unity in Malaysia, which implies that health goods are necessary goods. However, one must distinguish between *needs* and *metaneeds* in the matter of PHS. The metaneeds of PHS are not so compelling, urgent and necessary like the category of basic needs. A larger part of demand for PHS by the richer section consists of metaneeds, like attempts to slowdown the ageing, shipshaping the figure, cosmetic surgery, autonomous blood test and so on. The metaneeds are not so much induced by pathological requirements, and many of such needs (the pseudo demand) can be easily dispensed with. However, the rich people can afford the satisfaction of metaneeds, and they create the demand for these needs. Metagoods are, however, partly luxury goods. The privatised institutions cater to satisfy these metaneeds because these are the main sources of profit maximisation.

The public hospitals satisfy basically the primary needs arising out of morbidity , but privatised institutions supply both basic and metaneeds, increasingly the latter. The total resources being scarce in the economy, the diversion of crucial resources like skilled medical manpower to the privatised medical institutions to satisfy metaneeds (the pseudo demand) will create situations where more important basic health needs remain unattended to, resulting in loss of life and prolongation of the period of sufferings. Thus, free operation of market mechanism would divert scarce resources towards demand-based system at the cost of need-based priorities (Chan, 1998, p. 345). Indeed, the private sector hospitals with the same number of beds as public hospitals employ more doctors in Malaysia. Thus, higher requirement of medical personnel per unit of bed in the private hospital is seen by some as the manifestation of some kind of inefficiency.

The concentration of more doctors and skilled medical personnel is possible because the user fees charged by private hospital are much higher than those in public hospitals. So, because of higher margin of profit, some operational inefficiency can be covered up.

Third, privatisation has been found in many other cases of privatised services to be involved with *allocative inefficiency* in the sense that prices charged are much higher than the marginal cost. This is exactly going to be the case in the privatised medical institutions in the country.

Fourth, it is said that privatisation has reduced the administrative and financial burden of the government, and has also reduced the size of the public sector. While it may be true to some extent, it is not always a salutary sign to reduce the role of government, for if it does not get the opportunity to perform its responsibilities of welfare maximisation, and social selfare is going to be reduced. As a matter of fact, many concerned people strongly feel that privatisation in Malaysia has reduced the burden of the government but has increased the burden of the common people who are now to pay higher prices and higher tariffs for the public utilities (Ghosh, 1998, ch. 20).

Higher prices in the case of PHS generally do not reduce the demand because health services are found to be necessary goods in Malaysia, and their income elasticity of demand is less than one. As a matter of fact, the demand for health services is going up at an increasing rate in the country following longer life expectancy, and reduced death rate. The demand for public health services for gerentological uses would be indeed very high in the new millennium. All this will require more medical expenses and higher subsidy by the government.

Fifth, privatisation of medical services has been found to be unjust for the poor. The poor people should have minimal entitlement and empowerment for the medical services they receive. They confront with vertical and horizontal inequalities in the distribution of PHS in the privatised hospitals.

Being in the nature of *merit goods,* there is no harm in the privatisation of PHS provided double-pricing system is introduced in the privatised hospitals whereby the poor patients can get treatment on the basis of their low income and purchasing power. The rich patients may be made to pay more on the basis of their higher income. The poor should have proper empowerment and entitlement for the PHS.

Before effecting complete privatisation programme, it would be necessary to develop proper control mechanism to guard against price rise of the products and services, and the operational mechanism of dual pricing system must be found out and implemented to guarantee fair pricing, quality assurance and welfare commitment to the relatively poor section of the population. The government can introduce like low-income group housing, low-income group hospital.

To deal with liberalisation, the government will have to expand its regulatory and enforcement functions. At the low income level, the government will continue to emphasise quality and inexpensive health services. All this does not mean that the government will reduce its role but only that the emphasis will now change together with education and growing sophistication. People must be more aware of their own health and health care requirements. The government is supposed to continue to expand curative health services to meet the growing demand for comprehensive in-patient and outpatient services. New hospitals will be built and existing ones will be upgraded and be equipped with high-technology medical equipment and the latest available drugs. The main hospitals such as Hospital Kuala Lumpur will be decentralised to provide more efficient distribution of services and easier access by local communities.

The government cannot shy away from the social responsibilities of providing medical care and services particularly to the poor patients. If the government sheens its responsibilities the egalitarian dimension of PHS will go away. Thus, government intervention will be extremely essential at the outset to control price mark-up, oligopolistic strategy in the formation of pricing, and to ensure the prevention of *market failure.* Government intervention is supposed to provide the necessary *checks and balances.* As a matter of fact, privatisation is the offshoot of *government failure* in the provision of PHS. Thus, there must be better cooperation between the public and private sectors in the area of PHS, and privatisation must be complementary to the attempt of the public sector to provide best health care services.

PROBLEMATICS OF PUBLIC HEALTH SERVICES

Public Health Services in Malaysia have four major problem areas: problems relating to products, cost, distribution, and structural problems. Earlier discussions have tangentially touched upon some of the problems of public health services in Malaysia. In this section, at the cost of repetition, some of the earlier points along with some new problem areas would be identified.

One of the major problems is concerned with cost escalation not only of products but of the provision of public services. The product cost has gone up because of the depreciation of ringgit as an aftermath of financial crisis in the country, as most of the products are imported from abroad. There are, of course, various other reasons for cost proliferation of PHS. *First*, the doctors are prone to use branded drugs rather than generic drugs. Needless to say, the branded drugs are more expensive than generic drugs. *Second,* there does not seem to be strict control over the prices of drugs. More often than not, drug prices are several times higher than the costs of production, because the producers would like to increase the mark-up to a great extent as drugs are necessary commodities. The MNCs very much indulge in this practice of fleecing the consumers to extract surplus from the market. The burden of the government, therefore, has been growing up in Malaysia. But in terms of percentage of expenditure on health services, the burden seems to be extremely low in relative terms. The cost seems to be prohibitive in the case of consumers, and they are not empowered to look into or question the technique of billing. The private sector has no guidelines for drug listing and the uses of drugs. As a matter of fact, Malaysia has not yet been able to come up with a common national drug listing for both the private and public sectors.

In order to get relief from the excess burden of escalating cost, the government has advised the people for *self-medication* which can be defined generally as treating oneself or the family without prior consultation with a professional medical practitioner. It is believed that self-medication not only brings health benefit but also cost saving to both consumers and the government. However, the brilliant the idea maybe, it is likely to be very dangerous to the consumers because they do not have the required knowledge about the doses and the frequency of the use of various types of medicines and drugs. For instance, a consumer may think that Vitamin A is beneficial for eyesight. However, if Vitamin A is taken in pure form (not beta carotene) and in too high doses, there maybe the possibility of liver damage, apart from other longterm side-effects. Similar is the recent research on Vitamin C and *viagra*. A recent British Medical Journal Report (1998) comes out with the conclusion that continuous use of Vitamin C above 500 mg. may lead to some tissue damage, and may even produce carcinogenic effects. Little learning may be a dangerous thing. Self-medication, instead of proving less expensive, and beneficial to the consumers, may ultimately land them into trouble, and they have to pay higher prices later.

As for, health care products, it must be mentioned that the traditional drugs and medicines circulated in Malaysia do not generally undergo severe toxicological tests, and their quality is not standardised, as there is no strict quality control. The local drugs which are easily available on the roadsides and in informal markets, are not at all reliable. The pills for every ills are not really cost effective and safe drugs. The basic problem for product development, and product processing in Malaysian drug industry is that these are not backed-up by research, development and clinical trials. The country has no history of research culture in drug industry, nor is it helped by the experts from foreign countries on continuous basis for development and processing of drugs of international quality and standard.

Manpower shortage may perhaps be one of the reasons for such a state of affairs. And it is also responsible for low R&D activities in drug industries. Malaysia has always confronted with a shortage of qualified health manpower. The shortage will be felt very much in the millennium in medical professions. There would be shortages of medical professionals and allied health professionals by the turn of the century. The extent of the shortage can be appreciated from the following Table (Table 4)

TABLE 4 - SUPPLY OF SELECTED MEDICAL AND ALLIED HEALTH PROFESSIONALS

Category	Supply/Number			Requirements (based on norms)
	1990	1995	2000	2000
Medical Professionals				
Doctors	7,012	9,504	14,029	15,510
Dentists	1,471	1,791	2,243	2,909
Pharmacists	1,239	1,622	2,586	2,909
Ratio to population				
Doctors	1:2,569	1:2,177	1:1,658	1:1,500
Dentists	1:12,245	1:11,552	1:10,370	1:8,000
Pharmacists	1:14,538	1:12,756	1:8,995	1:8,000
Allied Health Professionals				
Dental Paramedics & Auxillary	2,137	2,720	4,097	6,361
Medical Assistants & Laboratory Technologists	4,093	5,392	8,287	9,842
Nurses	28,932	32,401	47,812	50,551
Occupational Therapists & Physiotherapists	234	410	811	911
Public Health Inspectors	1,007	1,418	2,019	2,695
Radiographers	508	537	1,049	1,297

Source: Seventh Malaysia Plan, p. 543

Shortages in the structural aspect of health care services will also be encountered in the country in the new millennium, particularly with respect to supply of hospitals, number of beds in hospitals, equipment and infrastructure in both urban and rural areas. The demand for these infrastructures is continuously moving up along with larger demand for public health services.

The distributional inequalities of PHS encompasses many dimensions, e.g. rural-urban inequalities, inter-state disparities, and inter-income group inequalities. It has sometimes been pointed out that rural health in Malaysia is quite satisfactory and is based on the principle of equity. A study has shown that in Malaysia, the poorest 20 per cent of population captures significantly more than 20 per cent of the subsidy only from rural clinics and midwives (Griffin, 1992, p. 130). Drawing on the data and information from Meerman's study (1979), Charles Griffin has concluded that subsidies are targeted in Malaysia to some important but relatively inexpensive services that benefit the poor disportionately. Although, it appears that the rural sector is consuming larger proportion of medical subsidy in the country because of their larger participation, one must not lose sight of the fact that these subsidies are with respect to low-cost products and services. The rural sector is relatively deprived of costly medical services, better and modern equipment, infrastructures, and medical attention. In the rural areas, there are lesser number of hospitals per unit of population. Population-doctor ratio is much higher in the rural areas compared to the urban sector. Moreover, the delivery of health services is much poorer in the rural areas. The proposed telemedicine is likely to help only the urban sector, and it may not reach the rural sector in the short run.

In terms of inter-income groups, the PHS are serving better the rich people in urban areas rather than the poor people in rural areas. Since the poor cannot pay high charges, they have to be satisfied with ordinary types of services and health care facilities. There are, again, many inter-state disparities in the distribution of health services in Malaysia. e.g. different states have different doctor-population ratios. Kuala Lumpur, for instance, has doctor-population ratio of 1:721, whereas for Sarawak, 1: 5175, Terengganu 1:4,226, and Kedah 1:4,277. If one compares bed complements per thousand population, one can find that Kuala Lumpur has 2.04 beds complements, Sarawak 1.52, Kelantan 1.05, Kedah 1.28, and Penang 1.99 Some of the states have achieved better health care facilities and services in terms of doctor-population ratio and number of hospitals per unit of population. One can also find sectoral differences in the endowment of health manpower in the country. For instance, in 1995, there were nearly 4,300 doctors in the public sector, compared with 5,000 doctors in the private sector. The supply of specialists, health care products and services are also unequal .between private and public sectors.

All these have resulted in unequal achievements in health indicators like infant mortality rate, and life expectancy. For instance, infant mortality rate has been found to be very low in Perlis (6.7), Negeri Sembilan (5.3), Johor (7.6); but it is very high in the states like Melaka (10.9), Perak (11.5), Sarawak (19.2), Trengganu (12.7), and Sabah (37.8).

CONCLUDING OBSERVATIONS

Health care management in Malaysia in recent years is going to be influenced by many new factors and forces. Many types of structural changes such as demographic changes, economic changes, epidemiological changes and the like will be important deterministic factors in public health services in future.

Improved health care practices in Malaysia have already been able to reduce the rate of mortality in the country. *Ceteris paribus,* this implies relatively higher rate of growth of population and larger stock of surviving people. The increase in life-expectancy and lower death rate of normal people will lead to larger number of ageing population. The changing demographic structure in the country will also witness more and more of ageing population in the age group of 65 and above. The percentage of ageing population will go up to 4.2 per cent and 6.1 per cent in the years 2000 and 2020 respectively. This will mean more dependency load, and higher medical expenditure and higher gerentological investment in the country. This type of investment expenditure is entirely unproductive, and is to be borne by the tax payers. However, although unproductive, it is an unavoidable cost, and every country has to bear such a cost. For instance, in developed countries, 30 to 50 per cent of total health care cost goes for the medical care of elderly people.

Malaysia is undergoing a period of epidemiological changes that resemble those of a developed country. The country is now having most of *capitalist diseases* which are mostly prevalent in DCs. The diseases such as AIDs, trauma, psychiatric diseases, mental aberration, schizophrenia, industrial hazards, drug addiction and drug dependence are becoming very prominent in Malaysia. Moreover, one can also observe the emergence of drug resistant pathogens and the resurgence of communicable diseases in the country.

The Ministry of Health in Malaysia has to implement the policy of *health for all* in the Seventh Plan, and *primary health care* has been chosen as the main strategy to achieve the objective. The Plan will also incorporate programmes to extend health care facilities to larger number of women, adolescent, elderly people and workers, apart from improved home nursing and rehabilitative services. Specialist services and drugs which are currently used in secondary and tertiary health care facilities will have to be made available at the primary health care level. This will involve not only extra monetary cost but also the services of specialists and skilled medical personnel.

The introduction of information technology in the field of public health services precisely through the device of telemedicine which aims at keeping people in the *wellness paradigm* is indeed a revolutionary change in the field of medi-care. It cuts across many physical distance barriers and sectoral boundaries in the way of health care services. All these will involve higher cost but probably less time for recovery.

At present, in the Malaysian health care management system, which is at its cross-road, trade offs between time (convenience) and cost seem to very crucial, and cost at both micro and macro levels is escalating very rapidly. This indeed is the main concern of the government, which has led to the introduction of privatisation and corporatisation of some part of public health services. However, *government failure* in the provision of such an important *merit good* as health care, notwithstanding the success of the government in many other fields, is sure to impinge on the maximisation of social welfare which it so fervently desires to promote in Malaysia.

REFERENCES

Chan, Chee Khoon (1996), "Health Care Financing" in Jomo, K.S. & Ng Suew Kiat (eds.), (1996).

Ghosh, B.N. (1998), *Malaysia: The Transformation Within,* Longman, Kuala Lumpur.

Gomez, Mary (1998), "Financing Malaysia's Health care System", *Medical Tribune,* 15 March.

Govt. of Malaysia (1996), *Seventh Malaysian,* Govt. Press, Kuala Lumpur.

Griffin, Charles C. (1992), *Health Care in Asia,* The World Bank, Washington, D.C.

Jomo, K.S. and Ng Suew Kiat (eds.) (1996), *Malaysia's Economic Development,* Pelanduk Publications, Kuala Lumpur.

Meerman, Jacob (1979), *Public Expenditure in Malaysia: Who Benefits and Why,* Oxford University Press, New York.

Sen, A.K. (1981), *Poverty and Famines: An Essay on Entitlement and Deprivation,* Oxford Univ. Press.

Suleiman Abu Bakar (1997), "Essential Drugs Concept: An International Prospective", Keynote Address delivered at the opening ceremony of the Seminar on the same subject at Penang in Sept.

Chapter 8

PRIVATISATION IN THE PHILIPPINES: A CRITICAL ASSESSMENT

Antonio Tujan (Jr.) and Jennifer Haygood

INTRODUCTION

Worldwide, private business is taking control over strategic government corporations and assets, public utilities, and the provision of even the most basic social services. Otherwise known as privatisation, this phenomenon is specially intense today in the underdeveloped countries of Latin America,, Africa, Asia, including the Philippines, and the former Soviet bloc countries.

From 1980 to 1992, a total of 6,832 sales of public assets and corporations have been made by governments, mostly in underdeveloped countries[1]. The World Bank recorded annual privatisation receipts increasing 30 times in these countries from 1998 to 1993 amounting to US $29 million. Meanwhile, a survey by the Organisation for Economic Cooperation and Development (OECD) reveals that privatisation receipts worldwide were expected to reach US$100 million in 1996 – reflecting a 50% increase over total receipts in 1995[2].

This frenzied rush over what might seem only as the harmless sale of public assets and utilities, and the transfer of control and delivery of social services to the private sector is, in reality, taking away from governments their regulatory functions for national and public interest, and their responsibilities of providing for the basic needs and services of their constituents and ensuring that their welfare is not compromised.

The result is not distribution but the concentration of wealth, power and resources to a select number of people and multinational corporations - those who already enjoy a large share of wealth in their countries and in the world. Very alarming indeed, are the social, political and economic implications of unbridled privatisation.

SAP(ING) ECONOMIES

The logic for privatisation is the same as that of liberalisation and deregulation. It aims to widen market access for vested business interests in the economies of the underdeveloped countries where the state plays a significant role in industry, agriculture, and in the provision of services, not to mention control and exploitation of natural resources. Liberalization of economies facilitates the entry of foreign players in all sectors of affected economies and the free flow of capital to and from economies by breaking down economic barriers (i.e., removal of imports and exchange controls). Deregulation, on the other hand, paves the way for removal of state controls and subsidies (social mechanisms set up to regulate prices and protect consumers as well as local producers and the national economy) over strategic industries (i.e., the oil industry, agriculture – in rice procurement and distribution). Privatisation is the sale or transfer of government assets and operations to private entitites. Privatisation has a very wide coverage, including real estate and similar assets, government owned or controlled corporations (GOCCs) or parastatals, social service institutions or agencies, and sometimes even key administrative, executive and police functions.

All three policies form part of the structural adjustment programs (SAPs) imposed by the International Monetary Fund (IMF) and the World Bank over the underdeveloped countries in the Third World and the former Soviet bloc countries. The SAP made sure that the country would be able to repay its debts through tight fiscal management reducing government spending through-cost-cutting and privatisation, including raising government revenues through taxation and sales receipts from privatisation, and opening the country to foreign investments and trade through liberalisation and deregulation. The concept of privatisation as part of the SAPs was introduced to underdeveloped countries in the early 1980s. During this time, many countries experienced severe economic strains brought about by increasing trade imbalances and mounting foreign debts. To make sure that underdeveloped countries paid their debts, the IMF and the World Bank offered more debts tied with economic conditionalities which the highly-indebted countries must follow.

PRIVATISING THE PHILIPPINE GOVERNMENT

The Philippines was among the first countries that succumbed to the SAPs in the late 1970s. Coupled with the huge foreign debt it had incurred, the economic and political crises experienced by the Philippines in 1983 to 1985 were used by the IMF and World Bank to push for privatisation in the country. In fact, the IMF was a key factor for the financial collapse in 1984 when it withheld the release of scheduled loan funds to pressure Marcos to implement fiscal, economic and political reforms. Presidential Decree No. 2030 under Marcos introduced privatisation as a government policy in the Philippines, but it was only under Cory Aquino that it was finally implemented. Since it started in 1987, privatisation here has taken many forms. Under Cory Aquino, the focus of the privatisation program was the sale of white elephants – assets and/or corporations owned by former Marcos cronies whose foreign indebtedness was guaranteed and assumed by government banks. Aquino later widened the scope of privatisation to include private sector participation in infrastructure and energy projects including water and irrigation. The Build-Operate-Transfer (BOT) Law was enacted to legitimise the entry of private business in vital government development undertakings and operations.

Under the term of Ramos, privatisation became more intensified. Most of the biggest sales occurred under the Ramos administration (i.e., Petron, the Philippine National Bank, the Manila Hotel, MWSS). The government also made a handsome profit from selling public lands such as the Fort Bonifacio. Ramos also expanded the scope of the BOT Law to include other schemes and to widen private sector choices of participation. The latest target of the government's privatisation program under Ramos is the public utilities sector starting with the sale of the Metropolitan Waterworks and Sewerage Systems (MWSS). The National Power Corporation (NPC was targeted for privatisation by year end or in early 1998[3] The forging of partnerships with the private sector in the provision of basic services is currently being assessed. Studies have been made on the privatisation of the health services. State colleges and universities as well as social security institutions are also being considered for privatisation. Indeed, privatisation in the country has taken on different modes but the logic remains the same. Echoing the IMF-World Bank's oft-repeated homily, the *raison d'etre* for privatising state assets and corporations, government operations and development undertakings are: (1) to improve efficiency; (2) to increase investments; (3) to broaden the ownership base; (4) to develop capital markets; and (5) to generate government revenues for priority government expenditures.[4]

Yet, what is clear to the public is the perpetually widening gap between the rich few and the masses of poor Filipino families as a result of the SAPs that reinforce the existing structural oppressive relationships between the elite and the economically dispossessed farmers and workers and as such, compound the structural inequities in the country. Privatisation has, for one, added more room for the creation of monopolies in the economy and provided for increased concentration of capital, wealth and resources to the local elite and the transnational corporations that dominate the economy. For another, debts assumed by the government to assure salability of its assets and corporations are shouldered by the poor workers and farmers in the form of higher indirect taxes covering a wider array of goods and services, and by decreasing government subsidies on health, education, and those government agencies that ensure wider access to public goods (i.e., the National Food Authority (NFA) for rice procurement and distribution). Higher prices for basic commodities resulting from repressive economic policies have further eroded the real value of workers' wages.

White Elephant Sale?

In the 20 years of Marcos dictatorship, a small number of comprado-landlord cronies, including relatives (the likes of Herminio Disini, Eduardo

Cojuangco, Ricardo Silverio, Roberto Benedicto, Cuenca) took advantage of their proximity to the Marcoses. They availed of loans from both local and foreign sources to prime up their businesses and put up new companies. These loans, without sufficient collateral, were granted with guarantees from the national government and often through Marco's behest. Thus, the behest loans. In 1985, 73% of the total foreign debt was actually Marcos debts or the so-called behest loans.[5] The interest of these cronies ranged from banking and finance to agriculture and manufacturing. At the same time, due to their close ties with Marcos, they were able to use government regulations and power to exact fees, dominate the markets, and create monopolies. A Senate Blue Ribbon Committee Report headed by former Senator Teofisto Guingona revealed how Marcos himself would get commissions or kickbacks from the business deals of his cronies in return for the economic favours he granted them.[6]

Meanwhile, Marcos embarked on the establishment of government presence in almost every sector of the economy such as oil, banking, sugar, and shipping. Government presence in these sectors was supposed to ensure domestic supply of basic commodities for mass consumption especially in times of crisis, and supply of inputs vital to industry. Thus, the creation of Philippine National Oil Company, the Land bank of the Philippines for rural credit, among others. These government entities later came to be known as government-owned or-controlled corporations or GOCCs. Many studies have already been conducted on GOCCs and the phenomenal growth during the time of Marcos increased from only 37 in 1967 to 303 by the end of his term.[7] The studies suggest that a lot of these corporations and subsidiaries only served to siphon off scarce government resources for personal aggrandisement of both bureaucrat capitalists in the government and vested business interest of Marcos cronies.

Government corporations put up for the original purpose of regulating the market and ensuring domestic supply of basic services and commodities should be differentiated from those that were merely absorbed by the government by virtue of loan default and/or foreclosure, or GOCCs which were set up by the Marcoses mainly to siphon off public funds. A large part of the capital infusion of crony-controlled companies were Marcos guaranteed loans. As such, they were technically government corporations. When these corporations went into bankruptcy in the early '80s, Marcos went to the rescue by infusing taxpayers' money to revive the corporations – but of no avail. Thee companies continued to suffer losses. In the end, crony-corporations defaulted on their loans. These loans were absorbed by the government financial institutions (GFIs), of which a large amount was shouldered by the Philippine National Bank (PNB) and the Development Bank of the Philippines (DBP). Marcos ordered these banks and other GFIs to turn these loans into government equity. These became the non-performing assets (NPAs) (now termed as transferred assets or TAs) in the form of: (1) capital equipment, whole plants/production facilities – physical form assets acquired through foreclosure; (2) financial – promissory notes and other financial claims versus a borrower-enterprise backed by mortgages of physical assets, guarantees (bonds); and (3) equity.

Barely a year after her proclamation as President, Cory Aquino created the Asset Privatisation Trust (APT) and the Committee on Privatisation (COP) under Presidential Proclamation 50, to facilitate the disposal of GOCCs and the NPAs or what is now known as TAs.

The APT absorbed all the NPAs/TAs. It is responsible for the sale of these assets and GOCCs marked for disposition by COP. In addition to the APT, 13 agencies like the National Development Corporation (NDC), the PNB and the Government Service and Insurance System (GSIS), among others, also serve as disposition entities.[9] The PCGG or the Presidential Commission on Good Government was responsible for disposing sequestered assets from the Marcoses and his cronies. Aside from identifying which assets are to be sold, the COP also monitors expenditures of the GOCCs.

The disposition of TAs and GOCCs is carried out either through public bidding of shares of assets, negotiated sale of shares of assets, direct debt buy-out (the APT lingo for debt-to-equity), or public offerings of shares of stocks (as was the case of Petron and PNB). Negotiated sales are resorted to when the results of the bidding are unacceptable. Direct debt buy-outs (DDBOs) allow debtors to buy back the debts incurred by the company.[10] In other cases, creditors are the ones that buy the debts at half the original amount.

Selling in Desperation

But selling these assets proved to be difficult because of the huge debts that went along with the assets. To ensure their saleability, Aquino infused public money to revitalise the GOCCs and TAs. As such, GOCCs and TAs were sold on a clean basis; that is, free of liabilities [11] In the cases where assets were sold to previous owners, government's unbooked exposure (interest on loans) is not included. [11] As a result, the difference between total selling price and government exposure for the first four years of its implementation under Aquino (1987-1990), privatisation cost the government a net loss of approximately P42 billion . (See Table 1)

TABLE 1: DISPOSED ASSETS BY INDUSTRY

Industry/a	No.	Selling Price	Govt. Exposure	Net Profit/ (Loss)
Agriculture	18	2,853,744,000	7,650,721,000	4,796,977,000
Manufacturing	124	8,135,324,000	---	18880692000
Mining	9	7,229,538,000	---	8825845000
Services	27	1,145,781,000	2,112,618,000	633,837,000
Trading	3	98,977,000	327,804,000	228,827,000
Utilities	33	974,310,000	7,966,976,000	6,992,666,000
Government Firms	16	3,699,226,000	4,680,819,000	981,593,000
Total	230	24,136,900,000	---	41,673,437,000
1992/b	24	3,821,258,000	6,317,475,000	2,496,217,000
1994/b	4	81,422,473	1,072,565,163	814,229,473
1995/b	4	2,389,992,451	5,868,424,322	3,479,431,871
Total		7,024,479,924	---	5,161,419,398
		31161379924	---	46,834,856,398

Sources: (a) Asset Disposition Yearly Report, 1987 – 1990; APT List of Disposed Assets as lifted from IBONFF, 30 April 1991;
(b) APT Report to the COA, 1992, 1994, 1995; includes only the fully disposed assets;APT first Quarter Report 1996.
Note: For 1994, government exposure includes unbooked interest of interest on loans.

In fact, sales through DDBO was the highest at 63 as of March 1996. Fully disposed assets totalled 259 during the same period (See Table 2). This desperate net-loss sale of assets continued under the Ramos regime. Available data for the years 1992, 1994 and 1995 (covering APT sales from fully-disposed assets alone) recorded P6.2 billion net losses for the Ramos government. Despite net-loss selling, the privatisation program was declared a success in 1994 when the Ramos government transferred $2 billion to the national treasury and produced the governments' first fiscal surplus in twenty years.[12] But the success of privatisation program in 1994 was due largely from the sale of government shares in Petron in the stock market.

TABLE 2: ASSETS DISPOSED BY MODE OF SALE (1987 TO MARCH 31, 1996 (IN THOUSAND PESOS).

Disposal Mode	No.	Settlement Price
Fully disposed	259	26,829,554
Bidding	61	4,911,321
DDBO-AV	25	1,502,507
DDNP-TP	38	3,679,077
Retrieval	12	989,158
Negotiated Sale	40	8,989,461
Non-APT Sales/a	43	2,297,515
Other Modes/b	40	4,460,515
Partially Disposed	63	6,616,357
Bidding	30	3,969,168
DDBO-AV	1	1,582
DDBO-TP	2	82,051
Retrieval		
Negotiated Sale	17	747,221
Non-APT sales/a	3	2,476
Other modes/b	10	1,813,859
TOTAL	322	33,445,911

(a) Government Financial Institution Sale
(b) Lease, rentals
Source: APT 1996 Q1 Report

Bankruptcy Sale

Bent on generating more revenues for debt repayment, privatisation under President Ramos took on a large coverage, even if it meant giving up even the country's national heritage and patrimony to foreign ownership and risking the interest of economic development and the welfare of the Filipino masses. More assets that were more profitable and, therefore, more attractive to foreign buyers, were put up for sale, not because they were non-performing assets, but because the government needed more revenues. Such was the case of the sale of Petron, For Bonifacio, the Alabang Stock Farm, the Manila Hotel and the aborted sale of the Tokyo properties.

Wider sectors of the economy previously not open to market-oriented private sector participation was opened up to profit enterprises as the government also looked at the utilities in a frenzied, thoughtless selling spree. Through Executive Order no. 37 of December 1992, newly-elected President Ramos expanded the coverage of the privatisation program to include assets and activities presently owned or undertaken by line agencies of the government.[13] Ramos also enacted into law two Republic Acts – 7661 and 7886, extending the lives of the COP and the APT. RA No. 7668 amended RA no. 7661 to extend the lives of the two disposition entities from 1995 to 1999. Executive Order No. 298 was also enacted to add other modes of privatisation of disposition of hard-to-sell assets. Under this EO, the APT may enter into joint venture arrangements in a business with a private person or entity for sharing of funds, land, resources, facilities and services. Thereafter, the joint-venture is privatised or turned over to the proper government agency. Other modes include the BOT schemes, management contracts, lease purchases and securitization.[14] Not through selling white elephants from Marcos crony corporations, but through bankruptcy sales did Ramos dramatically increase earnings from privatisation. And in the process, he achieved the reversal of the budget deficit. In 1994, the government earned P25 billion by selling Petron through the stock market. The 1995 sale of Fort Bonifacio alone amounting to P39.2 billion to the Metro-Pacific consortium comprised 22.56 per cent of total cumulative revenues of the government form 1987 to present (See Table 3) The government sold its 515 equity in Manila Hotel to a Malaysian-led consortium although the Supreme Court later overtuned this transaction

TABLE 3: NUMBER OF ASSETS/COMPANIES DISPOSED
(1987 – 1996 IN BILLION PESOS)

	Gross Revenue	No. of Assets/Co. Privatised
GOCCs	72.50	95
APT Assets	44.40	340
PCGG Assets	17.60	9
BCDA Assets	39.20	1
Total	173.70	445

Source: Committee on Privatisation
Note: The sale of Fort Bonifacio made by the BCDA in 1995 at P39.20 billion
and the sale of Petron Corp. in 1994 at P25 billion make up 37 percent of total
sales.

Not content with the sale of government assets and the country's national patrimony and heritage, and privatising development through BOT schemes, which include utilities project like the mass transit systems and the power plants, the government decided to sell off the utilities to earn megabucks. Most prominent are the sale of the MWSS and the impending sale of the NPC, both large utilities that would provide mega profits for private business. The MWSS was recently sold to the Lopez and Ayala groups, both of which were partners of TNCs in water utilities for US$7 billion, the biggest utilities privatisation deal so far in the world. This has sparked a controversy by its very size and significance to the Philippine economy, and is now subject to a temporary restraining order form the Supreme court. While the controversies have targeted the traditional Philippine comprador monopolies i.e., the Lopez and Ayala groups, what is relatively unknown is the fact that these local monopolies have teamed up with foreign global monopolies in a 60-40 sharing to snare the MWSS. Ayala's partner is infrastructure giant Bechtel of USA which has a tie-up with another giant, North West Water of the UNK, in all its international infrastructure projects.[1] Lopez's partner is the other waterworks global giant, Lyonnais des'Eaux of France, which has cornered practically all the water utilities privatisation projects in Australia and Southeast Asia.[15]

A Water Crisis?

In June 1995, R.A. No. 8041, otherwise known as the Water Crisis Act, was enacted into law. Its objectives were supposedly to improve supply and distribution, to finance the privatisation of state-run water facilities, and to curb water pilferage, illegal connections and leaks. The rate of loss of non-revenue water stands at 55 % more than half the average 2,500 million liters per day.[16] Obviously, the Water Crisis Act follows the footsteps of the Power Crisis Act which provides the Ramos administration the legal excuse to shortcut privatisation procedures and the leeway in awarding projects.

The Ramos government gives the following reasons for privatising the MWSS: to put an end to (1) the water crisis: (2) inefficient water supply delivery; (3) perceived graft and corruption, and (4) the 60% water loss due to theft and leaks[17] With its $250 million foreign and P900 million local debts, the MWSS can hardly be called liquid and profitable. Nor is it efficient. After 120 years of existence, the MWSS services only about 67% of the households in Metro Manila[17]. With privatisation, water service coverage is targeted to expand from the present 67 per cent to 85 per cent by the year 2001 to universal coverage by 2006. Water tariffs would be reduced resulting in savings of P7 million a day for consumers and the expansion of piped sewerage and septic tank cleaning service coverage from the present 75 to 835 by 2021.[18]

Making a Killing in Return

The government expects handsome concession and other fees. The winning bidders will pay an amount equal to the debt service of the MWSS annually to the government while budgetary outlay from the government to the MWSS would no longer be necessary. According to government documents, the MWSS privatisation program will be patterned after that of Buenos Aires in Argentina. Both apparently share parallel experiences.[19] Coincidentally, Lyonnais des Eaux SA of France, the partner of the Lopezes' Benpres Holding Corporation, led the consortium (Aguas Argentinas) that won the water contract for Buenos Aires.[1] Specialising in water services, this French multinational company has amassed profits in its various water services contracts. In Argentina alone,

Aguas Argentinas made a profit of US$25 million in 1994. This was only after 20 months in operation.[1] The main savings of the consortium came from the retrenchment of 3,830 workers from the total 7,500 workers – a 50% cut in manpower in the first three months.[1] The same fate awaited workers in the MWSS. Cost-cutting measures to ensure profits for the first years in operation of the winning combine and consortium would include the retrenchment of thousand of workers. Those who will remain will be hired on contractual basis for six months. From then, the new MWSS management will decide on the number of workforce to be regularised and the rest would eventually be retrenched.[20]

In the meantime, it would be worthwhile to note that the privatisation of state water supply in Buenos Aires, Argentina, has only benefited the few. Water is now more expensive but the service remains the same. On many days, there is no water in Rosario, Argentina's second largest city.[21] Back in its homebase, this French firm was alleged to have given bribe money amounting 21 million francs to the former Mayor Alain Carignon of the French City of Grenoble in exchange for a water privatisation contract. Corruption over the 1989 contract led to water prices rising threefold in 6 years. Mayor Carignon was found guilty and was fined 420 million francs ($85 million) in damages.[1]

Private Power Monopoly

With the sale of the MWSS, lawmakers are now busy finalising the law that would pave the way for the privatisation of the NPC. Slated have been privatised by end-1997 or early 1998, the NPC is now being groomed and prepared for the eventual takeover by private business. Congress is presently busy polishing the bill that would lay the groundwork for the privatisation of the NPC. House Bill No. 7964 provides for: (a) an unregulated and competitive bulk power generation component, with power producers selling electricity on long-term contracts; (b) a partially deregulated and non-exclusive transmission component with an NPC spin-off company serving as a common electricity carrier, but with the possibility of private sector firms and distribution utilities owning and operating transmission lines for their own use; (c) opening a window for the private sector to avail of Official Development Assistance (ODA) with continued government guarantees.[22]

The NPC shall be divested of its generating assets to ensure competition, supply, reliability and efficiency. Its monopoly in power generation and monopsony in the procurement of electricity shall cease.[22] The NPC presently has the monopoly in power generation in the country cornering more than half of the market (about 60%). The rest is provided by the independent power producers (IPP). The NPC alone buys the electricity from the other power producers which it sells to distributors or franchise holders. [22] The Manila Electric Company (MERALCO) owned by the Lopezes is the single largest distributor of electricity in the country. Other distributors are composed of smaller distribution utilities and electric cooperatives.[23] Meanwhile, the Lopezes through its Private Power Corporation have already penetrated the power generation subsector. There is no law barring the Lopezes from bidding for the NPC after it has won the MWSS with Ayalas. If it wins the NPC, power generation and distribution in the country will be under the control of the Lopezes.

PRIVATISING DEVELOPMENT

Other than the sale of government assets and corporations, private sector involvement in the development of infrastructure facilities (in power, irrigation, road construction, etc.) was maximised. In 1990, the Aquino government, in keeping with the economic reform policies stipulated in the multilateral Philippine Assistance Program (PAP), passed R.A. No. 6957. An Act Authorising the Financing, Construction, Operation and Maintenance of Infrastructure Projects by the Private Sector and Other Purposes. [23] This is more popularly known as the Build-Operate-And-Transfer (BOT) Law. Later in June 1993, the BOT Law was amended by R.A. 7718 (An Act Amending Certain Section of R.A. 6957) under the Ramos Administration. The amendment allowed full participation of the private sector in vital government development infrastructure programs and projects.[23]

How It Works?

While R. A. 6957 involved only two schemes – the BOT scheme and the build-Transfer (BT) scheme, R.A. 7718 added a host of other related schemes such as build-own-and-operate (BOO), build-lease and transfer (BLT), build-transfer- and –operate, contract-add-and-operate (CAO), develop-operate-and transfer (DOT), rehabilitate-operate-and-transfer (ROT), and rehabilitate-own-and-operate (ROO). The most widely used scheme is the BOT scheme. Under this scheme, a private firm, either local or foreign, enters into a contract with the government in the construction and financing of a given facility, and maintains it for its entire lifespan(usually up to but not exceeding 50 years), after which, the contractor turns it over to the government. During its term of ownership and operation of the facility, the contractor is allowed to collect user fees, rentals and charges not exceeding its original proposal or as negotiated and included in its contract bid. This will allow the contractor to recover its investment as well as operating and maintenance expenses. [23] (See Table 4 for a listing of other schemes and the salient features of the law). Contract bidders can either be a natural-born Filipino or a foreign entity. If the contractor is a corporation, at least 60% Filipino equity is required, unless otherwise approved by the government (meaning 100% foreign-owned firms may participate).[23]

Disadvantages from BOT Development

Priority government projects are identified in the Public Investment List (PIL). The PIL represents the approved disbursements for every year for new and ongoing projects. It is determined on the basis of yearly national budgetary outlay (in the case of National Government and GOCC financed projects) and on the Medium-Term Public Investment Program. The PIL helps proponent agencies and ODA donors ensure that implementation plans and fund disbursements are realistic.[24] This system allows creditor countries and private entities to select projects to apply for. In the process, the final decision on which projects are put on stream are based on the business considerations of the transnational corporations regarding the exposure and profitability of the project. Vital government infrastructure projects are implemented not on the basis of the over-all needs of the economy but on profit margins resulting in a hodge-podge of government development efforts and losing on effective programmatic approach in the process. For example, in the case of construction, operation and maintenance of toll roads, there are instances where roads that are economically justified but not financially viable cannot be constructed unless the government provides a revenue or traffic guarantee. Many urban roads proposed for BOT are treated as separate investments when they should be integrated into the entire road network in terms of access and egress. [25]

These guarantees, in the end, wipe out whatever advantages there are for the government from BOT schemes. Another example is the power sector, the first to be exposed to the BOT law. The arrangements have been based on reasonably standardised energy conversion agreements where NPC supplies the fuel and then purchases the power output. NPC also takes the risks of force majeure as well as the risk associated with foreign currency payments. This assumption of risks by the NPC partly explains why so many countries have signed up, many times larger than in any other country.[26] But more crucial issues against BOT are that, first, this scheme commercializes infrastructure development resulting in distortions mentioned above and higher costs such as in ports and toll road. Secondly, this scheme is inherently biased and assures profits for the transnational corporations which bring in capital equipment tax free beside other tax advantages. Filipino bidders who have to pay 30% for capital equipment besides EVAT and other taxes cannot compete with lower bids from TNCs. Thirdly, the government ends up more indebted than ever through loan guarantees for BOT Projects, instead of reducing direct government borrowing and spending. (See Table 5 and 6).

TABLE 4: VARIOUS SCHEMES FOR PRIVATE SECTOR PARTICIPATION IN INFRASTRUCTURE DEVELOPMENT AS PROVIDED IN THE AMENDED BOT LAW OR R.A. 7718.

BUILD AND TRANSFER(BT) A contractual arrangement whereby the project proponent undertakes the financing and construction of a given infrastructure or development facility and after its completion turns it over the government agency or local government unit concerned which shall pay the proponent on an agreed schedule its total investment expended on the project plus a reasonable rate of return thereon.
BUILD-LEASE-AND-TRANSFER (BLT) ..is authroised to finance and construct an infrastructure or development facility and upon its completion turns it over to the government agency... on a lease arrangement for a fixed period after which ownership of the facility is automatically transferred to the government agency or local government unit concerned.
BUILD-OPERATE-AND-TRANSFER (BOT) … undertakes the construction, including financing of a given infrastructure facility, and the operation and maintenance thereof. The project proponent operates the facility over a fixed term during which it is allowed to charge facility users appropriate tolls, fees, rentals, and charges not exceeding those proposed in its bid or as negotiated and incorporated in the contract to enable the project to recover its investment, and operating and maintenance expenses in the project. The project proponent transfers the facility to the government agency... at the end of the fixed term not exceeding 50 years. This shall include a supply and operate situation which is a contractual arrangement whereby the supplier of equipment and machinery for a given facility.... Operates the facility providing in the process technology transfer and training of Filipino nationals.

BUILD –OPERATE-AND OWN (BOO)

.. is authorised to finance, construct, own and operate and maintain an infrastructure or development facility, in which the proponent is allowed to recover its total investment, operating and maintenance costs plus a reasonable rate of return by collecting tolls, fees, rentals or other charges from facility users. Under this project, the proponent which owns the assets of the facility may assign its operation and maintenance to a facility operator.

BUILD-TRANSFER-AND-OPERATE

…..an Agency/LGU contracts out the building of an infrastructure facility to a private entity such that the contractor builds the facility on a turn-key basis, assuming cost overruns, delays, and specified performance risks. Once the facility is commissioned satisfactorily, title is transferred to the implementing agency. The private entity, however, operates the facility on behalf of the implementing agency under an agreement.

CONTRACT-ADD-AND-OPERATE(CAO)

…..adds to an existing infrastructure facility which it is renting from government and operates the expanded project over an agreed franchise period. There may be or may not be a transfer arrangement as regards the added facility provided by the project proponent.

DEVELOP-OPERATE-AND-TRANSFER (DOT)

…favourable conditions external to a new infrastructure project to be built by the project proponent are integrated into the arrangement by giving the same the right to develop adjoining property, and thus, enjoy some of the benefits the investments creates such as property or rent values.

REHABILITATE-OPERATE-AND-TRANSFER (ROT)

....an existing facility is turned over to the private sector to refurbish operate, and maintain for a franchise period, at the expiry of which the facility is turned over to the government. The term is also use dto describe the purchase of an existing facility from abroad, importing, refurbishing, erecting, and consuming it within the host country.

REHABILITATE-OWN-AND-OPERATE (ROO)

.... To refurbish and operate with no time limitation imposed on ownership. As long as the operator is not in violation of its franchise, it can continue to operate the facility in perpetuity.

Source: Republic Act No. 7718 and its Implementing Rules and Regulations

TABLE 5: GOVERNMENT GUARANTEED MEDIUM-AND LONG-TERM FOREIGN LOANS OF THE PRIVATE SECTOR TO FINANCE VARIOUS PROJECTS (1990-1996)

Project	Year	Amount of Loan
Smelting and Refining Facility	1990	US$ 27,500,000.00
Tandik Mini-hydroelectric PO	1993	AU$ 6,440,000.00
Project in Agusan River MERALCO		
Distribution project	1994	US4138,000,000.00
Various Telecommunications Projects	1994	US$ 15,022,627.36
Satellite Project	1995	US$ 65,739,600.00
Oleochemical Process Equipment	1995	US$ 30,000,000.00
Dry Process Cement Plant	1996	US$ 80,000,000.00

Source: Bangko Sentral ng Pilipinas

MORE DEBTS FROM BOT?

While the general idea for the privatisation of development initiatives was to reduce government spending especially on the availability of more loans, records from the Central Bank, the BOI and the DBM would show that government actually incurred more debts through counterpart funds and guarantees on loans made by its private partners in infrastructure and development projects. The amended BOT Law provided for direct government guarantees. Under Section 2, letter (n) ----of R.A. 7718, government or local government units will assume responsibility of the repayment of debt directly incurred by the project proponent (local or foreign) in implementing the project in case of a loan default. Of course, this would include interest payment on these loans. A high-ranking official of the BOT Centre consistently denied to this writer the existence of government guarantees on infrastructure projects, yet various news reports quoting pronouncements from the government of eventual removal of guarantees to private developers especially in the power sector indicate otherwise.

SELLING OUT AND COMMERCIALISING SOCIAL SERVICES

The country's social services have traditionally been privatized and commercialised because of government default. The lack of budgetary allocation for social services has resulted in very poor quality or non-availability of public education, health, housing, welfare, community development and other services. Budget for health care as a percentage of GNP has averaged only 0.16 per cent from 1979 – 1989. In 1991, this improved to 2.37 per cent but still compares unfavourably with Thailand at 3 per cent, Malaysia at 4 per cent, or China and India at 5 per cent.[27] The government's budget for education, touted to be a substantial share of the budget pie averages only 2.5 per cent of the GNP, the lowest in the region.[25] This government default in social services allows the takeover by private concerns which provide services for a hefty fee where services or services of quality are non existent. As a result, private enterprises have cornered a substantial share of social services, and in fact, provide the bulk of capital intensive services such as tertiary education and tertiary hospitals.

However, this situation is still not enough for the neo-liberal program of privatisation and commericialisation of the Philippine government. On one hand, the drive to reduce public spending for services as a way of reducing the budget deficit is a commitment to the IMF-World Bank. On the other hand, the neo-liberal concept of transforming government into an efficient enterprise means commercialising operations and services wherever possible and selling of inefficient, funds-draining operations and services. This translates to privatising whatever is left of tertiary education, tertiary and even general hospitals, and mass housing, for example. This also means commercialising the whole concept of social services in the name of efficiency and funds maximisation.

HOUSING FROM PRIVATE DEVELOPERS

While Marcos' housing program already relied on the private sector to supply the medium to high cost housing, it was President Aquino who initiated the private sector participation in the delivery of low-cost housing in her 6-year National Shelter Program. Under this program, private developers were required to develop a percentage of every project for low cost housing.[28] This program was also adopted by the Ramos government. Compared with the 14 per cent achievement rate under Aquino, the NSP under Ramos achieved an impressive 100.95 per cent of its target.[28] But this program suffered the same flaws as the previous one by its default in providing socialised and low cost housing for the homeless and its objective preference for the upper and middle classes. This can be seen in the amount of funding that went to the Community Mortgage Program which provides housing for the homeless and the lowest 30 per cent. Under the Ramos government, the CMP got the lowest budget of P807.57 million or 1.4 per cent of total NSP funds while the direct housing program which benefits the middle class got the bulk i.e. P35,153.50 million or 61.8 per cent of the total.[28]

While socialised housing suffers from a lack of funds, low-cost housing was privatised as flagship medium-rise projects of the Ramos administration and was developed as joint ventures between the National Housing Authority or other agencies with private developers. The Smokey Mountain Project is a joint venture between NHA and RII Builders. The Payatas-NDC mega housing project and the Home Along da Riles are both joint ventures with San Jose Construction.[29] Especially sine these are joint ventures with private developers, profitability becomes a paramount concern for every project and in the eventual costing of the housing units, making them inaccessible to many of the urban poor. In many cases, ground-floor commercial units are sold at higher commercial rates in order to compensate for lower prices of upper-level units. In other cases, the developer makes money from swaps of highly profitable commercial development for the housing project, such as the offshore reclamation and commercial port development component of the Smokey Mountain Project. [29] Pushing the burden of housing to the private sector, and privatising and commercialising low cost housing, while leaving the Community Mortgage Program for distributing and improving squatter communities unfunded, reduce the effectiveness of the National Shelter Program. As a result, housing becomes less and less accessible to the urban poor now numbering 3.5 million in Metro Manila and 15 million nationwide, according to the Presidential Commission for the Urban Poor. [28]

PRIVATISING HEALTH

In the early 1996, government announced plans to privatise four government speciality hospitals: Philippine Heart Centre, Lung Centre of the Philippines, National Kidney Institute and Philippine Children's Hospital. Prospective buyers have already signified their interests in these hospitals. For example, the Association of Philippine Physicians in America have made queries on the terms of sale of the Philippine Heart Centre. Another entity, the MCA Holdings and Management Corporation, a Filipino firm with strong links with Canadian partners, expressed its intention to participate in the privatisation of the four Medical Centres.[30] Concerned groups and individuals fear that with the privatisation of the operations of these speciality hospitals, costs for the services offered by these hospitals would shoot up and marginalise the indigent patients. Their fears are not unfounded. The importance of the four speciality hospitals or medical centres in the country can best be appreciated when one realises the nature of their clientele. A study commissioned by the DOH reveals that the percentage of charity cases in the four hospitals is quite substantial at 55 per cent for the Heart Centre and 70 per cent for the Kidney Institute. For the Lung Centre, the rate of charity cases, while undetermined, can more or less be quantified by the distribution of lung diseases especially tuberculosis, cancer and chronic obstructive pulmonary diseases which are most prevalent among those in the lower socio-economic classification[30] Once these hospitals are privatised, it cannot be assured that the benefits enjoyed by the indigent or poor patients would continue. For example, a USAID funded DOH study on the privatisation of the medical centres suggests that for the Philippine Heart Centre, a privatised operation and/or management would minimally expect to recover the costs for each indigent patient treated as this would exceed the centre's current out-of-pocket cost (individual-privately-financed medical service). A privatised heart centre would not continue to provide the current level nor volume of indigent services as the hospital would need to increase the percentage of private patients to assure a profit. The heart centre is already operating at near optimal levels. Any increase in private patients would necessitate a reduction in indigent patients.[31] The same study suggests that government researches usually done at no cost to the public would stop once these hospitals are privatised. Government would lose control of its specialised research facilities and resources, including the indigent patient base. Government influence over physicians to conduct research of public value would also be lost. Any loss of public health research commissioned by the government is unique only to the country and thus directly affects the health of the nation.

A Poor Man's Hospital No More

While the privatisation of the medical centers is still being planned out, certain government hospitals are already undergoing various stages of privatisation. The Fabella Medical Centre, a Philippine government-run maternity and children's hospital, is one such case. Formerly Maternity and Children's Hospital, Fabella, provides free maternity and children's care and caters to families belonging to the lowest income brackets. In the few cases that the hospital charges the patient, the highest charge would depend on the income status of patients- at least 10 per cent of the total fees collected in private hospitals are charged to users.[32] Established since 1920, Fabella is just one of the few hospitals specialising in maternal and pediatric care for the economically disadvantaged. Sadly though, the hospital did not escape the profit orientation being encouraged among public hospitals. It will be turned into a private general hospital and relocated to Muntinlupa in the south of Metro Manila.[33] Meanwhile, increasing health expenses are felt by the indigent patients of the Philippines General Hospital (PGH) – the premier government general hospital. Budget constraints have allegedly hampered the hospital's capacity to expand its services to indigents. Now poor patients often have to pay fees which are being exacted on out-patient services. In addition to this, there has been a 60 per cent increase in the hospital's laboratory fees in the last three years.[33]

Commercialisation of the PGH also means hiring contractual workers with contracts ranging from 3 to 12 months. Since July 1, 1996, PGH has hired 228 contractual workers, like nurses, pharmacists, medical technicians, physical therapists, X-ray technicians, clerks and utility workers.[33] Another form of privatisation of the health sector is the collectivization of local hospitals, that is, privatising ownership or management of hospitals to cooperatives. This was already been implemented in some local hospitals in Davao. [34]

JUSTIFYING PRIVATISATION

Government justifies its privatisation program for the health sector in that it intends to focus on promotive and preventive health care, leaving the more expensive curative health care to the private hospitals. The National Health Plan for 1995 to 2020 specifically identified chronic degenerative diseases and socially-related conditions as the emerging leading causes of death other than cardiovascular diseases and cancer. These diseases have rapidly escalated in the last 30 years. Such diseases require investment in the more expensive curative health care. As they are, government health services are mostly aimed towards low income groups while private enterprises in health care concentrate on middle-income and upper-income groups. Leaving curative health care to private business would be tantamount to leaving the large number of poor Filipinos unattended and increasingly marginalised as private health care is significantly higher than what government charges.

Experiences of other countries that embarked on privatisation of health services are not altogether encouraging. For instance, as a result of contracting health services out, areas of British hospitals are left unclean. For example, lifts transporting patients are left unclean for months. There are not enough staff to perform duties and the presence of untrained staff in ward contribute to the problem. Meanwhile, there is a marked increase in public expenditure costs. Already, patients are being refused treatment in previously publicly-owned hospitals. Patients are forced to travel miles to receive treatment.[35] In Japan, the health care system had become inaccessible to elderly and chronic disease patients. The Medical Service law amended in 1992 realigned health-care units by functionality. It puts a limit on the period of stay in hospitals for the elderly and chronic disease patients, and introduced discriminatory treatment of patients. A plan has been implemented to close 74 (one third) national hospitals and sanatoriums in 10 years.[36]

PRIVATISING EDUCATION

Unlike the other social services, education plays a unique role in the expansion of the business opportunities of foreign and big local corporations. Aside from being a field for commercialisation, education serves as the foundation for the replication of the labour force and the perpetuation of exploitation. The debt-driven economy is mirrored by a poorly financed educational system. The allocation of the government is simply not enough as evidenced by the annual shortage of classrooms, textbooks, and teachers. While elementary and secondary schools are mostly public, institutions for higher learning are increasingly privatised, thus marginalising the poor majority. The private sector runs 80 per cent of the 1,200 colleges and universities. [37] Meanwhile, the Education Act of 1992 deregulated private schools, giving them the prerogative to raise tuition fees even without government approval. The sustained drop in the enrollment rate of students is only reflective of the existing poverty in the face of the increasing cost of education.

To address the deteriorated quality of the educational system resulting from lack of funding (or more precisely, misallocation of the national budget), past and present governments embarked on programs, the main thrusts of which are, nonetheless, towards privatisation. While the private sector has found business in education, the crucial part is that the private sector now has the free hand to re-orient the curriculum to its advantage. Here lies the central issue in government neglect and privatisation efforts. For instance, PORDED and SEDP, meant to improve facilities and student achievement, succeeded in changing the curriculum to develop manpower for the export-oriented manufacturing dominated by TNCs. PRODED was funded with $100 million loan from the World Bank and SEDP was funded with P250 million from various multilateral banks such as the ADB and JICA. [38]

Under the Ramos government, the Philippine educational system was undergoing the most painful reorientation and restructuring. Following the GATT Master Plan, the functions of the Department of Education had been spun off with the creation of three governing agencies-the Department of Basic Education, the Commission on Higher Education (CHED) to take charge of the tertiary education, and the Technical Education and Skills Development Authority (TESDA). Under the plan, private business schools were greatly encouraged, especially with regard to the drafting of the school curriculum.[39] Basic education consisted of English, Science, Mathematics and value formation, specifically obedience and docility. Under the TESDA, vocational-technical education was carried out by private institutions in response to fast-changing needs of industries due to technological advances. Apprenticeship and in-plant training, or what is otherwise termed as the dual training system combining in-plant and school training system, was also implemented. Likewise, the private sector was allowed to determine the school curriculum to suit the needs of their businesses. [39]

Under the CHED, the national budget for education was substantially reduced. Government intends to rationalise state colleges and universities (SCUs) and socialise tuition and other fees for SCUs and other public educational institutions to generate income. In effect, the well-off students were to subsidise their poor schoolmates.[39] An interview with CHED reveals that government plans to adopt to corporate set-up in the management of public schools where sponsors from the business sector will pay the operational cost of running the school. Services that can be privatised include scholarships and research undertakings.[40] Under the CHED, government plans to close non-viable campuses and delete courses considering no long attuned to the demands of a globalised economic system. Examples of such courses are social sciences and the arts.[39] Lastly, representatives from industries can actually sit in the boards of SCUs, making certain that the privatised and commercialised educational system yields returns on their investments.

ADVANTAGES OF PRIVATISATION?

The neo-liberal discourse had provided quite a list of justifications for privatisation.

1. Efficiency or better management from privatisation will increase productivity and improved services.

The oft-repeated argument is that privatisation will end the axiomatic problem of bureaucratic inefficiency. This problem becomes an easy target for money lenders who are looking into fiscal restraints and ending budget deficits. And this becomes even more significant for international moneylenders when in many developing countries, large public enterprises borrow heavily and absorb capital from the financial market. But while a number of privatised firms in the Philippines enjoyed a turnaround, it remains unclear whether this is really due to privatisation. There is no substantiated evidence whether or not private sector operation and management of former public enterprises for profit proves more efficient and financially viable.[9] AUN document on privatisation says the same from the experiences of several countries. For example, while most privatised industries in Britain have grown since privatisation, it is clear that this has more to do with the nature of industries concerned than with the nature of their ownership. The privatised firms which have grown rapidly since privatisation (especially in the telecom) were also growing rapidly before privatisation.[41] Numerous studies of ownership effects on performance have not come up with the unanimous conclusion that private control and management is indeed more efficient than public control and management. There are not exact sets of indicators that would effectively compare performance of the public and private enterprises. If ever, these are usually unrepresentative. [42]

In the same light, using profitability as a measure of efficiency for both private and public enterprises would naturally put the latter at a disadvantage. This is especially true when public enterprises created were performing regulatory functions and provide support services especially in times of market failures. For example, the Philippine National Food Authority (NFA) was meant originally to subsidise farmers and protect the grains industry from monopoly interests (cartels). By buying a substantial share of production, it is expected to influence the prices of grains and make it available for the poorer sectors of the country.[42] Profitability cannot be a standard of comparison since private enterprises are out to make profits. On the other hand, public enterprises (at least in theory) are set up to provide support for the economy and the general welfare of the people. In times of market instability, public enterprises are used to pump-prime the economy through their investments. Moreover, they assure the affordability and continued supply of such basic commodities such as rice, sugar and services such as education, health, housing.

2. Fiscal Stability Ensures Absence to Debt

Selling burdensome government assets and corporations are supposed to relieve government of providing subsidies to these cash-strapped entities and thus, lower spending pattern. At the same time, it would reduce the financial burden on governments for wages, operating costs, and debt servicing. True enough for the Philippines, the gains at face value of its 1994 privatisation efforts were substantial enough to contribute to the government's P18.1 billion surplus. Part of the amount was channeled to the servicing of the country's foreign debt. But, as shown earlier, most of the sales made by the government were bankruptcy sales other than the fact that these assets were sold free of liabilities. To this day, a large amount of the government's budget for debt servicing are eaten up by interest and amortisation payments for the liabilities assumed from the ailing crony corporations. (See Table 7).

Table 6 shows that from 1987 to 1995, interest and amortisation payments for assumed liabilities amounted to P261.90 billion roughly equivalent to 27.24 % of the country's total debt burden and 36% of total foreign debt from 1987 – 1995. It comprises 46.3% of amortisation payments on debts during the same period. Of course the figure does not include government infusions for operational and maintenance expenses for the transferred assets.

The immediate advantages of selling off non-performing assets are obvious. Selling bankrupt corporations and assets unload government of unnecessary costs of maintaining such assets. At the same time, returns from the sales provided additional revenue for government, no matter how minimal. But the downside is tremendous when we look at how this argument has been abused in selling off more than just non-performing assets, but also government corporations which are profitable and key economic players in a desperate bankruptcy sale. Selling off profitable corporations like Petron is contradictory to the objective of cutting off losses and earning more revenues. Selling off corporations which provide a key role in economic development like the utilities simply means handing over economic sovereignty to foreigners. Selling off properties and corporations which embody national patrimony and heritage like Manila Hotel is mercenary, no matter if government is bankrupt or not. And when government guarantees profitability to foreigner in selling off non-performing corporations free of liability, then indeed, such short-sightedness smacks of subservience to foreign monopoly capital.

TABLE 6: IDENTIFIED BOT-PROJECTS WITH GOVERNMENT GUARANTEED LOANS

Project Name	Agency	Proponent	Scheme	Project Cost In US$Million (Estimated Cost)	Donor	Loan Amount
Limay Bataan Combined Cycle Gas Turbine Power Plant Bloc	NP C	ABB/Maru beni/Kawasaki Consortium (Swiss/Japan)	BTO	300	Japan Eximbank	150.8 15
Limat Bataan Combined Cycle Gas Turbine Power Plant Block B	NP C	ABB/Maru beni/Kawasaki Consortium (Swiss/Japan)	BTO	300	Bayeris ch	53.75 0
Makban Binary Geo. Plant	NP C	Ormat Inc. (USA)	BTO	16	Citicor p	19.50 0
Mindanao Diesel Power Barges	NP C	Mitsui/BW ES (Japan/Denmar k)	BTO	200	Indosue z/ICO	50.00 0

Source: CCPAP-BOT Centre, October 1996

Antonio Tujan (Jr.) and Jennifer Haygood

TABLE 7: DEBT BURDEN OF THE NATIONAL GOVERNMENT (IN BILLION PESOS)

	1987-92			1993-95			1996			1997		
	Domestic	Foreign	Total	Domestic	Foreign	Total	Domestic	Foreign	Total	Domestic	Foreign	Total
A Total Interest Payments	242.10	102.60	344.90	175.70	65.80	241.40	60.20	18.70	78.90	56.00	18.20	74.20
Regular Accounts	212.20	58.50	270.70	169.70	50.60	220.30	57.30	15.50	72.80	54.30	15.40	69.75
Due to Assumed Liability	30.00	44.10	74.10	5.94	15.20	21.00	2.90	3.20	6.10	1.70	2.80	4.50
B. Principal Amortization	114.60	101.90	216.50	62.60	80.60	143.20	17.40	27.20	44.60	17.04	26.40	43.50
Regular Accounts	58.50	54.60	113.10	24.91	46.50	71.50	12.90	19.90	32.90	13.80	18.10	31.90
Due to Assumed Liabil	56.10	39.00	95.10	37.60	34.00	71.70	4.50	7.30	11.80	3.20	8.30	11.50
TOTAL DEBT BURDEN	356.70	219.90	576.70	238.30	146.40	384.60	77.60	45.90	123.50	73.00	44.60	117.70

Source: Department of Budget and Management

3. Increased competition results in wider access and cheaper public service

Another "economic" argument for privatisation and liberalisation of utilities and social services is that this will result in the entry of more players, lower production and delivery costs, and thus provide wider access and cheaper prices for the public. Reality, however, tells a different story. Profit, rather than service, is the paramount motive, so accessibility is secondary to profitability. For instance, since the privatisation of the water supply in the United Kingdom, water prices have risen. Users who once paid $150 per year for water are now charged between $250 and $800 per year for the same service. As a result, two million users were late in payment of their bills in 1994. Each month, 1,000 customers are cut-off from water services[21] In Abidjan, Cote d'Ivoire, the proportion of people connected to water supplies dropped from 57 per cent in 1977 to 47 per cent in 1983. The state water company contracted with a subsidiary of Bouyges of France to manage Abidjan's water system in 1977. The number of new connections fell from 8,000 a year in 1977 to 2,300 in 1982. [21]

THE COSTS

Experience has shown that the impact of the SAPs have never been felt by the rich and the privileged. It is the masses of the poor that have always borne the inhumanity of such programs. SAPs never brought the development promised for decades now. Instead, they have compounded the misery of the poor and perpetually doomed them to immiserisation. Privatisation, just like the policies of liberalisation and deregulation has only added to the rising unemployment, depressed wages amidst high costs of living, landlessness, rising mal education and malnutrition as a result of budget cuts on welfare services in the underdeveloped countries like ours.

1. Unemployment

The World Bank does not provide data on the important issue of the impact of privatisation on employment. In a sample of 40 underdeveloped countries, state enterprises in 19991 accounted for 4.1 per cent of all jobs. The privatisation of airways and ports and railway firms in Chile cut down the number of jobs by more than 70 per cent in each case. In Ghana, the 42 largest public enterprises employed 241,000 people in 1984, but only 83,000 people after their restructuring. [43] In Philippines, there are no exact data on job losses as a result of privatisation of state enterprises. But the privatisation of MWSS alone had displaced more than 5,000 workers. In the meantime, contractualisation of labour as a mechanism of privatised firms to cut on costs is imminent. The devolution of the country's health sector has resulted in contractualisation of health workers. Budget constraint also poses threats to security of tenure of the workers. There is now an increasing army of contractual workers and the unemployed.

But this is nothing new in a globalised world economy. Government officials have repeatedly admitted the trend towards contractualisation of workers with only a few regularised for managerial positions.[44] Cases of labour standard violations are also rampant. In the UK for example, take home pay for health workers have been cut up to 50 per cent. There is massive use of casuals and poor conditions of work. Hours of work and annual leaves have been cut and overtime work is left unpaid.[35] In Japan, health workers especially nurses are forced to work overtime. This has resulted in deaths among workers in the night shift.[36] There are more telling stories. It is one thing that private business is laying off workers and hiring contractuals for increased profit returns. It is another thing when it is your own government that lays the foundation for worker's exploitation.

2. Marginalised access to social services

Unemployment and low family income unfavourably affects the state of nutrition and the capability of families to avail of health services. Continued poverty also manifests itself in the growing number of street and working children. Low education breeds ignorance regarding health promotion and disease prevention. Inadequate housing facilities results in the formation of slums or squatter colonies which are often characterised by overcrowding, poor environmental sanitation, and so on.

REINFORCING MONOPOLY CONTROL

While privatisation had its roots in public debt management, most especially in the case of bankrupt crony corporations whose behest loans were absorbed by the government, privatisation in its full implementation is not about solving a country's debt problem. It is a component of the neo-liberal program of restructuring economies and giving the upper hand to private monopoly enterprises in the name of the free market. Privatisation is not so much about efficiency, nor is it about redistribution of wealth or broadening of the ownership base. Neither is privatisation the rechanneling of government funds for more productive ventures. Privatisation means the expansion of business for transnational corporations and the local elite, especially to lucrative but heretofore forbidden sectors of utilities and social services, or to exploitation and control of resources and national patrimony.

In the end, what privatisation has achieved is the further concentration of wealth and resources into the hands of foreign monopolies and the local elite. The sale of utilities and social services, the sale of state corporations controlling national patrimony, the transfer of infrastructure development through BOT's to the private sector – these have resulted in the opening of countries for foreign trade and investment and the rapid increase of opportunities for foreign investments. In the case of increased concentration of wealth within countries by local private groups, experiences similar to the Philippines have been evident in many underdeveloped countries. In Mexico for example, an already extreme concentration of wealth was intensified through provatisation. A group of some 35 businessmen who already controlled nearly a quarter of Mexico's GNP took a leading part in virtually all of the privatisation of Mexico's public utilities. [45]

In Chile, between 1975 and 1979 most of the local banks were sold for a song to a handful of families that already dominated Chile's finance and industry.[45] In Philippines, Ayalas and the Lopezes have well-established foreign connections. Their partnerships with foreign multinationals have given them leverage for capturing the more juicy business ventures in the country. The World Investment Report for 1996, for example, reveals that a significant part of increases in foreign direct investments (FDI) in 1994 and 1995, alone were attributed to mergers and acquisitions made possible by the privatisation opportunities opened up for foreign participation, (See Table 8).

TABLE 8: SELECTED CROSS-BORDER MERGERS AND ACQUISITIONS BY TNCs WITH VALUE OF ABOVE $1 BILLION

Acquiring Company	Home Country	Acquired Company	Host Country	Value (US $B)	Industry
United Communications Industry PLC (via Total Access PLC)	Thailand	Inter city Paging Service LTD	Sri Lanka	2.8	Telecommunications
Central & Southwest Corp.	United States	Seaboard PLC	United Kingdom	1.9	Electricity Distribution
Southern Company	United States	S. Western Electricity	United Kingdom	1.7	Power Station and Distribution
Texas Utilities Co	United States	Eastern Energy	Australia	1.6	Electricity Distribution
Telsource (consortium led by Koninklijke PTT Nederland NV & Swiss Telecom	Netherlands	SPT Telecom	Czech Republic	1.5	Telecommunications
Sodexho S.A.	France	Gardner Merchant	United Kingdom	1.1	Catering

Source: UNCTAD, (Based on Data Obtained from KPMG, taken from the 1996 World Investment Report by the World Bank)

Antonio Tujan (Jr.) and Jennifer Haygood

TABLE 9: FDI FROM PRIVATISATIONS IN DEVELOPING COUNTRIES, 1989 – 1994 (IN US$ MILLIONS, PERCENTAGE

Region	1989	1990	1991	1992	1993	1994
North Africa & Middle East FDI from privatisation	1.00	0.00	3.20	19.20	302.00	121.90
Share of region's FDI inflows	0.10	0.00	0.20	0.90	8.00	3.30
Sub-Saharan Africa FDI from the privatisation	13.80	38.20	11.10	49.80	573.50	262.00
Share of region's FDI inflows	0.40	3.50	0.60	3.30	31.80	8.80
East Asia & The Pacific FDI from privatisation	0.00	0.70	77.10	522.70	1156.50	982.00/a
Share of region's FDI inflows	0.00	0.01	0.40	1.90	2.50	1.90
South Asia FDI from privatisation	0.10	10.60	4.20	41.80	16.20	14.10
Share of region's FDI inflows	0.02	2.30	0.90	6.70	1.90	1.10
Latin America & The Caribbean FDI from privatisation	183.30	2461.50	3264.30	2414.50	1373.00	3695.00
Share of region's FDI inflows	2.20	27.70	21.20	13.60	7.10	15.00
All developing regions FDI from privatisation	198.20	2511.00	3359.90	3048.00	3421.20	5075.00
Share of region's FDI inflows	0.70	7.50	8.10	6.10	4.70	5.90
Central and Eastern Europe FDI from privatisation	461.50/b	488.90/b	1868.20	2656.90	2931.90	1121.00
Share of region's FDI inflows	"	"	76.30	71.00	52.50	19.00

Source: World Bank, *Privatisation Database & World Bank*, 1996 as taken from 1996 *World Investment Report of the World Bank*

Concentration of wealth further maximised through the formation local and foreign tie-ups, the object of which is to facilitate the entry of foreign monopoly corporations and likewise establish its monopoly position in the local economy. In effect, monopolies are formed through which firms avoid the costs of competitive tendering. Tenders often lead to higher prices and fosters corruption. Many deals in infrastructure development projects and big ticket privatisation items are laden with graft and corruption. On one hand, compradors profit from providing TNCs with local partnerships, bureaucrats exact their share from graft and corruption. The reason why bureaucrats are also very aggressive in privatisation and BOT projects is because these provide them with easy earnings from corruption, sometimes amounting to 10 per cent of contract price. The transnationals, on the other hand, understand that this is the price they have to pay for taking over lucrative state monopolies and natural resources. Because of this, corruption is widespread in privatisation projects worldwide.[1] But this is worth it. The annual turnover of most public utility firms amount to more than one billion pounds or roughly $2.67 billion.

Furthermore, with underdeveloped economies already tied to the economies of the industrialised countries and so patterned in such a way that they are made dependent on foreign capital and industrial inputs from these highly developed countries, efforts towards the development of a self-sustaining, self-sufficient industrial economy are doomed as the basic foundation for the development of such an economy are left under the control of largely foreign interests whose loyalty lies not in the host country but in their home countries. Of course, it is to the best interests of the TNCs and imperialist countries to keep underdeveloped countries at their mercy otherwise there would be no markets for their surplus capital and industrial and consumer goods.

REFERENCES

1. The Privatisation Network: The Multinational Bid for Public Services. Published by the *Public Services Privatisation Research Unit* (PSPRU), January, 1996

2. The ECOLOGIST, Volume 26, No. 4, July/August 1996 pp. 145 – 153

3. Interview with NPC Employees Union, February 20, 1997

4. Update on Philippine Privatisation Program (As of Dec. 1996), Committee of Privatisation.

5. IBON Facts and Figures, 15 May 1989.

6. Executive Summary of the PCGG Position Paper on Behest Loans, PCGG Research Department, The Teofisito Guingona Papers, July 20, 1989.

7. Briones, Leonor M. The Role of GOCCs in Development, 1985.

8. Asset Privatisation Trust Annual Report

9. Manasan, Rosario G. Public enterprise Reform: The Case of the Philippines, Discussion Paper Series No. 95-01, PIDS, May 1995.

10. *IBON Facts and Figures*, 30 Apr. 91.

11. Interview with Director Danilo Daniel, PCGG Finance Administrator, May 1996.

12. Dean Gonzalo T. Santos, Jr. The Philippine Privatisation Program, Centre for International Private Enterprise, 1995.

13. Commission on Audit, Financial Report on the GOCCs, Volume II, 1994.

14. *Asset Privatisation Trust*, First Quarter Report, 1996.

15. Public Services Privatisation Research Unit (PSPRU).

16. *Business World*, February 19, 1997.

17. Violeta P. Corral, "Asian NGO Coalition (ANGOC): MWSS Privatisation", 7 February 1997.

18. Dr. Angel Lazaro, MWSS Administrator, Round Table Discusion on MWSS Privatisation, Feb. 20, 1997.

19. Water Supply Sector Reforms in the Philippines: The Government's private Sector Participation Initiatives, February 5, 1995

20. "The Ten Most Asked Questions About the Privatisation of the MWSS," MWSS Papers Presented during The Round Table Discussion on the Privatisation of the MWSSs, February 20, 1997.

21. *Third World Network News and Features*, 95/1317

22. House Bill No. 7964, "The Omnibus Electric Power Industry Act"

23. Interview , CCPAP-BOT Centre, May 5, 1996

24. Medium Term Public Investment Program (MTPIP), 1993 – 1998.

25. *Philippine Public Expenditure Management for Sustainable and Equitable Growth,* volume II, Department of Budget and Management, September 1995 (Country Report to the World Bank).

26. "Philippine Power Sector, Focus on Private Sector Participation," Excerpts from World Bank's Green Cover Draft study by Jamie Sopher/Industry and Survey Industries Division, July 1994.

27. *Philippine National Health Plan,* 1995 – 2020.

28. IBON Special Release, April 1996

29. League of Urban Poor for Action

30. Mercado, Remigion, "Privatisation of the Specialty Medical Centres, A Cause for National Concern" (Unpublished)

31. Department of Health, Study 2: *Feasibility Studies on the Privatisation of the Four Specialty Hospitals,* HEI/HCI

32. Interview, May 7, 1996.

33. *IBON Features,* August 19, 1996 p. 4

34. *Alliance of Health Workers* (AHW), May 1996

35. Privatisation Alert, Health Services Union of Australia

36. Report to the NGO Forum Workshop on the 4th World Conference on Women, Yasuko Tomiie

37. *Sunday Chronicle,* 2 June 96.

38. *IBON Facts and Figures,* 30 Nov. 90.

39. The State of Education, Ramon Guillermo, CONTEND, A lecture, IBON Office, Dec 96

40. Interview with Commissioner Mona Valisno, CHED

41. Role and Extent of Competition in Improving the Performance of Pes, United Nations, New Delhi, India 1989/ {proceedings of a UN Interregional Seminar on Performance Improvement of PEs, New Delhi, India, 12 – 19 April 1989.

42. Ha Joon Chang and Agit-Singh, Public Enterprises in Developing Countries and Economic Efficiency, August 1992, UNCTAD Discussion Papers.

43. The Private Sector Lending of the W3 Group, "Issues and Challenges", Peter Bosshard from the Berne Declaration, Jan 1996

44. *New Internationalist,* Sept. 1994.

Chapter 9

PRIVATISATION IN SINGAPORE: A HOLISTIC VIEW

Rama Ghosh

INTRODUCTION

The concept of privatisation became increasingly popular in developing countries since the mid-eighties when a number of such countries introduced privatisation of public enterprise, deregulation, and liberalisation in various fields of economic activities. In the course of time, privatisation was regarded as an important means to introduce viability and efficiency of enterprises. The practice of privatisation became popular in many countries e.g., U.K., U.S.A., Japan, Canada and so on, and the idea percolated to the less developed countries (LDCs) quite recently through perhaps the success stories of multi-national corporations.

There are many motivating factors for privatisation. First, in LDCs, there was growing dissatisfaction with the slipshod performance of state enterprises which mainly ran on losses, and there were excess capacities and unnecessary price escalation. In some public utility industries, there were alternate periods of over supply and under-supply. Some industries were too slow and sluggish to meet up consumers' demand. Second, the public enterprises were not

economically efficient – neither production efficiency nor distribution
efficiency. It was believed that the application of market principle would induce
economic efficiency and price reduction. Third, privatisation pressure came
from various active groups of controller of industries who thought that it would
lead to more freedom and internationalisation of market which may also
generate better market power. Lastly, the pressure for privatisation in newly
industralising countries like Singapore, South Korea and Taiwan came from the
World Bank which was championing the case of capitalism as a condition for
the grant of loans to these countries.

Singapore at the initial stage of her industrialisation did not, however, feel
the dire need for privatisation as it was doing splendidly well in the act of
economic management through the state machinery. In the eighties, when most
of the countries were submerged in the morass of recession, Singapore was
having a growth rate of nearly 10.5 per cent and the wage growth rate was
approximately 19 per cent (Chan, 1982). And this high rate of growth
continued unabated till the end of 1984. Thus, Singapore was late comer in the
field of privatisation.

WHY PRIVATISATION?

As a matter of fact, two important initial ideas coming from the
government were responsible for the move towards privatisation in Singapore.
First, as a fast developing country, Singapore needed the expansion,
modernisation and strenghtening of its capital market. But all these
improvements were impossible without the help of local and foreign private
capital. The government did not and could not want to take the financial burden
of capital market development on modern lines. Singapore, before privatisation
was introduced, had been doing extremely well in capital market management
but it wanted to do even better and had the ambition of becoming the leading
international financial centre.

In terms of the number of listed companies market capitalisation and shares
listed Singapore was the best in the ASEAN region in 1986 (Far Eastern
Economic Review January 1986, p. 44). Second, the Singapore wanted to share

the growing responsbility of workers' welfare expenditure with the private employers and wrokers themselves. One of the important reasons for the transfer of responsibility to private employers and workers was to lighten the financial burden of the state and also to introduce a system of private welfarism in place of state welfarism. (Lim, 1983).

However, this philosophy of transfer of responsibility through privatisation was not fully relished either by the private sector employers or by the workers. The private employers were reluctant to bear the additional cost and the workers thought that the private sector would make discrimination and would not be able to bear the brunt of growing housing requirements and escalating medical costs of employees.

But in spite of doubts and misgivings, the programme of privatisation was carried through subsequently in various stages. As a matter of fact, after 1985, privatisation was accorded high esteem and was regarded as the saviour of the sinking economy of Singapore. It is to be noted that 1985 Singapore experienced all the bad effects of recession in the same way as the other ASEAN economies, with large disemployment, loss of purchasing power, loss of business confidence, negative economic growth and dwindling market power. In the mean time, the number of public enterprises grew substantially from 29 in 1969 to 429 in 1985 (Low, 1991, p. 56). Some of these state-owned enterprises long before had ceased to be cash cows and gradually became problem children while some enterprises became dodo unit requiring immediate divestment.

On the other end of the spectrum, the operational costs including wages started escalating, and Singapore which is essentially an outward-looking economy became suddenly less competitive in the international market. This created a fear of psychosis in the government and business circles. Moreover, the domestic demand also reduced considerably in view of uncertainty both in the product and in the labour markets. Recession in many expanding industries including construction, and the higher propensity to save for the rainy days and unforeseen contingency reduced domestic effective demand. The economy was completely in a state of static limbo. All macro economic fundamentals started showing abnormally discouraging signals.

Moreover, the neighbouring countries including Malaysia resorted to direct trading practices bypassing Singapore. All these led to the conviction that the role of government in the country both as an entrepreneur and as a controller of the economic system has become counter-productive and it was responsible for the economic downturn of 1985 (Chan, 1986).

It was in this type of prevailing atmosphere that the government decided to use the private sector as the engine of growth and decided to privatise the industrial sector through a gradual and selective process.

There were a few important motivations for privatisation. First, in the fast developing economy of Singapore, the expectation of the people for subsidised social and public services was growing substantially both in depth and range. The demand for public goods and merit goods was constantly going up as these constituted the main elements of better standard of living for the people. Second, the working population of Singapore were heavily dependent on the state for basic social reproductions like education, public utilities, health care services and so on. This was mainly responsible for a high turn-over rate in private companies. And such companies were in difficulty to find and retain labour force that was committed, disciplined and loyal. Third, it was thought that privatisation will create better working conditions and amenities for the working class, and will reduce the turnover rate. Lastly, the government was financially too weak to meet the growing demand for subsidised social and medical care for the growing population of the country. The government, therefore, decided to divest itself of the loss-making operations and functions through privatisation.

Objectives of Privatisation

There were many important objectives that were kept in mind for the privatisation program in Singapore. The major objectives are given below.

First, to make the capital market the leading institution in the region. This would make sure both internalisation and internationalization of capital for the growing economy of Singapore. Second, it was necessary to expand the private sector for gaining competitive efficiency including both production efficiency and allocative efficiency. While production efficiency would minimise cost and increase output allocative efficiency would ensure that consumers are able to get the products at minimum possible prices. Third, as far as possible it would be necessary to reduce competition between the private sector and the public sector. It was realised that such a type of competition is unhealthy and self-defeating in the longrun.

Fourth, the state wanted to reduce to its minimum the impact of crowding out of private investment from the competitive sector. A reduction in government investment in some competitive sectors may help to reduce rate of interest and thereby ensuring larger private participation with higher economic efficiency. Finally, the state had the desire to gradually contract its wings and ultimately withdraw from the mundane commercial activities which would be made free for the private sector, and a number of companies were recommended for privatisation (vide Appendix 2).

PROCESS AND PROGRESS OF PRIVATISATION

Singapore's decision to introduce privatisation did not arise only out of the consideration of inefficient state enterprises. The degree of inefficiency was low in general and was not something of immediate concern. However, it was one of the reasons though not the only reason. Government companies in Singapore, as observed by the Chairman of the Economic Committee (1985), thrived and prospered in fair competition with the private sector companies. The state enterprises also contributed substantially to the growth and development of the economy of Singapore. However, the government was perfectly happy for them to be owned and managed by the private sector. In any case, the state was ready to divest itself of these companies for fair prices to the private sector. This attitude of the government was present in the late seventies, much before the period of official privatisation of 1985.

The official decision to privatise public companies was taken up during the period of recession of 1985, and obviously it was difficult to divest these companies to the private sector which was adversely affected by the lean business market. Be that as it may, the private sector felt that the government was too dominant and omnipotent, and the crowding out effect was one of the important considerations for the introduction of privatisation in Singapore (Low, 1991).

Singapore's privatisation process was mainly the process of divestment. The Public Sector Divestment Committee (1986) was formed to prepare guidelines, conditions and modalities for privatisation. The following were the major terms of reference of the Committee (PSDC) (Ng and Toh 1992, p. 52).

a)   To prepare guidelines and time-frame for privatisation;
b)   To set-up modalities and conditions for privatisation;
c)   To formulate the program to divest government managed companies.

The Committee which submitted its report in 1987 proposed a ten-year time frame to divest government stake in the equity of more than 600 government companies and 39 statutory boards. However, initially only 7 out of 39 statutory boards were selected because these were monopolistic in nature posing problems for privatisation (Pelkmans and Wagnar, 1990). PSDC identified the following main four major forms of privatisation (Low, 1991, p. 108):

1)   Liberalisation or deregulation whereby competition by and in the private sector is encouraged through the relaxation of government rules and regulations;
2)   Privatisation of ownership involving sales of shares or assets;
3)   Privatisation of production in which government buys goods and services rather than manufactures them;
4)   Privatisation of financiing where the government relies on consumer charges rather than tax revenue to finance operations.

In the case of privatisation, divestment in government-linked companies involved three major holding companies: MND Holdings, Temasek Holdings Limited and Sheng Li Holdings (Ng and Wagner, 1989). These three holdings were involved in the divestment program through the sale of their equity to the private sector. The private sector, needless to say, constitutes private individuals and/or institutions.

Divestment process of privatisation was applied to many public-owned enterprises in Singapore (vide Appendix I). The divestment of government-linked companies having a paid-up capital of more than S$100 million and where government equity share is substantial include: Singapore International Airlines, Neptune Orient Lines, Singapore Aerospace and so on. In the cases of these government-linked companies, divestment was only partial and in some specific cases, the shares were floated in several separate branches for proper streamlining and easy management. Complete divestment was practised in the cases of a few giant petrochemical industries, such as, Ethylene Glyocols, Phillips Petroleum and the Polyolefin.

As for the key public utilities like Telecom and Electricity Generation Board, the government had to be very careful and cautious because of the following considerations: (i) these monopolies would require government control and supervision even after their privatisation (ii) the ability and suitability of investors to invest in these huge companies, (iii) revenue maximisation from the sale of shares of these public utilities was not in the priority list of the government. These are some of the reasons why the privatisation of Singapore Telecom was protracted.

The need for regulation of monopolistic companies such large statutory boards even after privatisation arises out of the fact that they earn an average return on equity of 12 to 15 per cent per year over a ten year period: 1976 – 86 (Vide Table I) whereas the rate of return earned was only 11 per cent by large private sector companies of comparable size operating in the competitive market during the same period. If one applies the criterion of earning on total funds invested, it is found that the three monopolies earned higher return (11 per cent) than similar sized firms under competitive market conditions (Ariff, 1989, pp. 97 – 98).

TABLE 1: OPERATING AND RETURN RATIOS OF PUBLIC MONOPOLIES (1976 – 86)

Monopolies (Statutory Boards)	Operating Rations		Return Ratios	
	Gross Margin	Sales Total Assets	Return on Investment	Return on Equity
Telecom Authority of Singapore	0.34	0.31	0.11	0.15
Public Utilities Board	0.22	0.34	0.07	0.14
Port of Singapore Authority	0.42	0.27	0.11	0.12

Source: Mohamed Ariff, op. Cit, p. 98

The divestment programme of PSDC identified the following seven boards for privatisation

a) Singapore Telecommunications (ST)
b) Singapore Broadcasting Corporation (SBC)
c) Port of Singapore Authority (PSA)
d) Commercial and Industrial Security Corporation (CISC)
e) Public Utilities Boards (PUB)
f) Jurong Town Corporation (JTC)
g) Civil Aviation Authority of Singapore (CAAS)

All the above seven boards do not qualify equally for privatisation. For instance, because of the sensitivity of SBC, it was not thought to be privatisable JTC and CISC were privatisable but they were not attractive to investors. The privatisation with respect to other boards started off since 1987. Telecom was the first to be privatisedm, and in other cases, incremental approach was practiced. PSA was the board which was corporatised very recently in Singapore. PUB was corporatised in 1995 and Singapore Power Pvt. Ltd. took over the operations of gas and electricity. PUB, however, remains as the water authority of Singapore. However, the corporatisation had mainly two objectives of (i) providing efficient services to consumers and (ii) encouraging competition in the electricity industry. The electricity and gas operations were controlled by five specialised subsidiaries in Singapore.

Between 1985 and 1990, 25 government-linked industries were privatised in Singapore. Out of these, 23 companies were very efficient in their performance. Hence, they became the most suitable candidates for privatisation. Of the 25 companies, 4 were fully owned by the government, 7 partly owned, and 14 were partly privatised owned companies. But in spite of privatisation, till 1995, the influence of the government in the industrial sector was dominating not only with respect to the number of industries but also with regard to its overall control and supervisory power. As a matter of fact, the Policy of divestment did not in any way imply the reduced role of government in Singapore because of the concept of *rolling privatisation* (Ng and Toh, 1992, p. 52). In the context of privatisation in Singapore, rolling privatisation implies not only the identification of suitable privatisable industries, but also a strategy of continuous re-investment of resources obtained from the sale of government-linked companies in new priority areas.

Another interesting aspect of the privatisation exercise in Singapore is the privatisation of most efficient industries. However, in many other Asian countries like India, Indonesia and Pakistan, this is not the usual practice: the opposite strategy is very common. That is, mostly the loss-making inefficient industries are the ones to be privatised at the first instance. Secondly, the government considered certain key-industries such as defence and defence-related industries and other strategic services as not privatisable in Singapore. The policy seems to be quite sensible as it gives first priority to national security and protection to sensitive national issues.

In the course of time, privatisation was extended to cover social reproductions like health and education facilities. In the public health care management, the government introduced in 1989 a system of cost-sharing which is a mixture of individual responsibility and government subsidy. Under this system, the patients will pay a part of the medical expenses which are necessary, and for the extra demand (meta demand) for better services and facilities, they need to pay more. The principle is applied to all classes of patients. The public health care system provides 20 per cent of primary health and 80 per cent of hospital care, and vice versa condition for the private system.

However, the whole exercise of privatisation of health services can be looked upon as the manifestation of *government failure* in the provision of public health services. The basic rationale for the introduction of privatisation in the area of public health services (PHS) was in line with World Bank's idea (1993) relating to investment in health. World Bank considers health care as a *Private good*, and therefore, thinks that the primary responsibility for health care lies in private individuals (Ghosh, 2000, Chp. 2). Thus, considered, privatisation of health policy is based on two complementary principles: (i) the reduction of state intervention and public responsibility, and (ii) the promotion of diversity and competition. The question of social welfare is regarded as the responsibility of the private domain, and the government wants only to intervene when the private sector will not or cannot respond. There are two other adjunct principles for the privatisation of PHS. First, the public sector is generally inefficient and inequitable, whereas the private sector is more efficient and more equitable since it must conform to market dynamics of free choice and competition. The limit of responsibility of the government in the case of privatisation is to look after those public activities which are targetted to the poor people.

Privatisation was also introduced in the case of another merit want, the education system, in 1989. Initially, the concept encompassed the granting of independent status to schools. To start with, the new programme was introduced to two government-aided schools and a government school. The basic objective of privatisation of education was not primarily to reduce the financial burden of the government but to provide more autonomy and operational flexibility so that the quality of education may be improved (Low, 1991, p. 167).

The introduction of privatisation in the realm of education was in a sense the manifestation of government failure to provide quality education at affordable cost. The failure of the government was not only with respect to the quality of education but also with regard to the quantity of highly skilled manpower which the country needed for his technological development and information-based industries. Moreover, one may not agree with Linda Low's observation that privatisation of education was not to reduce the financial burden of the state. As a matter of fact, the tacit presumption in favour of privatisation was the reduction in the financial burden. This is partly true both for the health and the education sectors. These services after privatisation have experienced higher fees and charges but reduced government subsidies.

A few points by way of summing up may be presented here. Privatisation in Singapore consisted of not a few uniform principles but a number of asymmetrical exercises. There are the following types of privatisation principles which have been adhered to in Singapore:

First, for some strategic industries like defense, the privatisation exercise has not at all be recommended.

Second, in some efficient, suitable and big industries like petrochemicals, the government's stake in equity has been completely divested.

Third, for important public utilities like Telecom, the government has been retaining regulatory control and holding the majority stake. Such a step is necessary because the public utilities in   general would retain their monopoly status even after privatisation and these provide services which are very essential for human life.

In general, the government will have a triplistic role in the context of privatisation. The role of the government will come to a naught in the case of industries which are completely divested. Second, the role of the government has been reduced in the case of contracting out services. Third, the role of the state has considerably gone up in the case of privatised public utility industries which yield substantial externalities.

On the whole, it can be said that the role of states in the Southeast Asian countries including Singapore and Malaysia has considerably reduced in the wake of privatisation. In the pre-privatisation period, the power of the state in these countries was very strong, supreme and absolute. The visible hands of the state were noticeable in cases of policy formulation and policy implementation during the period of absolute state capitalism. However, after privatisation through the introduction of multinational capitalism and marketisation, the reduced role of state can be seen in the areas of employment, income and output, in the shares of GDP, and also in the field of education, health and trade regulations. The growth of market power, technocracy and liberalised regime, has enormously delimited the power of state in the Southeast Asian countries. And Singapore is not an exception. The change in the social structure and aspirations for a society with higher degree of freedom and a more comprehensive system of democracy has visibly reduced the power of the state.

In fact, the collapse of the ideological iron and bamboo curtains, as the Prime Minister of Singapore observes, has brought new and serious sources of polarisation. The social structure that had supported four long decades of capitalist regime and growth were now in a complete flux (Wheelwright, 1999, p. 405). The disembedded economies of these areas in Southeast Asia have been witnessing the declining power of state since the days of privatisation, and more particularly since the financial crisis of 1997. Indeed some of the states in Southeast Asia have been witnessing political transition through the process of what may be called *creative destruction* for a better society. Social business cycles are in operation in such transitional economies.

IMPLICATIONS AND EFFECTS OF PRIVATISATION

The impact of privatisation should be analysed in terms of efficiency and equity criteria. There are various types of efficiency, e.g., engineering efficiency, allocative efficiency and so on. As in many other countries, privatisation in Singapore has been able to achieve efficiency in production and delivery in terms of time. That is, after privatisation, many industries, (e.g., telecom) were able to produce and distribute the services and products with much less time than was necessary earlier. Thus, some industries after privatisation achieved time efficiency.

In the same way, it is argued that some privatised industries, e.g., telecom could create additional demand for its products to a significant extent. For instance, the number of telephone lines which was 998,000 in 1989 – 90 increased to 1,246,000 in 1993 – 94. However, such a type of conclusion has to be interpreted with caution and circumspection. The increase in the demand for telephone lines may be due to many reasons other than being the effect of privatisation. The demand might have escalated due to increase in population, increase in the number of industries, higher per capita income of the people and so on. As a matter of fact, after the introduction of privatisation in 1987, economic growth rate in the city state went up consistently every year excepting in 1995 and 1996. The economic slowdown in these two years culd be due to decrease in demand for electronic products. How should one interpret the correlation between privatisation and higher economic growth? One possible explanation is that higher economic growth has been made possible because of increase in efficiency due to privatisation. But correlation may not necessarily be taken as the causal explanation. Higher rate of economic growth might have been possible through higher domestic investment, higher degree of total factor productivity, larger dose of foreign direct investment and the induction of better technology. All these factors may be made operational without privatisation.

However,, it is argued that the divestment exercise in the Singapore stock market has been responsible for the increasing inflow of foreign investment in the manufacturing sector between 1990 and 1993 (vide Table 2).

TABLE 2: FOREIGN INVESTMENT IN SINGAPORE'S MANUFACTURING SECTOR ($ MILLION)

	1990	1991	1992	1993
Food, beverage and tobacco	799	858	896	966
Textiles	106	88	77	77
Clothing, made-up textiles and footwear	101	85	84	67
Leather and rubber products and natural gums	74	88	85	99
Wood products and furniture	112	102	103	99
Paper and paper products	519	618	687	711
Industrial chemicals	2722	3016	3287	3800
Other chemical products (except plastic)	706	6687	761	871
Petroleum and petroleum products	5841	6222	7073	7937
Plastic products	386	407	448	501
Non-metallic mineral products	387	418	467	463
Basic metal industries	140	109	103	104
Fabricated metal products (except machinery and equipment	1223	1362	1431	1523
Machinery (except electrical machinery)	1409	1536	1700	1859
Electrical/electronic machinery, apparatus, appliances and supplies	8076	8675	9668	10625
Transport equipment	804	832	906	1019
Precision equipment and photographic and optical goods	564	591	659	683
Other manufacturing industries	164	140	127	148
Total	24133	25831	28565	31498

Note: Data have been revised according to the Singapore Standard Industrial Classification, 1990 edition

Source: Economic Development Board

As earlier, one can well argue that larger inflow of foreign capital may not be significantly influenced by domestic privatisation policy. The inflow of foreign investment may be influenced by political and economic stability, availability of educated, disciplined and loyal labour force and so on. Singaporean labour force, according to the evaluation of Business Environment Risk Intelligence, is the best in the world (Govt. of Singapore, 1995, p. I). It is also sometimes argued that Singapore's competitiveness which is quite high by any international standard is mainly due to its success in privatisation. But many will agree to differ with such a sweeping generalisation.

However, all these are not to deny the importance and signification of privatisation in the case of Singapore. What is necessary is that while analysing the impact of privatisation, one needs to be discreet and careful. It is true that privatisation has considerably economised the time element in production/delivery, reduced wastage and costs. For instance, the introduction of privatisation in the Public Utility Board (PUB) reduced capital expenditure to support the development programmes of PUB to a very significant extent in all the component projects of water, electricity and gas from S$1,362.7 million in 1994 to only S$52.2 million in 1996 (vide Table 3) This is not a mean achievement by any standard.

TABLE 3: PRIVATISATION AND CAPITAL EXPENDITURE OF PUBLIC UTILITIES BOARD

Year	Nature of Privatisation	Capital Expenditure(S$ in million)
1994	Pre-corporatisation period	1362.7
1995	Partly corporatised	728.2
1996	Fully corporatised	52.2

Source: Annual Reports of PUB
* The capital expenditure is related to the development projects for water, electricity and gas.

The impact of privatisation in Singapore on the whole has remained successful. It has enhanced the engineering and operational efficiency and quality of services/products in many cases. In the wake of privatisation, Singapore Airlines and Singapore Telecom were adjudged as the two top companies in Asia out of ten outstanding companies in the assessment made by the *Asian Business* in 1993. Nevertheless, one should not forget the darker side of the privatisation paradigm.

While privatisation has reduced the private cost, it has in some cases increased the social cost through retrenchment and disemployment of quite a number of employees. Privatisation, moreover, has not been able to achieve allocative efficiency, for the prices of products have gone much beyond the marginal cost, and in many cases consumers' surplus has been drastically reduced. As a matter of fact, mere change in the ownership of means of production does not *ipso facto* guarantee enhanced efficiency . Privatisation might have decreased the burden of the government but it has correspondingly increased the burden of the common people in the Southeast Asian economies (Ghosh, 1998, p. 172). It has also led to the concentration of market power and monopoly power in a few hands. It has converted government monopoly to private monopoly

CONTEMPORARY ISSUES

There are many lurking contrmporary issues relating to privatisation in Singapore. Some of the major contemporary issues may be briefly mentioned here. One of the most serious issues is the balance between equity and efficiency. Most of the countries of Southeast Asia are facing this problem (vide Gouri, 1991). It is no less important for Singapore. Between 1987 and 1995, privatisation in Singapore created technological unemployment for 764 employees (Hussin, 1993), and many more of such cases might have gone unreported. An attempt to increase the so-called efficiency has intensified the problem socio-economic inequity. It would be difficult to say whether the achievement is socially and economically desirable or not.

A section of workers has always remained critical of privatisation in view of the problems it creates in the labour market. Privatisation has introduced the fear psychosis of possible job loss and a feeling of constant insecurity particularly in the minds of unskilled and semi-skilled workers. The workers have to remain all the time serious, cautious and tensed in the regime of privatisation.

In the case of Singapore, the initial resistance to privatisation came from the bureaucratic class but it had to give in ultimately in the power war with ministers and politicians (Milne, 1991). Because of the non-collusive nature of the programme, privatisation was delayed and could not be very progressive at least in the earlier stage in Singapore. However, in spite of *initial inertia,* the government was able to work out the mode of privatisation which could be made operational without much difficulty. Strong political influence has been an important determinant for the success of privatisation in some of the ASEAN countries including Singapore and Malaysia (Milne, 1991, pp. 329 – 332).

The real issue towards the continuous success of privatisation has been skill development and trianing the manpower. Two basic problems have been encountered in this direction. First, qualified teachers and also trainees are not available in sufficiently large amount. Second, the investment required for training and skill formation has never been adequate. The original skill base of Southeast Asian countries including Singapore is indeed very low. Skill constraint is a serious issue standing in the way of success of privatisation in Singapore. Human capital formation by the private sector has remained limited due to paucity of funds and also due to the fact that training is often highly correlated with turnover rate.

Another basic issue relating to privatisation in Singapore is the escalating price of privatised goods and services. The popular feeling is that the increased prices of these products and services have more than off-set the increase in efficiency and productivity. And the common people are unable to enjoy the fruits of privatisation. As the losers often outnumber the gainers, the final outcome is neither real Pareto optimal nor potential Pareto optimal (as envisaged by Kaldor-Hicks criterion).

Connected with this, is the issue of privatisation of social reproductions like public health services (PHS) and education. Privatisation of these areas means perceptible welfare loss to the people and the dimunition of the power and responsibility of welfare state. Moreover, it is feared that the entry of the private sector in the arena of education may not only imply higher cost but also dilute the quality of education. It may look upon education as *non-merit good* having private benefits and no social obligations. Many are afraid that corporatisation will bring in completely new ethos of marketism which, along with resource crunch, will adversely affect research and expansion of social knowledge. Privatisation of education in the name of efficiency, unless proper care is taken, may lead to many undesirable consequences.

The growth of crony capitalism and monopoly power is another serious dimension of privatisation in the Southeast Asian region. Privatisation has entrenched the system of pure capitalism whose only aim is to maximise *surplus extraction*. The social benefit of privatisation has remained extremely limited in a country like Singapore . In many of the privatised companies, the share of the government is rather large. And the surplus extracted by the government is often used as cross-subsidy to help other industries and sectors. While the purpose is benign, government behaviour is often not transparent and the money may be used not in the projects of national interest. The way the surplus is used can be questioned and becomes an issue,as is evident in many Southeast Asian countries.

CONCLUDING OBSERVATIONS

The tempo of privatisation has indeed remained slow and sluggish in Singapore. Over a period of ten years from 1987 to 1997, only 600 industries were privatised in the country. And some of these industries are not yet fully privatised. In future, therefore, it is expected that privatisation exercise will continue to be an important agenda for government action.

The slow progress in privatisation might have been the result of initial disapprobation from bureaucracy, working class and even a section of the employers. While such a negative psychosis is no longer explicit, the privatisation programme has been facing many challenges from many quarters. Some of these challenges pertain to the maintenance of socially acceptable balances between: (i) equity and efficiency, (ii) price and quality (iii) marketism and social welfare, (iv) monopoly and competition, and (v) growth of political favouritism and distributive justice. The attainment of proper balances in these respects will call for appropriate trade-offs and compromises.

The financial crisis of 1997 and its aftermath put a temporary set-back towards the growth of privatisation. The financial crisis is a pointer to the limits of free market philosophy. Under such a situation, the progress of privatisation has to be very cautious and pragmatic. The proposal for privatisation in Singapore came from the government quarters unlike in many other countries where privatisation has mainly been the result of the initiative from the private sector.

Although the financial crisis was only a short term phenomenon, and the worst had already bottomed out, in the immediate post-crisis period, the government needed to proceed with transparency, accountability and justifiability. The crisis was really a testing time for the government. The Prime Minister of Singapore has already realised that the old ideology and social system are now in the midst of great change (*International Business Asia*, 31 March 1995). All this may give rise to a new political business cycle in future where privatisation may not be accorded a red carpet treatment as in the past.

APPENDIX I

DIVESTMENT OF GOVERNMENT LINKED COMPANIES, 1985 – 90

GLC	Paid-up Capital $m*	Date	Govt's share	
			Before $	After $
Singapore Press Holdings Ltd	243.0	Oct 1985	0.06	0.0
Cerebos Singapore	8.8	Nov 1985	45.0	0.0
Mitsubishi Singapore Heavy Industry	100.0	Dec 1985	44.0	0.0
S'pore Airlines Ltd	619.7	Dec 1985	100.0	63.0
PT Cerval Food Ltd.	415.0	July 1986	22.5	0.0
Dowty Aviation Services Ltd.	2.0	Sept. 1986	5.7	0.0
National Iron & Steel Mills Ltd.	63.0	Sept. 1986	19.7	0.0
United Industrial Corp Ltd.	159.5	Sept. 1986	10.9	0.0
S'pore Airport Duty Free Emp Ltd.	41.5	Oct 1986	20.0	0.0
Resource Development Corp. Ltd.	25.0	Dec 1986	100.0	30.0
S'pore National Printers Ltd.	9.5	Jan 1987	100.0	63.0
Neptune Orient Line	169.0	May 1987	62.0	52.0
Sembawang Maritime Ltd.	70.0	May 1987	50.0	0.0
Sembawang Shipyard Ltd.	150.0	Jun 1987	74.0	64.0
S'pore Airlines Ltd.	619.7	Jun 1987	63.0	55.0
Chemical Industries Ltd.	15.1	Jul. 1987	22.9	0.0
Jurong Shipyard Ltd.	100.0	Aug. 1987	43.1	16.2
Singmarine Industries	77.0	Sept. 1987	61.4	30.9
DBS Land	586.4	Sept. 1987	44.7	21.0
Parkland Golf Driving Range	0.8	Oct. 1987	60.0	0.0

Ltd.				
Sugar Industries of Singapore	16.0	Dec. 1987	40.0	0.0
Hitachi Electronic Devices Ltd.	30.0	Aug. 1987	15.0	0.0
Neptune Orient Lines	372.2	Jul. 1988	52.0	44.5
Van Ommeren Terminal (S) Pte. Ltd	52.3	Oct. 1988	8.0	-
Yaohan S'pore Pte. Ltd.	18.0	Nov. 1988	15.0	-
S'pore National Printers	19.0	Nov. 1988	63.0	51.0
Phillips Petroleum S'pore Chemicals	165.0	Dec. 1988	25.0	-
Keppel Corporation	315.0	Jan. 1989	58.5	52.2
Intraco	75.0	Feb. 1989	26.7	10.0
Denka S'pore Pte Ltd.	14.0	Mar 1989	20.0	-
Ethylene Glyocols S'pore Pte Ltd.	186.6	Apr. 1989	50.0	-
The Polyolefin Co. Pte Ltd.	109.2	Apr. 1989	25.0	-
Petrochemical Corp of S'pore	686.7	Apr. 1989	50.0	20.0
Acma Electrical	55.73	Mar 1990	0.2	-
Singapore Aerospace	150.0	Aug 1990	100.0	66.7
Singapore Shipbuilding & Engineering	40.4	Aug 1990	88.6	60.2

*unless otherwise stated

Source: Thynne in Thynne and Ariff, eds., 1989, Table 2(5), pp. 44 – 45 and Ministry of Finance

See also, Linda Low (1991, op. Cit., pp. 194 – 195 (Appendix 6.1)

APPENDIX 2

COMPANIES RECOMMENDED FOR PRIVATISATION

Companies recommended for listing

First tier companies

Under Temasek Holdings

1. Jurong Shipyard Ltd
2. Singapore National Printers Pte. Ltd*
3. Singapore Offshore Petroleum Services Pte Ltd.
4. Singapore Pools Pte Ltd.
5. Yaohan Singapore Pte Ltd.

Under MNDH

6. Resources Development Corp Pte. Ltd.

Under Statutory Boards

7. Changi International Airport Services Pte Ltd.

Second-tier companies

Under Temasek Holdings

8. DBS Land Ltd
9. DBS Finance Ltd
10. MMGU Insurance Pte Ltd.
11. Sembawang Towing Co. Pte Ltd
12. Shing Loong Finance Ltd
13. Singapore Airport Terminal Services Pte Ltd.
14. Singapore Avaiation & General Insurance Co. Pte. Ltd.

Under Statutory boards

15. Container Warehousing & Transportation Pte Ltd.

Companies recommended for reduction in shareholding + Listed companies

Under Temasek Holdings

16. DBS Bank Ltd.
17. Keppel Corporation Ltd.
18. Neptune Orient Lines Ltd.
19. Sembawang Shipyard Ltd/Sembawang Holdings Pte Ltd
20. Singapore Airlines Ltd.

Unlisted Companies

Under MNDH

21.   International Development & Consultancy Corp. Pte. Ltd.

Under Statutory Boards

22.   SBC Enterprises Pte. Ltd.

23.   SPECS Consultants Pte. Ltd.

Companies recommended for total privatisation

Listed Companies

Under Temasek Holdings

24.   Acma Electrical Industries Ltd

25.   Chemical Industries (FE). Ltd.

26.   Intraco Ltd.

27.   National Iron & Steel Mills Ltd#

28.   United Industrial Corporation Ltd#

Unlisted Companies

Under Temasek Holdings

29.   Dowty Aviation Services Pte. Ltd.

30.   Hitachi Electronic Devices (S) Pte Ltd.

31.   Sembawang Salvage Co Pte. Ltd.

32.   Singapore Airport Duty-Free Emporium Pte Ltd

33.   Van Ommeren Terminal (S) Pte. Ltd.

Under MDNH

34.   Construction Technology Pte. Ltd.

Under Statutory boards

35.   GATX Terminals Pte. Ltd.

36.   Jurong Environmental Engineering Pte. Ltd.

37.   Setsco Services Pte Ltd#

38.   Singapore Airport Bus Services Pte. Ltd.

39.   Suzue-PSA Cold Storage Pte. Ltd.

Under Ministry of Education

Educational Publications Bureau Pte. Ltd#

---

*The company has since been public listed.

+ Only eight and not nine are listed here.

 # The company has since been divested.

Source: Linda Low (1991), op. Cit. Pp. 158 – 159, and Singapore Ministry of Finance, *Report Sector Divestment Committee.*

REFERENCES

Ariff, Mohamed (1989), "A Financial Management Perspective" in Thynne, Ian et al. (eds.), op. Cit.

Chan, Heng Chee (1982), "Singapore in 1981: Planned Changes and Unplanned Consequences", *Asian Survey* February.

Chan, Heng Chee (1986), "Singapore in 1985: Managing Political Transition and Economic Recession", *Asian Survey,* February.

Ghosh, B.N. (1998), *Malaysia: The Transformation Within*, Longman, Kuala Lumpur.

Ghosh, B.N. (1999), "Privatisation: The ASEAN Experience" in Ghosh B.N. (ed.) *Privatisation: The ASEAN Connection,* Utusan Publication, Kuala Lumpur in 1999.

Ghosh, B. N. (2000), *The Three Dimensional Men: Human Resource Development in Malaysia.* (In Press).

Gouri, Geeta (ed.) (1991), *Privatisation and Public Enterprise*, Oxford and IBH Publishing, New Delhi.

Govt. of Singapore, (1995) *Singapore,* Ministry of Information and Arts, *Singapore.*

Hussin, Mutalib (1993), "Singapore in 1992: Regime of Consolidation and Toist", *Asian Survey,* February.

Lim, Linda (1983), "Singapore's Successes: The Myth of the Free Market Economy", *Asian Survey,* June.

Low, Linda (1991), *The Political Economy of Privatisation,* McGraw Hill, Singapore.

Milne, R.S. (1991), "The Politics of Privatisation in the ASEAN States", *ASEAN Economic Bulletin,* Vol. 7, No. 3.

Ng, Chee Yuen and Toh Kim Woon (1992), "Privatisation in the Asian Pacific Region", *Asian Pacific Economic Literature,* Vol. 6, No. 2.

Ng, Chee Yuen and Wagner, N. (1989), (eds.), "Privatisation and Deregulation in ASEAN", *ASEAN Economic Bulletin*, March, Vol. 5, No. 3.

Pelkmans, J. and Wagnar, N. (1990), (Eds.), *Privatisation and Deregulation in ASEAN and the EC,* EIPA and ISEAS, Singapore.

Thynne, Ian et al. (eds.) (1989), *Privatisation: Singapore Experience in Perspective*, Longman, Singapore.

Wheelwright, E. L. (1999), "Global Corporate Capitalism", in Anthony Phillip O' Hara (ed.), *Encyclopedia of Political Economy*, Routledge, London and New York.

Chapter 10

PRIVATISATION IN THAILAND: AN OVERVIEW

Dawood M. Mithani & Pairat Watcharaphun

INTRODUCTION

Privatisation is not a rigidly defined concept. It may mean different things to different people. Interpreted in a narrow sense, the term is commonly associated with the sale of assets of public undertakings for the private ownership - called divestiture, or denationalisation i.e., a change of ownership from state to the private sector. In a broad sense, privatisation refers to any shift in activity from the public to the private and its process covering several modes and methods. In other words, privatisation is a process of transferring the government assets or functions to the private sector. In today's mixed economies privatisation implies reducing the size and role of the public sector and enhancing that of the private sector. It is a process towards increasing market-orientation of the mixed economy. The main objectives of privatisation, in general, are as follows:

- Reducing the size of the public sector and consequently government's budgetary liabilities;
- Improving the efficiency and performance of the state enterprises;
- Increasing the degree of market-orientation.

- Getting bureaucrats out of business, or inflicting business culture in lieu of bureaucracy in the management and operation of the public sector undertakings.

- The process of privatisation may be characterised by different modes in different context, such as:

- Withdrawal, that is, government withdrawal from providing any specific public utility - (e.g. water supply, electricity supply, social overheads, and so on).

- Divestiture, that is, selling the public assets to the private sector. It implies transfer of ownership of an undertaking from the government to the private sector.

- Joint Venture. It refers to establishment of a new joint public-private venture. It gives a triangular approach to the mixed economy: consisting public sector, private sector and joint sector.

- Contracting out. The government assigning the contract to the private contractors to provide certain services for the government. It is a cost-saving and efficiency-improving device.

- Franchising, that is, bestowing monopoly privilege to the private enterprise (the lowest bidder) to supply a particular public utility. The government simply regulates price in this case and the buyers have to deal directly with the private franchisee.

- Farming out. Thailand, in particular, used this form of privatisation for raising the revenue. Under this device, monopoly privilege is conferred to the highest bidder private enterprise to secure a fixed amount of revenue (e.g. tax collection). The bidder earns excess collection as the profit.

- Leasing. Under this system, the public enterprise is leased out to the highest bidding private operator for a fixed period of time.

- Vouchers. These refer to coupons of value given by the government to qualified citizens that are to be used to purchase a public utility in open market. The service is rendered by the private sector. The government, however, shoulders the responsibility of funding for the service.

- Grants. These refer to the subsidies given by the government to selected private firms for producing certain essential services.

- User charges. Under this concept, the price of public utility is determined in terms of a fee, a toll, or a charge. In this system, the government provides services like a private enterprise.
- Liberalisation. It refers to deregulation. It is a narrowed down meaning of privatisation which implies the removal or relaxation of government regulations or bureaucratic obstacles to permit market forces to play freely.

Privatisation is a burning issue in Thailand. It is proposed as one of the remedial measures for recovery under the IMF loan conditionally to overcome the recent (1998) economic crisis of the country. The present paper intends to provide an overview of the issues pertaining to privatisation in Thailand.

Pre-Privatisation Period: A Historical Perspective

hence, it used to have a greater degree of market-orientation in the post War II era. Nonetheless, Thailand's economy emerged with an extension of the public sector. For in those days, the spirit of economic nationalism was high and craving for the minimisation of foreign influence on Thai economy. In 1953, the Thai government enacted a state organisation bill in order to promote a rapid growth of the state enterprises. During the fifties, several state enterprises were established to support the industrial growth, to augment domestic consumption and to maintain national security.

Economic significance of state enterprises in Thailand is manifested It is interesting to note that unlike most of the Asian countries, Thailand considered state activity as secondary to market activity; by its high rate of expansion (nearly 24 percent per annum) during the period 1981-1985. Furthermore, recurrent expenditure of the Thai public sector increased from 9.5 percent of GDP in 1970 to 18.0 percent in 1983 and reached to a peak of 20.7 percent in 1985. Likewise, the ratio of capital investment of public sector to central government's capital expenditure went up from 32.5 percent in 1970 to 86.8 percent in 1983 and with a quantum leap to 171 percent in 1985. This implies capital investment of public sector has expanded at a much faster rate than that of the central government's spending over the years. Nonetheless, it played relatively a smaller role in employment generation. In fact, the employment expansion of state enterprises registered a 177 percent increase as against that of 197 percent by the central government during the period 1970-1982. In recent years, however, relatively more generation of employment in public sector is envisaged due to its growth and policy restriction on the expansion of employment in the government sector (not exceeding two percent annually) (see, Dhiratayakinant, 1991).

Thai public sector captured its dominance in major growth sectors such as power, transport and communication, and manufacturing. Its expansion aimed at: controlling prices, generating budgetary revenue and moulding the economy in tune with the government policies.Its role was to implement large-scale investment projects and to carry out the activity related to national security and public health (Ramang Kura, 1991:1-2).

Since 1957, however, the Sarith Thanarath's government gave a brake to the growth of public sector expansion and introduced a strategy to privatise certain less crucial and loss-making state enterprises. The process of privatisation,however, remained slow since the subsequent governments remained much inactive on the issue. It was only during the regime of the Prime Minister Preim Thinasulanontha, the issue of privatisation was resumed with determined policies incorporated in the Sixth National Economic and Social Development Plan of the country (Bhisithvanich, 1991: 15).

GENESIS OF PRIVATISATION IN THAILAND

By and large, the first five national development plans (1961-1986) in Thailand categorically mentioned that the government would limit its expansion of the public sector and will abstain from intervening in the free market economy. Thailand in this way embarked upon the essence of privatisation much ahead of the Thatcher government in Great Britain and ASEAN neighbours. The term privatisation was, however, popularised in the country since the early years of the fifth national development plan (1982-1986) with the adoption of a set of privatisation policies by the Council of Ministers in October 1983. The program was emphatically inducted into the sixth national development plan (1987-1991). During this period, in Thailand 33 public sector companies have been privatised.

Major factors which prompted reforms of public enterprises through privatisation in Thailand are:

- Lack of adequate domestic finance. There has been increasing difficulty for many public sector undertakings to finance the required investments on their own.
- Losses. Most of the public enterprises incurred heavy losses, which means there were negative returns on government investment.
- Rising external debt. In view of widening fiscal gaps, the government relied heavily on external borrowings resulting in rapid expansion of the external debt during the eighties and mid-nineties.
- Inefficiency. Like most developing countries, public sector undertakings in Thailand were marked for the growing inefficiency in internal management, outlook and performance. Lack of vision, absence of business culture and growing corruption carried their adverse effect in ruining the Thai public enterprises.
- Political interference. Undue political interference and lack of autonomy further worsened the fragile economic situation.

In Thailand, privatisation is largely referred to as a means of improving the overall-efficiency through market-orientation by reducing the proportion of government sector and expanding that of the private sector in the economic arena. Under the privatisation policy in Thailand, the emphasis was placed on the improvement of the performance and efficiency of the state enterprises. The following measures have been suggested in this context (see, Dhiratayakinant, 1991):

- Improvement in the existing management;
- Change in management team;
- Improvement in marketing facilities;
- Transfer or liquidation of existing public sector enterprises;
- Joint public-private venture.

OBJECTIVES OF PRIVATISATION IN THAILAND

Objectives of privatisation programme in a developing country such as Thailand may be looked upon in two ways: general and specific.

The general objectives of privatisation programme include:

- Readjusting the public-private sector mix in the economy;
- The expansion of private sector as an engine of growth;
- Increasing the degree of competition in the economy;
- Lowering the growth rate of public expenditure as well as borrowings by curtailing the operations of the loss-making public sector undertakings through transfer; and
- Improving the efficiency of the public sector undertakings.

Ostensibly, the framework and content of privatisation programme tend to depend on the mix of the overall goals that is to be realised.

Specific objectives, on the other hand, have to be spelt-out in the case of the particular privatisation programme. Specific objectives may be varied, such as:

- Reducing the cost of producing a particular public utility or service,
- Improving the working and performance of a specific public undertaking,
- Eliminating the political interference in a particular public enterprise,
- Reducing the financial burden of the government in providing certain public utilities,
- Reducing foreign debt of state enterprises,
- Inflicting professionalism in the management of a particular government enterprise, and
- Providing a particular public utility in response to greater consumer demand.

The Sixth National Economic and Social Development Plan of the country spelt out the following norms for privatisation:

- The government would encourage private equity participation in public sector investment projects;
- To lease or franchise partly or wholly manufacturing or infrastructure-related public enterprises to the private sector to carry out their operations;
- To liquidate or sale to private sector those state enterprises which have continually failed in their operations;
- The government will retain the revenue-generating as well as social-welfare oriented state enterprises; and
- The government will expand the role of public sector in heavy industry projects which involve huge finance and high technology,

MODES AND CHARACTERISTICS OF PRIVATISATION IN THAILAND

Thai policy-makers have adopted the following modes of privatisation:

Divestiture, as a form of privatisation, has been assigned very little scope in Thailand. Only a small number of state enterprises have been liquidated.

1. Under farming out, the government bestowed the private monopoly in producing liquor and channel of distribution activities.
2. Franchising has been a most favoured form of privatisation adopted in the country. For, it allows the state enterprise to remain in existence and provides an opportunity to lay down the conditions for franchising. Thai government preferred to franchise forest, and tin mines.
3. Leasing has been popular in Thailand for idle or less efficiently utilised properties of the state enterprises. The government allowed private sector to take over such government assets for a certain period of time. At end of the lease period these have to be returned to the government (e.g, the collection of highway tolls).
4. Contracting-out has been favoured in the case of large public utilities and infrastructures. It has proved to be an easier and cost-savings device for the Thai government.

5. Public-private joint ventures have not become quite popular in Thailand owing to lack specification of clearly delineated role of government and private partners in the policy matters. In recent years, Thai state enterprises have been brought to stock market for trading stocks to private enterprises which is attracting or raising funds from private sector or foreign investors to expand state enterprises' activities or transactions. For example, Thai Airway International Public Company Ltd, Telephone Organisation of Thailand are now under this category of privatisation.

6. Thai government also recognises liberalisation, i.e., relaxation of rules and regulations as a means to provide greater flexibility and facilitating improvement in management of the state enterprises under the process of privatisation. Liberalisation , however, has received only a lip service on the practical side, even in the nineties. Plethora of rules and regulations have obstructed the smooth working of the state enterprises and restricted the improvement in their overall operational efficiency and performance.

Besides, in Thailand, an unusual (and less agreeable) concept of privatisation is introduced by the government officials. This is referred to as 'self-privatisation' meaning administrative improvement by a state enterprise through adoption of modern business and management techniques. Self-privatisation is incorporated as a part of privatisation policy of the Thai government (Dhiratayakinant, 1991).

Table 1 portrays an idea of types of state enterprises and their privatisation modalities envisaged by the Thai policy makers.

TABLE 1: CLASSIFICATION OF THAI STATE PUBLIC ENTERPRISES WITH APPLICATION OF PRIVATISATION MODALITIES

Type of State Enterprises	Privatisation measure
1. High income generating public enterprises	Retain public ownership: No divestiture Management contract
2. Public Utilities	Retain public ownership: No divestiture Contracting-out, joint venture
3. Infrastructure	Retain public ownership: No divestiture Contracting-out, franchising, leasing
4. Special policy orientation	Retain public ownership: No divestiture Contracting out, sale of equity shares with government retaining majority
5. Promotion orientation	Retain public ownership: No divestiture Contracting out.
6. Trade, manufacture and service	Liberalisation (special privileges repealed) Leasing, franchising, sale of equity share, sale of public enterprise and liquidation (when private concerns can do better than existing public enterprises) Privatisation begins with the worse cases and works upward; first turns them into limited company.

(Source: Dhiratayakinant, 1991: 711)

It clearly shows that divestiture is least favoured under privatisation programme in Thailand. We may recapitulate that in Thailand, privatisation assumes the following features:

1. Using private discipline in government organization or state enterprise. Reorganising the advisory and executive committees by inviting experts or managers from the private sector to join as members.
2. A government or state enterprises makes a contract deal with the private entrepreneur. Under contracting-out system the government and state enterprises give a lease to private sector in areas such as electricity

producing, tin mining, high way, or allowing the private telephone company to set up the individual homephone.

3. Transferring of ownership from government or state enterprises to private sector. Such ownership transfer may be in the form of a sale of government services or transaction to private sector through a mechanism of a private placement, public offering, employee buy-out or management buy-out.

4. By liberalisation, the process is meant to reducing a proportion of government services and to increase that of private sector. This may lead to a reduction of monopoly or abolition of monopoly.. For example, Tobacco sector and Telephone services have been liberalised in Thailand.

The major purpose of stimulating privatisation is meant to increase work efficiency and productivity, thus, reducing operating costs.

A major propelling force behind privatisation is the fact that the government cannot handle all state enterprise debts. Particularly, the expansion of the entire range of infrastructures involves huge expenditure which cannot be met by limited fiscal resources. Assistance of private resources ,thus, becomes unavoidable. Other reason for privatisation is the transfer of private technologies or linkage synergy. As a matter of fact the expansion of privatisation in Thailand, 1980 onwards, has been attributed to the limitation of monetary and fiscal policies of the government in sustaining the activities of the public sector.

In Thailand there is a great deal of confusion prevailing about the true nature and meaning of privatisation. Though there was an indication of privatisation as an important planning objective incorporated since the First National Economic and Social Development Plan, concrete steps in this direction were lacking in the country, in comparison to the neighbouring ASEAN countries such as Malaysia, Indonesia and Singapore. Over the years, hardly any attention is paid by the government on the issue of privatisation with a serious consideration. There has been a conspicuous absence of long term policy and programme with a vision and zeal in this regard. Political instability has also contributed to a lack of concrete efforts required to undertake a major privatisation programme.

PRIVATISATION PROGRAMME

Various privatisation reform measures such as liquidation, sales of state enterprises, private management contracts and leasing were suggested in dealing with the inefficient public undertakings. The order of priority was assigned in terms of continuously loss making state enterprises in the manufacturing and commercial related field. State enterprises which are efficient and profit-making, especially in the fields of infrastructure or welfare were placed in the bottom of the ascending order (Ng, Chee Yuen and Toh Kin Woon, 1992: 53).

In addition, the Thai government was determined to refrain from establishing any new state enterprise in the area where private firms could do the job effectively. It also determined not to expand the existing enterprises that compete with private sector barring the activities related to public interest and national security. Besides, state enterprises which have been set up for a specific purpose were to be liquidated or transferred to the private sector once the purpose is fulfilled (Virabhongsa Ramangkura, 1991: 3).

During 1980s, Thai state enterprises such as Alum Organisation, Chol-buri Sugar Corporation, Gunny-bags factory, and mining organisation were liquidated. The government reduced it share-holding in the case of Krung Thai Bank, Marble Company, Northeast Jute Mill Company and Paper Plant Factory. Bang-Pa-In Paper Mill and Narayanaphan Company are no longer public enterprises. Joint-venture is introduced in the case of hotels and golf courses belonging to Tourism Authority of Thailand. The government run United Thai Hotel and Travel company gave its hotel rebuilding task to private enterprise under the joint-venture.

It is interesting to note that railway catering services and affiliated hotel services of the State Railways of Thailand are franchised. In addition, their vacant land is leased out for construction. Similarly, the Bangkok Mass Transit Organisation (BMTO) also franchised few routes which are operated with air-conditioned and non-air-conditioned buses. Furthermore, crane operation service at the Port Authority of Thailand was also franchised.

On the other hand, Telephone Organisation of Thailand contracted-out its telephone installation service. Thailand Tobacco Monopoly and Petroleum Authority of Thailand contracted-out cleaning services to the private enterprises. Waterworks Authority contracted-out water pipe works. Similarly, certain types of maintenance services of the Electricity Generating Authority of Thailand and the Bangkok Mass Transit Organisation was contracted-out. Airport Authority of Thailand contracted-out duty free shops, and cleaning services. From 1995, private companies were constructing major expressways and were entitled to share in toll revenues with the government.

By 1996, some thirty-one small-scale state enterprises unrelated to major economic activities were liquidated through leasing, franchising and sale of shares. Besides, the private sector was invited to participate in the management of seven undertakings, three state enterprises were contracted out and 17 were rehabilitated (Ng, Chee Yuen and Toh Kin Woon,1992: 53).

Presently, there are 83 state enterprises manned by 3-4 hundred thousand employees in Thailand. Their aggregate assets are valued at billion bahts (Phuraya, 1998: 85). There is a strong case for furthering the privatisation process; because every year at least 10 state enterprises turn out to be loss-making units. In 1996, for instance, 16 state enterprises incurred the loss of over 4,553 million bahts. In 1997 budget, the government had to make provision of about 20,000 million bahts to 23 state enterprises. Among other things, the Bank of Thailand established the Financial Recovering and Development Funds to improve and take over four middle commercial banks (Anatta, 1998:39).

In its process of privatisation, unlike its neighbouring country Malaysia, Thailand has been rather slow and gradual in reducing the relatively smaller role of the state in its economic arena. The progress of privatisation has been steady without causing abrupt changes in the structural order. This may be attributed to Thai's market ideology that has always remained pivotal in the policy formulation. Gains from privatisation in Thailand so far has been moderate in direct improvement in efficiency and financial gains. Its impact on economic growth, equity, political stability and social consequences has been rather insignificant.

PRIVATISATION MASTER PLAN 1998

Thai government had to give its commitment for launching upon a privatisation programme in its Letter of Intent submitted to the IMF while seeking its financial help during the recent 1998 economic turmoil. In that year, the Chuan Leakpai government in Thailand came out with a master plan for privatisation.

The Master Plan of Chuan Leakpai government is regarded as the strategic document that determines the direction and extent of privatisation in reforming the state enterprises in the country. It is a good reference document for official units, state enterprises, investors, the officers of the state enterprises as well as general public in knowing the nature, object, process and intention of the government in launching upon privatisation. It spells out a step towards increasing the role of the private sector into the state enterprises. Thai government is committed to establish the Policy Committee of the Privatisation Programme. The committee shall study the possibility to privatise some more state enterprise quickly and ensure that the reformation is based on a strong footing.

Currently, it has been reported that there are 59 state enterprises, under the sole government control, consisting of five main departments: Telecommunication and Transportation, Water Supply, Power and other state enterprises (in the sectors such as industry, social, technology, trading and services, agriculture and financial institutions). Under the present move (as per the Master Plan), privatisation in Thailand relates to the reformation of state enterprises. It consists of the adjustment of organisational structure, organisations which are taken care by the related official departments and related laws. Under the privatisation criteria, the government determines the rationales and the profits of the privatisation in financial and social terms.

In the social context, while promoting the liberal market, the government sets the units to protect the right of the people, to control or interfere whenever the people are exploited by the private sector. Further, there are laws such as the determination of pricing and protecting of the Monopoly Act, Labour Protection Act and the legal criteria for foreign enterprises and taxation, Thai Constitution 1998 Act 49, Civil and Commercial Laws need suitable amendments to facilitate smooth privatisation process.

The Master Plan of privatisation in Thailand lays down that 50% of the income from privatisation will become part of national revenue. This has to be used for agriculture, education, public health, labour welfare and rural development. The rest (50%) of the income will be utilised as public loans for financial institutions.

It has been stated that the Privatisation Master Plan (PMP) will have the focus on the reformation of telecommunication enterprises and their privatisation to unfold the liberal market. The privatisation of Radio-Television of Thailand has been emphasised. Separation of the postal enterprise from the telecommunication has been suggested by the planners. A new telecommunication Act is envisaged to set up an independent supervisory body on telecommunications The PMP envisages to privatise Metropolitan Water Supply Organisation and find the alliance or partner to joint-investment to manage and execute by hire contract. The government intends to set up an independent organisation to control and supervise water supply management in the country.Privatisation is also assumed for ill state enterprises in the transportation sector. The models of privatisation will be tuned by the policy, supervision and operation envisaged by the transportation ministry. An independent supervisory body is to be created for this sector as well. In the power sector, electricity supply restructuring is envisaged through privatisation of the state-owned electricity plants. In the case of natural gas supply competitive market is to be restructured: (i) by dividing the transit enterprises and trade enterprises of PTT and (ii) introducing third party into gas pipe system. Privatisation of PTT as a whole has been suggested. The Master Plan also envisaged privatisation of 42 state enterprises in the following key sectors, namely, banking industry, agriculture, and science and technology.

According the Master Plan, privatisation implies transfer of responsibility and increasing role of the private sector in the functioning areas of state enterprises. It involves sale of the assets or share (i.e. transfer of ownership), concession, leasing, hiring of the private executive in the services, and deregulation with a view of promoting a liberalised, and competitive market. The Plan envisaged furtherance of liberal competition through privatisation for the period 2003 – 2006,which is described as the liberal market period in Thailand.Furthermore, the PMP suggests developing the investment plan to encourage private investors to invest in the state enterprises or to develop new projects.

CONCLUDING OBSERVATIONS

The process, instruments and policies of privatisation may be viewed in two dimensions, viz: macro-privatisation and micro-privatisation. Macro-privatisation implies a general reduction of state involvement characterised by a direct sale of assets of the public enterprises. Liberalisation (involving deregulation) is another facet of macro-privatisation which is associated with a gradual transformation of the role of the state from producer state to regulator state and finally to facilitator state in a mixed economy. Micro-privatisation, on the other hand, relates to the operational dynamics of state enterprises for the improvement of efficiency and performance. In Thailand a leaning towards micro-privatisation such as leasing or sub-contracting as against macro-privatisation such as sale of public sector assets is predominant (see, Geeta Gouri, at.el., 1991).

In comparison to several other Asian countries, Thailand has a strong market-orientation and relatively lesser dominance of the public sector. The Thai government, however, recognises that privatisation is a key instrument for efficiency and engine of growth. Prior to the economic crisis of 1998, privatisation had remained only a political-oriented phenomenon and lost its meaningful economic significance in the country.

In Thailand, privatisation is basically understood as the transfer of state enterprises. There are six major issues of privatisation in Thailand: (1)law reformation; (2) extent of the role of the government; (3) entry of new private enterprises in the areas governed by the state enterprises; (4) bringing the universal standard methods; (5) adjustment of the supervisory body; and (6) Supervision and evaluation of private companies.

Under its privatisation process, Thailand has moved from facilitator state to a welfare state by regarding private sector as core sector of the economy. Under the revived phase of privatisation, the Thai government confirmed its strong faith in market ideology and efficiency.

In Thai economic planning, thus, a greater role is assigned to the private sector initiatives, and the public sector's scope was limited to the traditional areas of the state functions, such as natural monopolies. The government had expressed its consistent faith in the market economy and intervened only in apparent cases of market failures such as provision of public goods.

In spite of despite categorical announcement of privatisation policy and norms prescribed under the PMP, there has been a lack of transparency in the official approach towards the scope and extent of privatisation in the country. Clear direction, formal and procedure for the privatisation policy and programme are conspicously absent. As a result, the management of the public sector enterprises have always been in utter confusion and peril. Since the government used to face strong labour resistance against divestment move, other modalities of privatisation, such as leasing, franchising, contracting-out and joint ventures have been adopted in the process.

Privatisation is assumed to be an efficient and effective way to improve upon the present economic situation in Thailand. It is supposed to reduce the public expenditure, promote efficiency in operations, attract investors, assist in shelving the government's debt burden and bring about stability of Thai finance companies, besides inflicting open free competition in the market.

So far, only a few developing countries have reformed their public sector enterprise successfully in meeting laudable goals of privatisation. Needless to say, Thailand is not in this list. Indeed, privatisation is essential to boost the real economic growth of a country. The Thai government and policy makers, therefore, should have a focus on this issue in rebuilding the economy in the wake of quicker recovery phase.

A main drawback or hurdle in the privatisation process of the country is that the government has failed to liberalise the rules and regulations imposed on public enterprises. The existing state enterprises in Thailand should be given more autonomy in decision-making for effective functioning and greater efficiency.

Furthermore, privatisation is not a sufficient condition to ensure competition. It should have been accompanied by an effective competition inducing policy which is devoid of monopoly growth. There is a need to encourage new entry and ensure a level playing field with a better technical standards among the competitors in the whole gamut of market network.

Provision of effectively corporatised government sector is an essential condition for the success of privatisation. Privatisation as an engine of growth in any developing country including Thailand should mean that the growth of private sector is accelerating not just by means of the privatisation of public sector enterprises but more through the magnitude of new entries of indigenous as well as foreign entrepreneurs in the free market economy. Mere conversion of public monopoly to private monopoly will vitiate the whole purpose of privatisation. Thai entrepreneurs should be well prepared to meet those upcoming challenges and grab opportunities emerging at the threshold of the new millennium.

REFERENCES

Analta, Raeka (1998), 'The Privatisation of the State Enterprise's Bank: The Difficult Solution', *The Commercial Bank,* June. (in Thai)

Bhisithvanich, Suphachai (1991), 'The Privatisation', *The Journal of Comptroller-General's Department*, January- February (in Thai)

Chandhtarasorn, Voradej (1991), 'The Transfer of the State Enterprise to the Private Enterprise', *The Journal of Comptroller-General's Department* ,March-May (in Thai)

Dhiratayakinant, Kraiyudht (1991), 'Privatisation of the Bangkok Metropolitan Transit Organisation: A case study', in Geeta Gouri (ed.) *Privatisation and Public Enterprises: The Asia-Pacific Experience,* Institute of Public Enterprise, Hyderabad.

Dhiratayakinant, Kraiyudht (1991), 'Privatisation of Public Enterprices: The Case of Thailand', in Gouri Geeta (ed.) *Privatisation and Public Enterprise: The Asia-Pasific Experience,* Institute of Public Enterprise, Hyderabad.

Dhiratayakinant, Kraiyudht (1989), 'Privatisation: An Analysis of the Concept and Its Implementation in Thailand', The Thai Development Research Institute Foundation, Bangkok. (in Thai)

Geeta, Gouri (1991), *Privatisation and Public Enterprise: The Asia-Pacific Experience,* Institute of Public Enterprise, Hyderabad.

Ingavatas, Poonsin (1989), 'Privatisation in Thailand: Slow progress amidst much opposition', *Asian Economic Bullent*, March.

Ng, Chee Yuen and Toh Kin Woon (1992), 'Privatisation in the Asia- Pacific Region', *Asian Pacific Economic Literature,* November.

Phuraya, Kreingkrai (1998), 'The Dissection of Privatisation: From State to the Private, Who Earn, Who Lose?' *The Analysis*, June (in Thai)

Phuakhaw, Panadtha (1993), 'The Privatisation', *The Journal of Comptroller General Department,* July-August (in Thai)

Ramangkura, Virabhongsu (1991), 'Privatisation in Thailand', *Bank of Thailand Quarterly Bulletin,* June, (1 – 6)

Thai-ari, Phipat (1998), *The Criteria of the Privatisation in Thailand,* Chulalonkorn University Press, Bangkok. (in Thai)

Weerawarn, Amnoui (1991), 'The Privatisation: The Financial and Opportunity Alternatives', *Economy*, October.(in Thai)

Chapter 11

TRANSACTION COSTS, THE STATE AND PRIVATISATION: THEORETICAL ISSUES AND THE ASEAN EXPERIENCE

Shankaran Nambiar
International College, Penang

INTRODUCTION

The debate on privatisation has, mostly, been waged on the basis of efficiency. It has been argued that enterprises that are privately owned will be more efficient because they are more market-oriented than state-owned enterprises. Another argument that is raised in support of privatisation is based on the informational complexities faced by state-owned enterprises. In other words, state-owned enterprises in planned economies do not accurately set the prices of their produce because they do not directly respond to free market forces. In market economies the question of price-setting is slightly different because enterprises do interact with the market; but the price is set not just on the basis of cost considerations (say, the marginal cost, or some 'fair' price) but in view of equity principles, too.

In this paper we emphasise the notion of transaction costs. It is postulated that the state plays the role of transaction costs minimiser. When the objective of transaction costs minimisation is sacrificed this is done only to secure a higher goal, that of securing an equitable ordering that satisfies public efficiency. There is no attempt to prescribe a minimalist role for the state, although those who propose free market efficiency would forward such a recommendation. Indeed, if state participation reduces transaction costs, then state participation is supported.

The next section of this paper discusses the difference between the market and the firm. By doing so the foundations of the transaction costs approach is put in place. The third section discuss the notion of transaction costs before the transaction costs framework is outlined in the fourth section. The fifth section applies the transaction costs framework to the state. The sixth section briefly reviews the experiences of some Southeast Asian (ASEAN) countries, after which the seventh section examines these experiences using the transaction costs analysis. Finally, some concluding remarks are made.

THE MARKET AND THE FIRM

Coase (1937), in discussing the nature of the firm, established a fundamental difference between firms and the market. While the market is pervasive and makes exchanges between agents possible, the market has an important role to play in the allocation of resources. The market employs the price mechanism as a signal that facilitates the flow of resources from and to competing economic activities. ensuring that factors of production are used in the best possible manner. The primary position that the price mechanism occupies in the state of affairs governed by the market gives way within the firm.

The firm is as much concerned with efficiency as the market is; and the firm is as much concerned that resources are put to their best use as the market is. This does not result in the firm using the price mechanism as a device to direct the flow of resources. Rather, within a firm exchanges are decided by command: the top of the hierarchy in the firm being the entrepreneur, who directs the use of raw materials, the manner in which the time offered by workers is utilised, or, for instance, which department or line of production takes precedence over the other. Workers do not bid for raw materials and agree to buy them from a department within the firm at a mutually agreable price, neither do different lines of production compete with each other, on the basis of who can offer the best price, for semi-finished products.

The 'entrepreneur-co-ordinator', in Coase's terms, determines how resources are to be used and how the production process is to proceed. The price mechanism is too cumbersome to be used within the firm and, in fact, "these market transactions are eliminated and in place of the complicated market structure with exchange transactions is substituted the entrepreneur-coordinator, who directs production" (Coase, 1937:338). Coase points out that although contracts are not eliminated when a firm is established, the number of contracts that need to be made in using factors of production within a firm are greatly reduced. This is where the hierarchy wins over the market.

DISCUSSING TRANSACTION COSTS

Arrow (1969:48), probably, first used the term transaction costs, meaning by it the "the costs of running the economic system." Williamson (1985:19) is in concurrence with Arrow's use of the term when he suggests that transaction costs are as ubiquitous as friction is in physical systems. Elsewhere, Williamson (1979:233) indicates that transaction costs involve 'opportunism'.

The insights of Arrow and Williamson are developed more concretely by Dahlman (1979) who defines transaction costs to include search and information costs, bargaining and decision costs, and policing and enforcement costs. Pivotal to this delineanation of transaction costs is the idea of the exchange process, which is implicitly recognised as consisting, in the first instance, of the search for information regarding the availability of goods and services, their characteristics, quality, prices. The second stage of the exchange process requires some comparison on the basis of which a decision is made. Finally, once a decision is made to enter into a contract, mechanisms must be instituted to ensure that the contract is binding; that adjudication is possible in the event of doubt or uncertainty regarding the content or interpretation of an open contract; that adherence to a contract can be compelled; and, that breach of contract can be effectively punished.

Information, whether it takes the form of informational asymmetries or simply be the lack of it, is an important component of the exchange process. It need not be over emphasised that informational constraints can impede the formation and maintenance of contracts. Indeed, information and contracts lay the foundation for transactions, without which exchange would not be possible. Contracting, nevertheless, is fraught with impediments.

Aside from the problem of 'adverse selection', existing contracts may not conform with the needs of efficient production and exchange. The mismatch between existing contracts and contractual forms that support efficient production and efficient production and exchange will result in disequilibria. However, as Datta and Nugent (1989:35-36) note, "the time required for the elimination of such disequilibria may vary considerably (perhaps in proportion to the social costs of such changes), in general and in the long run, the competition (actual or potential) among alternative contractual forms can be counted upon to restore equilibrium."

Further sources of change that are thrust upon contracts include risks arising from fluctuations due to exogenous factors (changes in weather, luck, market conditions) and risks due to opportunism (shirking, cheating). Once techniques of production become entrenched and factor substitutability is narrow, resources have more limited alternate use and bargaining takes on a larger significance. It then becomes necessary to determine the right forms of contract. Similarly when there is greater specialisation of labour, contracts become more susceptible to change because labour can be used in different ways. When more and rapidly changing inputs become necessary for production, contracting costs have the potential to increase.

In view of the pervasive nature of contracts, Datta and Nugent (1989:37-38) propose a framework that is fairly similar to Dahlman's in that they, too, include the costs of obtaining information, the costs of negotiation, the costs of communicating the provisions to an agreement, the costs of monitoring and enforcement. These costs are termed ex ante costs as distinguished from ex post costs. Ex post costs include legal costs, costs associated with renegotiations and in inducing partners of a contract to settle disputes and resume their cooperative ventures. Ex post costs are introduced because comprehensive contracts cannot be determined with a view to all possible contingencies and also because contracts are neither self-adapting nor self-enforcing mechanisms.

THE TRANSACTION COSTS FRAMEWORK

Having outlined the nature and constitutents of transaction costs, it will now be possible to survey the transaction costs programme. Fundamental to this approach is the objective to minimize the costs of transactions that are relevant to an economic entity. The operationalisation of this approach depends on three assumptions: 1. bounded rationality, 2. asset specificity, and 3. opportunism. If any of these three conditions is not met, then contracts can function effectively, and, presumably, the market can tbe relied upon to act as a resource-allocator.

Let us consider the condition of bounded rationality. It is assumed, and entirely reasonably, that economic agents do not have full knowledge of all events, outcomes and prices. For instance, if an agent could anticipate a set of contingencies, then he would seek to cover for those possibilities when drawing up the contract. There would be no need for renegotiation (and the cost thereby incurred), if an agent could have successfully anticipated the occurrence of an incident that has thrown the initial contract into disarray because, say, certain sources of risk that were not thought of have now come to pass.

The second assumption, asset specificity, relates to investments that have very specific uses, or to factors of production that do not have a high degree of substitutability. A committment to a particular investment could be found to be misguided, resulting in the need to assess and consider new alternatives. Switching from one technique of production to another involves a variety of costs, something a firm would want to avoid or at least minimize.

Finally, agents are assumed to seek their own self-interests with guile. By this is meant that individuals would reveal a preference structure where the maximisation of their utility functions would take precedence over the demands or requirements of any given contract. In other words, opportunistic behaviour is one where an agent places his own utility function above that of the principal's. Manifestations of opportunism are seen when an agent seeks to deceive, mislead or cheat the principal.

Kay (1993:243) expresses the functioning of these three assumptions very clearly when he enumerates the consequences when one of the assumptions is not satisfied. In the first case, when the bounded rationality assumption is relaxed, problems arising from asset specificity or opportunism can be dealt with through comprehensive contracts since complete knowledge (through all time) is available. In the second case, if the assumption of asset specificity is removed then mistakes in investment can be easily rectified since alternate contracts would resolve what might otherwise be a crisis. The last case involves the relaxation of opportunistic behaviour, in which instance honest and sincere individuals would attempt to correct mistakes in investment or unpredicted changes in a mutually satisfactory manner.

Most economic contexts would find all three assumptions present. Two decision rules then become necessary. The first would be to arrange transactions in such a way as to take cognisance of informational inadequacies, given, especially, the challenge of opportunistic behaviour. The second, and broader, rule would be to try to minimize all transaction costs. The earlier rule entails devising checks and controls, and a system of rewards and fines so as to discourage violations of contracts; but more importantly it requires organising a set of transactions that best handles the constraints that are known to exist and those that can be anticipated. Of course, a costless set of transactions is preferred, failing which, any rational economic entity will attempt to keep transaction costs as low as feasible.

The nature of transactions, their frequency and costs, among other things, will decide the kind of economic organisation that must be selected. Certain transactions are best conducted within a firm whereas others are best left to the market. Likewise the state rather than the market may be better suited for a particular class of transactions. Again, central planning will favour certain transactions that the free market will not. With this we now turn to an examination of how the state can be viewed from the transaction costs perspective.

TRANSACTION COSTS AND THE STATE

The Weberian state is conceived as consisting of four elements: a) a differentiated set of institutions, b) a locus of power that extends from the centre, c) an area over which dominion is expressed, and d) monopoly over legitimized violence (Mann, 1986:48). It must also be noted that for Weber the bureaucracy had an intimate role to play in the running of the state because the "state's ability to support markets and capitalist accumulation depended on the bureaucracy being a corporately coherent entity in which individuals see furtherance of corporate goals as the best means of maximizing their individual self-interest" (Evans, 1992:146).

The Marxian view of the state carries three strands. One perspective emphasises the role that the state has to play as the as the representative of the dominant class, and thus sees the state as an instrument that supports their interests. The other perspective, that can be called the 'Bonapartist balancing act' (see Poulantzas,1972), derives from Marx's analysis of Louis Bonaparte's attempts to set different classes (the capitalists, petite bourgeoisie, peasantry and proletariat) against each other, with the ultimate objective of enhancing the state's own power.

The neoutilitarian political economists, for whom the theory of rent-seeking is the cornerstone of their analysis, envisage a minimal role for the state, prescribing that it be limited to "protecting individual rights, persons and property, and enforcing voluntarily negotiated private contracts" (Buchanan, Tollison and Tullock, 1980:9). Unlike the neoclassical economists who completely ignore the state, the neoutilitarian economists, using the individual optimization framework, discuss the workings of the state (Buchanan, Tollison and Tullock, 1980; Colander, 1984; Niskanen, 1971). Their research projects have centred around the functioning of the bureaucracy and voting processes. Another active area that has engaged their attention has been the dynamics of securing political support, which concerns incumbents who have to lure political supporters with economic incentives. If these incentives are not provided (in the form of licenses, jobs, contracts) then support will be swayed in directions unfavourable to the incumbents. However, by allocating resources to preferred supporters (present or potential), the market mechanism is superseded. A natural consequence would be for groups to lobby for special

advantages, such as licenses, subsidies and protection against competition, that
will enable them to earn rents (Kreuger, 1974). Rent-seeking will thus
encourage directly unproductive economic activities that could very well have a
welfare-decreasing impact on the economy (see Bhagwati,1982).

    Without entering into a lengthy debate as to the relative merits or demerits
of the different models of the state, it is acceptable to extract, as a core, the
principle activities of the state. Essential to the functioning of a state is the need
to: 1) maintain law and order, 2) maintain infrastructural and institutional
facilities, 3) determine economic policy, and 4) participate in economic
redistribution (see Mann, 1986:120-122). All of these activities require, to
varying degrees, the intervention of the state. The neoutilitarian school will
argue that a policy of issuing licenses, for example, will encourage bribery and
corruption among bureaucrats, thus lending credence to the perception of the
state as an inefficient intervener. The experience of rent-seeking behaviour will
run against Dugger's (1993:189) assertion that the state "is best seen as a
transaction cost minimizer, not as an inefficient intervener."

    The state, irrespective of the theoretical perspective chosen, is an entity that
is associated with a large number of transactions. But, the manner in which the
state is involved with the transactions depends on the nature of the state in
question.

Neoclassical/neoutilitarian economists would advocate a minimal state,
whereas the Marxist economists would propose an interventionsist state.
Across the spectrum of possibilities, at one end we would have a state that
directly participates in all the transactions surrounding the activities of a state,
classified under four heads as mentioned earlier. At the other extreme would be
the state that, perhaps, merely oversees the transactions that have to be
executed in order that state functioning can progress unhindered.

    A naive interpretation of the transaction costs framework would produce
the view that transaction costs are minimised if the state were to undertake all
transactions. Definitely, state planning and state control of resources would
minimise transactions. There are benefits to centralisation, but what overweighs
the decision against state planning and resource allocation are the informational
constraints invoked by the exercise of setting shadow prices. Much of the
failure of socialism has resulted from the difficulty of assessing actual needs
and responding effectively to the demand situations. The socialist model was

based on the assumption that relative scarcities could be accurately reflected in the computed prices. Lange (1936) had hoped that Walrasian prices could be incorporated in a planned system.

The role of the bureaucracy was overlooked in Lange's model. In a typical planned economy such as Hungary, Kornai (1990:155) observes: "the bureaucracy is busy intervening in all dimensions of economic life. Intervention into price formation is only a small part of its hyperactivity." In such a system, the firm's efficiency is compromised by virtue of being dependent on the bureaucracy, on one hand, and the market, on the other hand. An interventionist, and pervasive bureaucracy would clearly add to transaction costs.

Kornai's (ibid:21-29) idea of a 'soft' budget constraint is a useful tool in further supporting the argument that a planned economy need not necessarily be a transaction cost minimizer. A softening of the budget constraint occurs when a firm in a planned economy can rely on the state to bail it out should its earnings fall short of actual expenditure. In other words, the firm expects with high subjective probability that any excess of expenditure over earnings will be paid for by the state, and this anticipation of external assistance is incorporated into the firm's behaviour. As a consequence of the softening of the budget constraint, the price responsiveness of the firm declines, 'constructive destruction' in Schumpeter's sense ceases to have any significance, and excess demand for output builds up.

First, in the presence of excess demand, consumers would resort to arrangements of their own to procure goods, making side payments that would fuel corruption and generate a black market. Second, if old and inefficient products and production processes are preserved, that would reduce transaction costs in so far as the emergence of new firms is restricted, but transaction costs would be increased in attending to breakdowns and maintenance costs, not to mention the loss in economies of scale and scope. Third, in the absence of price responsiveness, firms would not react promptly and appropriately to changes in interest rates, exchange rates and input prices. When opportunity costs are ignored buyers may end up paying more than is necessary.

As far as equity is concerned planned economies hold the promise of ensuring that equity can be better served than in the free-market system. Transaction cost economics is based on the assumption that agents pursue their own interests with guile under the constraints imposed by bounded rationality. If this assumption is operationalised it only implies that agents have successfully achieved their own interests in the most efficient manner, but without necessarily having included the interests of external parties in their calculation. The problem of externalities would, thus, be poorly addressed. The global welfare function might possibly suffer. Dugger (1993) distinguishes between lower and higher efficiency. The earlier is with respect to the private interests of agents, and the latter to all interests, whether or not those interests are directly involved in an agreement. He further explains the implications of the distinction:

If the self-interests of parties to a private ordering conflict with the interests of the public, the private ordering possess efficiency potential only with respect to the private interest, not with respect to the public interest. The logic and the assumptions of transaction cost economics force us to conclude that the efficiency potentials of private orderings are lower than the efficiency potentials of public orderings (Dugger, 1993:209).

If agents representing private interests had to negotiate and bargain with those representing public interests, then the costs of arriving at a equitable solution would be high. But if private interests were allowed to prevail, the interests and rights of others would be eroded, and the larger good would not be served. The state is well placed to arbitrate and secure both equity and the larger good of society, imposing the transaction costs that would be well below those that would be incurred if the parties concerned had negotiated and bagained on their own.

The foregoing arguments indicate that the state can act as a transaction cost minimizer. That does not mean that the state is meant to supersede the market or the firm. Any such supersession may be deleterious and only lead to a 'shortage' economy. The decision to lay claim to production by the state, or to delegate production to the free-market firm must depend on the global context of the economy. It is pointless if the production of an essential input such as steel is in the hands of the state, if the outcomes of such a decision are perpetual shortages, slow delivery, corruption, poor quality and constant industrial relations problems. At the other extreme, to privatise health care will result in insurance companies gaining more power, in physicians maximising their costs (by performing more tests and procedures than necessary) and in patients 'searching' for good but inexpensive physicians. Aside from the loss of equity, privatising health care, from a transaction costs approach, need not, at first glance, be an optimal solution. In the next section we discuss some instances of privatisation. By discussing these cases we will gain some understanding into the interplay of forces that have resulted in the private sector production of goods. This will enable us to comment on the advisability (or otherwise) of such initiatives.

PRIVATISATION IN SOUTHEAST ASIA

Indonesia

Privatisation was slow to be implemented in Indonesia. The initial resistance to privatisation was overcome when, in 1986, oil prices declined. The decline continued for several years and so privatisation was forced upon the economy.

The first steps in the movement towards privatisation came with changes to shipping activity and policies relating to trade (Pangetsu and Habir, 1989; Pangetsu, 1991). These included simplifying customs and port procedures, deregulating rules on shipping routes and relaxing licensing requirements. In relation to trade, tariffs were replaced by non-tariff barriers so as to reduce the cost of production for exporters.

In 1991, although the government expressed the view that the financial sector was to be deregulated, new regulations were introduced (Parker, 1991). These regulations were directed at restricting the creation of new branches and increasing control and reporting requirements.

If the move to privatisation has been cautious in Indonesia, perhaps, as mentioned by Ng and Toh (1992:47-49) it is because of the fear that an economy open to market forces will lead to the increased influence of Chinese Indonesian business and foreigners. A second reason could lie in the 'embedded affinity for socialism' (Simandjuntak, 1991 in Ng and Toh, 1991), a view that emphasises the leading role that the state is expected to play in the development process.

Malaysia

The Malaysian government's aim of achieving 'Malaysia Incorporated' was sought to be reached through privatisation efforts. The first document towards initiating this movement was the government's Guideline on Privatisation, issued in 1982. The objectives of privatisation were meant to facilitate the development of infrastructure, without burdening the government; to promote competition, efficiency and productivity; to reduce the size and presence of the public sector; to stimulate private entrepreneurship; and, to encourage Bumiputera entrepreneurship. A further step was taken in 1987 when the idea of a privatisation masterplan was mooted. The purpose of this plan was to clarify and refine the objectives and strategies of the privatisation guideline.

The record for the implementation of privatisation has been impressive in Malaysia. The Malaysian Airline System, Telekom Malaysia, Tenaga, the Malaysian International Shipping Corporation, and the North-South Expressway are among companies that have been privatised. Certain segments of the government health care system have been privatised and more recently tertiary education has been actively privatised.

Md Salleh (1991:618-620) enumerates several approaches that have been adopted to execute the privatisation process. One approach has been to sell a minor part of the shares in companies to the public, with the rest remaining in the hands of the government, while retaining the existing management. A second approach has been to separate a component sector within a Ministry to a state-owned company, changing the legal status of the sector, but with state ownership remaining, though now over a freshly created legal entity. The third approach has been to allow public listing of companies that were formerly public-owned. The fourth approach has been to permit the private sector to compete in activities that were previously the monopoly of the government. The fifth approach involves the sale and leasing of assets owned by the government. The sixth approach is more protracted. In this approach ventures are provided for by the private sector and after a period of operating and collecting revenues from the venture, it is then transferred to the government. The last approach is one where municipal and local governments contract out some of their jobs to private companies.

The government's objective to privatise does not neglect the earlier committment to ethnic equity. In consonance with the New Economic Policy (NEP) that aims to raise Bumiputera participation to at least 30 per cent of total corporate ownership, the government has stipulated that any privatisation venture must include a minimum of 30 per cent of Bumiputera participation. Should individual Bumiputera investors be unable to participate, then Amanah Saham Nasional would contribute on behalf of the Bumiputera community.

It is inexplicable, however, why the government has chosen to privatise monopolies. Enterprises like MAS, MISC and Telekom face little competition within their respective industries. These enterprises are assured of making profits regardless of their new ownership structure. The Port Klang Container Terminal was a profit-making entity, but its profits increased three-fold subsequent to privatisation. TV3 and NTV7, however, entered the industry long after the state-run channels were established, and, yet, were able to introduce an element of competition into the industry.

Philippines

The move towards privatisation was initiated by President Marcos and carried through more fully by President Aquino. In tracing the development of privatisation Briones (1991:662) observes that during the Marcos era public enterprises grew rapidly, their focus being in the construction of massive infrastructure projects. This positive development came to a close in the later years of Marcos's rule when hundreds of public enterprises were bankrupt. In addition, government-owned or controlled corporations were misused for purposes of directing resources from public to private hands.

Two important agencies that were founded by Aquino to execute the privatisation process were the Committee on Privatisation and the Asset Privatisation Trust. The Committee was expected, among other things, to lay policy guidelines on privatisation, and to evaluate the sale or disposition of non-peforming assets (NPAs) or public enterprises. The Trust was required to sell or divest NPAs and public enterprises that were identified by the Committee. In effect, the Committee functioned at a broader policy level and the Trust, as an implementative agency, was responsible for the disposition of NPAs and government corporations.

The seriousness of intent with which privatisation was approached is obvious from the fact that the privatisation policy was directed at the government corporate sector, non-performing assets, and even at the bureaucracy. Indeed, the size of the entire bureaucracy was sought to be reduced. In fact, the privatisation policy has been so extensive that crucial areas in which the government played a role have witnessed the withdrawal of the government. These include development banking and even extended to social services, education and health.

The switch to privatisation has been expensive because of the costs involved in transferring assets and enterprises to the government before they were privatised (Briones, 1991:681). The government also had to bear losses in servicing debts. As a consequence of the immense financial pressure thrust upon the government, valuable funds have been reduced for health, social welfare and education.

Thailand

The privatisation process in Thailand seems to have been trigered off by the inability of state enterprises to finance their investments. This, in turn, resulted in these public enterprises relying on external debt. The high external debt made it necessary for the government to pursue privatisation (Ramangkura, 1991). It was in the sixth national development plan (1987 - 1991) that privatisation gained in importance, although the idea was fairly popular well before that time.

Privatisation took various forms in the 1980s (see Dhiratayakinant, 1991:707). One approach was to liquidate public enterprises. The Mining Organisation, Alum Organisation, Thai Airway Maintenance and Chol-buri Sugar Corporation were among the companies that were liquidated. In the case of the Krung Thai Bank, for instance, the Ministry of Finance reduced its ownership of shares in that corporation. Another mode of privatisation was for the government to enter into a joint venture with private enterprises. This was the modality employed with the Tourism Authority of Thailand, the United

Thai Hotel and Travel Co. and the Bang-Pa-In Paper Mill. More popular measures were to contract out certain parts of services offered by public enterprises. The Thailand Tobacco contracted out its cleaning services, as did the Petroleum Authority of Thailand. The Electricity Generating Authority of Thailand and the Bangkok Mass Transit Organisation contracted out some of their maintenance services. Franchising or leasing was practised with enterprises such as the State Railway of Thailand, the Bangkok Mass Transit Organisation and the Port Authority of Thailand.

In assessing privatisation, Dhiratayakinant (1991:709) summarises the sequence of measures taken by the government before a public enterprise is liquidated. First, an attempt is made to change the management team. Alternately, the government tries to improve existing management or marketing. If that too fails, then the government attempts to initiate a joint public-private venture with the private partner holding the majority of the shares. The final resort is to transfer or liquidate the existing public enterprise.

At a policy level, the Thai government has viewed public sector borrowing for investment purposes with caution. Rather than borrow the government has tried to circumvent the problem by encouraging private sector participation, either through private equity participation or by leasing or franchising the project to the private sector. Liquidation or sale of projects to the private sector is considered only in the case of public enterprises that have continually failed. However, the government is committed to undertaking heavy industries involving huge financial resources and high technological capabilities as well as social welfare oriented public enterprises.

TRANSACTION COSTS AND PRIVATISATION

The privatisation experience of some of the ASEAN countries we have discussed show that privatisation can take varying forms. Privatisation in its extreme form would imply the complete sale of public enterprises to the private sector or the independent operation of an enterprise that formerly was in the public sector domain. Privatisation in its most dilute form would occur in instances where segments or activities within public enterprises are contracted-out or leased to the private sector. Between these two forms various possibilities can be practiced.

Thailand has a definite policy of selling public enterprises that have repeatedly been unsuccessful. To run an enterprise that is loss-making is undoubtedly inefficient. It is only rational under such circumstances to seek a private enterprise that can take ouver the public corporation. This privatisation exercise would require search costs, selecting one of the many firms that may have applied to take over the public enterprise; evaluation costs, in determining the price at which the enterprise can be sold; and restructuring costs, i.e. the costs of changing accounting, information, organisation an human resource systems. It is worth the while to pay these costs if the firm can be successfully run as a private enterprise.

It is unproductive for the state to support an ailing firm. When a sick firm receives state support a soft budget constraint, Kornai's sense, applies. A softening of the budget constraint causes imprecise responsiveness to price signals, a reaction that leads to loss of profits and overemployment of labour in public enterprises and resource shortages in the economy. Contracts will ahve to be reneged or not made at all. The latter implies lost opportunity costs and the earlier compensation and legal costs. Indonesia's reluctance to submit to privatisation and Philippines's misuse of public enterprises in the 1980s do not in any way minimise transaction costs. They only add to transaction costs by distorting the budget constraint.

Private enterprises are definitely subject to hard budget constraints, but being exposed to hard budget constraints is not a guarantee that transaction costs are minimised. It is true, for example, that TV3 in Malaysia emerged in an industry that previously was within the domain of a public enterprise. TV3 was profitable soon after its inception; but by approving the establishment of this station, transaction costs were not necessarily being minimised. RTM, the state-run corporation, could very well have used its existing fixed capital to expand the range of services it was providing. The extra costs incurred in offering a new channel would have been more than offset by the extra revenue generated by a commercially-oriented channel airing market-geared programmes directed at the urban middle class. Even marginal additions to capital and equipment would have been justified since entertainment programmes targetted at the urban middle class had not been fully exploited by RTM.

If an enterprise has been under state-ownership, and has been operating efficiently and earning profits, it is difficult to reason why such an enterprise would need to be privatised. One possible reason could be found in the need to reduce the size of the bureaucracy. Another reason could rest in the need to subject the enterprise to a hard budget constraint. This would be an acceptable reason only if the state had been accomodating the enterprise's expenditure. Otherwise, transaction costs are increased by shedding rather than retaining the firm under the state's ownership. Given this line of argument, shedding MAS or Telekom in Malaysia increases transaction costs.

A variant of the above argument is the decision to make or buy. The state can, for instance, engage in constructing infrastructural resources, such as road-building, or it can permit a privately-owned corporation to build and, subsequently, purchase the constructed road from the private corporation. This explains the rationality of leaving the responsibility of constructing the North-South Expressway in Malaysia to a private enterprise, with the agreement that after a period of time the ownership of the expressway will be transferred to the government. In the interim period the revenue collected from tolls will go to the firm that constructed the expressway.

In most ASEAN countries the government is actively privatising many of its non-core actvities. In Thailand, the Petroleum Authority of Thailand has contracted out its cleaning services, just as the Electricity Generating Authority of Thailand and Bangkok Mass Transit Organisation have contracted out some of their maintenance services. In Malaysia the local municipal councils have contracted out garbage collection, and some of the non-core services (such as, waste disposal and laundry services) at government hospitals have been privatised. Though not significant these measures help to reduce transaction costs.

Unfortunately, the Philippines has had to reduce its allocation of funds for health, development banking and education. The Malaysian government is trying to withdraw from its traditional support for education with plans to corporatise public universities, by encouraging the establishment of private universities, and by permiting foreign universities to establish branch campuses in Malaysia. Within the health sector the Malaysian government is encouraging private hospitals and planning to introduce health management organisations. Although these measures will reduce transaction costs they ignore considerations relating to higher efficiency.

CONCLUSION

We can apply the transaction costs framework to the state's decision to buy or make. If the state's corporations are highly dependent on certain inputs, say, steel, for example, then the state would reduce transaction costs if it assigned the production of steel to a corporation directly under its control. A state that is actively engaged in the manufacturing sector would find it beneficial to take over the production of necessary inputs rather than to leave their production to the private sector. Thus there is little incentive to privatise and the transaction costs framework shows the rationality of the decision, though it, perhaps, be against our intuition.

Similarly, the state can be faced with the decision to retain an enterprise that it owns or release it to the private sector. Again, if by retaining the enterprise transaction costs are added to, but, by contrast, releasing the enterprise to the private sector results in a reduction in transaction costs, then the state will choose to privatise the enterprise. From the transaction costs perspective we see that the decision to privatise is not one which has a standard solution: to privatise at all costs. Instead, we find that the decision depends upon the context.

The state can be motivated by vested interests rather than by the objective of minimising transaction costs. The choice to hand licences to cronies or to use state-owned enterprises as instruments for laundering money simply go against any exercise to minimise transaction costs. Vested interests and cronyism are issues that interact with the state's decision to privatise. However, these are questions that need further investigation.

A state can relinquish its control over certain enterprises and privatise them, provided that they are run by industrial leaders who have established a high level of credibility within the economic system. Trust comes to play a role in this option. Although the enterprise is now privately owned, the government knows that it will be efficiently operated. The government may have had previous arrangements with these industrial leaders who would have demonstrated their willingness to cooperate. The government can, therefore, release the burden of operating the enterprise and yet expect its objectives to be complied with by the new owners of the enterprise. This is another situation which we have not examined, but which presumably has permeated into the calculus of policy makers.

REFERENCES

Arrow, K.J. (1969), "The Organisation of Economic Activity: Issues Pertinent to the Choice of Market Versus Nonmarket Allocation," in *The Analysis and Evaluation of Public Expenditure: The PPB System*, vol.1, US Joint Economic Committee. Washington, US Government Printing Office

Bhagwati, J.N (1982), "Directly Unproductive, Profit-seeking (DUP) Actvities," *Journal of Political Economy*, 90(5).

Briones, L.M. (1991), "Privatisation in the Philippines: Policy, Experience and Impact," in G. Gouri (ed) (1991), *Privatisation and Public Enterprise: The Asia-Pacific Experience*, New Delhi: Oxford and IBH.

Buchanan, J.M., R.D. Tollison, and G. Tullock (eds) (1980), *Toward a Theory of the Rent-Seeking Society*, Texas: Texas A&M University Press.

Coase, R. H. (1937), "The Nature of the Firm," *Economica*, 4(4).

Colander, D.C. (ed) (1984), *Neoclassical Political Economy*, Cambridge, Mass.:Ballinger.

Dahlman, C.J. (1979), "The Problem of Externality," *Journal of Law and Economics*, 22(1).

Datta, S.K. and J.B. Nugent (1989), "Transaction Cost Economics and Contractual Choice: Theory and Evidence," in Nabli, M.K. and J. Nugent (eds) (1989), *The New Institutional Economics and Development: Theory and Applications to Tunisia*, Amsterdam: North-Holland.

Dhiratayakinant, K. (1991), "Privatisation of Public Enterprises: The Case of Thailand," in G. Gouri (ed) (1991), *Privatisation and Public Enterprise: The Asia-Pacific Experience*, New Delhi: Oxford and IBH.

Dugger, W.M. (1993), "Transaction Cost Economics and the State," in C. Pitelis, (ed.)(1993), *Transaction Costs, Markets and Hierarchies*, Oxford: Basil Blackwell.

Evans, P. (1992), "The State as Problem and Solution: Predation, Embedded Autonomy, and Structural Change," in S. Haggard and R. Kaufman (eds) (1992), *The Politics of Economic Adjustment*, Princeton, N.J.: Princeton University Press.

Kay, N.M. (1993) "Markets, False Hierarchies and the Role of Asset Specificity," in C. Pitelis, (ed.)(1993), *Transaction Costs, Markets and Hierarchies*, Oxford: Basil Blackwell.

Kornai, J. (1990), Vision and Reality, Market and State, Hertfordshire: Harvester Wheatsheaf.

Kreuger, A.O. (1974), "The Political Economy of the Rent-Seeking Society," American Economic Review, 64(3).

Lange, O. (1936), "On the Economic Theory of Socialism," Review of Economic Studies, 4(1)

Mann, M. (1986), "The Autonomous Power of the State," in J.A. Hall (ed) (1986), State in History, Oxford: Blackwell.

Md. Salleh, I. (1991), "The Privatisation of Public Enterprises: A Case Study of Malaysia," in G. Gouri (ed) (1991), Privatisation and Public Enterprise: The Asia-Pacific Experience, New Delhi: Oxford and IBH.

Nabli, M.K. and J. Nugent (eds) (1989), The New Institutional Economics and Development: Theory and Applications to Tunisia, Amsterdam: North-Holland.

Ng, C.K. and T.K. Woon (1992), "Privatization in the Asian-Pacific Region," Asian-Pacific Economic Literature, 6(2).

Niskanen, W.A. (1971), Bureaucracy and Representative Government, Chicago: Aldine-Atherton.

Pangetso, M. (1991), "The Role of the Private Sector in Indonesia: Deregulation and Privatization,"The Indonesian Quarterly, 19(1).

Pangetso, M. and A.D. Habir (1989), "Trends and Prospects in Privatization and Deregulation in Indonesia," in Ng C.K. and N. Wagner (eds) (1989), "Privatization and Deregulation in ASEAN," ASEAN Economic Bulletin, 5(3).

Parker, S. (1991), "Survey of Recent Developments," Bulletin of Indonesian Economic Studies, 27(1).

Poulantzas, N. (1972), Political Power and Social Class, London: New Left Books.

Ramangkura, V. (1991), "Privatization in Thailand," Bank of Thailand Quarterly Bulletin, 31(2).

Simandjuntak, D.S. (1991), "Process of Deregulation and Privatization: The Indonesian Experience," The Indonesian Quarterly, 19(4).

Williamson, O.E. (1979), "Transaction-cost Economics: The Governance of Contractual Relations," Journal of Law and Economics, 22(2).

Williamson, O.E. (1985), *The Economic Institutions of Capitalism*, London: Macmillan.

NOTES ON THE CONTRIBUTORS

B.N. Ghosh, Ph.D.(India), M.CIM. (UK), GFCR (Harvard) is a Professor of Economics, School of Social Sciences, Universiti Sains Malaysia, 11800 Penang.

G.S. Gupta, Ph.D.(Johns Hopkins), is a Professor of Economics and Finance, Indian Institute of Management, Ahmedabad (India).

Mohamed Eliyas Hashim, is a Graduate Student of MPA Programme in the Universiti Sains Malaysia, 11800 Penang.

Moha Asri Abdullah, Ph.D. (London), is the Deputy Director in the Centre for Policy Research, Universiti Sains Malaysia, 11800 Penang.

Mohd. Isa Bakar, Ph.D. (Iowa State), is an Associate Professor in the Centre for Policy Research, Universiti Sains Malaysia, 11800 Penang.

Richard Allen Drake, Ph.D. (Michigan State University), is an adjunct Research Associate in the Department of Anthropology, Michigan State University, United States of America.

Mohamad MD Yusoff, Ph.D. (Michigan State University), is an Associate Professor, at School of Communication, Universiti Sains Malaysia, 11800 Penang.

Antonio Tujan (Jr.) is the Executive Director of IBON Foundation Inc. and currently of the Institute of Political Economy, Manila, Philippines.

Ms. Jennifer Haygood is a Senior Researcher of IBON Foundation Inc. Manila, Philippines.

Rama Ghosh, Ph.D. (India), is a Lecturer in Economics, DAV College for Men (Punjab University), Chandigarh (India).

Dawood M. Mithani, Ph.D. (India), is an Associate Professor, Graduate School, Universiti Utara Malaysia, Kedah (Malaysia).

Pairat Watcharaphun, MBA (Jacksonville State University) is Head of the Dept. of Finance, Faculty of Management Sciences, Prince of Songkhala University (Thailand).

Shankaran Nambiar MA (Delhi School of Economics), is a Lecturer in Economics, International College (Sydney University), 11900 Penang.

INDEX